SCHEDULED CASTES EDUCATION

SCHEDULED CASTES EDUCATION

(Issues and Aspects)

N. Mishra

Kalpaz Publications

Delhi-110052

SCHEDULED CASTES EDUCATION
[*Education*]

ISBN: 81-7835-074-2

Published in 2001 in India by
Kalpaz Publications
C-30, Satyawati Nagar
Ashok Vihar, Delhi - 110 053

Laser Typeset at Alphabet, Delhi
Printed at Mehra Offset Press, New Delhi.

Content

Introduction

Education is regarded the most powerful instrument for emancipation and empowerment of Dalits or for that matter, any class of people lagging behind in the social hierarchy. This was realised as far back as the process of Dalit advancement featured on the list of agenda of the reforms and leaders in the social and political spheres of life. Jyotiba Phule in the initial stage of Dalit movement realised this and worked towards creating facilities for advancement of Dalit education.

Various social reformers as also the British Government stressed upon spread of education among the weaker sections of society in the early part of nineteenth century. Their efforts resulted in many schools being established in Dalit areas. Hostels were also set up to accommodate the students. Due emphasis was provided to the education of girls as well. What hindered the growth of education in those days was the crunch of resources as well as shortage of teachers who would devote themselves to educating Dalits.

Efforts were made to meet the shortage of funds by raising donations ; and government also funded running of some schools. As to the problem of teaching staff, attempts were made to prepare the teachers from among Dalits itself as teachers from higher castes naturally stayed away from taking the responsibility owing to social stigma attached with the Dalit community. But then, there were not many among Dalit who were well educated and out of those who were qualified, only a small percentage of them took up the role of a teacher whereas most of them moved to the greener pastures. In this scenario only substandard teachers were available to accomplish the difficult task which required delicate handling.

Another problem which was as serious, if not more, as any other was that boys and girls who needed to be educated were to be literally driven out of their houses to the schools. Economically weaker as this section of society is, they use every possible resource at their command to enhance their income, children included. While education .was there to better their lot in the long-term, it needed short-term sacrifices to achieve that goal. Depressed as they were, perhaps they did not understand or could not afford to bear this short-term loss. They used their children as workers and help them each their livelihood. Young girls shouldered the burden of looking after the household while their mothers were away working in the fields. Even those who were persuaded to join school found it unattractive while other forces also compelled them to pull out; often dropped out of the school in the initial stages itself. Once dropped out, they were lost out to the field of education and could never be attracted back to school.

Thus, the problem remained and increased the burden on society to carry the illiterate lot with it and huff and puff on it way to progress. But we cannot complain because the problem was society's own making having its roots way back in the ancient Hindu history and it was back to society to bear the burden and workout ways and means to rectify the injustice of the past.

Untouchability was cleverly created cage for confining the so-called untouchables to their low status. They had no right to admission in the schools, learn Sanskrit and acquire knowledge. Therefore, Dalit movement was primarily focussed towards regaining the right to education as a *sine qua non* for their total emancipation.

Following are the important events and achievements of the Dalit emancipation in this respect in chronological order.

1. In August 1848 Mahatma Phule, the great social revolutionary started the first school in Pune for the girl students. He opened the first school for the students of untouchable communities in Pune in the year 1852. In 1856 the number of such schools rose to three and the number of students became 300. Altogether eight teachers were teaching in those schools. In 1858, he opened a hostel for the poor untouchable students in Pune wherein 25-30 students were provided accommodation every year.

2. In June 1856, at Dharwad, in the then Bombay Province, a Mahar, untouchable boy was refused to be admitted in the school on the ground of untouchability. Thereafter, the Bombay Government had to declare that all the schools receiving government grants should be open to all the students irrespective of their caste or creed. This was declared in the year 1858.
3. In 1865, Shri Shashipad Bandopadhaya (Bengal), a staunch Brahmo established a school for the poor labourers and the untouchables at Baranagar near Calcutta.
4. On 19 October 1882, Mahatma Jyotirao Phule submitted a memorandum to the Education Commission, Bombay headed by Mr. Hunter in which he pleaded the government to make primary education compulsory for the children of the untouchables. Further he advocated separate schools for them as they were not allowed to sit along with the caste Hindus due to caste prejudices.
5. Since 1883, separate schools were being started for the students of the untouchables in Baroda State. Mangudkar (1976) state that in 1910 the number of such schools rose to 297, and the number of students studying in these schools rose to 13,703.
6. In 1886, John Rathinam, an untouchable leader, set up a Model School in Thousand Lights area of Madras for the untouchable students and in 1899 established one hostel for them.
7. Pandit C. Tyodhi Dass started many schools in Madras city in 1889 with the help of Colonel Olcott, Mary Balbare and Annie Besant.
8. In 1890, separate schools for the Panchamas (Untouchables) were opened in the Mysore princely State at Mysore, Bangalore and Anekal.
9. In 1891, separate primary schools were set up for the Pariahs.
10. Colonel Olcott opened his first school for the untouchable students in Madras in 1894; second school in 1898 and third school in 1899. In 1901, 384 boys and 150 girls were getting education.

11. In 1895, Januji K. Khandare opened a free hostel for the students of the Depressed Classes at Akola in Maharashtra. He received the land for this purpose from the government, built the building at his own. It was the first ever hostel in Vidarbh.
12. Mangudkar (1976) states that in 1897, Raosaheb K. Rangarao, the Secretary of Brahmo Samaj, Mangalore set up his first school for the untouchable students in Mangalore.
13. In 1904, Ayyan Kali set up a school at Katakala near Venganoor in Kerala for the students of the untouchables.
14. The Maharaja of Kolhapur promulgated an ordinance on 28 November, 1906 to start night schools in Kolhapur for the untouchable students.
15. In 1906, M.L. Audiah established a school at Secunderabad for the students of the Depressed Classes. It was named after Sir William Barton, the then Resident of Hyderabad.
16. Shahu Maharaj of Kolhapur started a school in Kolhapur for the girls belonging to Chambhar and Dhor untouchables on 4 October 1907.
17. With the efforts of Chhatrapati Shahu Maharaj of Kolhapur a school for Mahar students was opened at Udagaon on 1 May 1909.
18. In 1910, Kalicharan Nandagavali built a school building at his own cost at Gondia in Bhandara district (Maharashtra) for the girl students of the untouchable community.
19. The Depressed Classes Mission of India established by Maharshi V.R. Shinde undertook the task of opening schools for the untouchables from the year 1911.
20. Pandit Palaniswami started Dravid School in 1917 in Madras for the untouchable students.
21. Mrs Jaibai Choudhari, a staunch lady social worker at Nagpur set up a school named Chokhamela School, at Nayabasti, Nagpur in 1922. It aimed at imparting education exclusively to girl students belonging to the untouchables.
22. The Arya Samaj opened a school for the benefit of *Bhangi* children in 1923 in Jodhpur.

23. M.R. Jaikar moved a resolution in the Legislative Assembly on 23 February 1928 recommending to the government "to provide special facilities for the education of the untouchables and other depressed classes and also for opening all public services to them specially the police." The resolution was adopted with minor changes.
24. On 14 June 1928, Dr. Babasaheb Ambedkar established the Depressed Classes Education Society to spread education among the untouchables.
25. Under the Poona Pact, 1932, it was agreed to earmark a reasonable sum for providing educational facilities to the members of the Scheduled Castes in every province.
26. The *Harijan Sevak Sangh* started giving scholarships to the students of the Depressed Classes since 1936-37. It gave scholarships to 94 students in that year.
27. By 1939, there was an institute called The Jatav Men's Educational Institute at Agra, which was running five schools for boys and one for girls in Agra district.
28. In June 1941, the *Harijan Sevak Sangh* opened one Harijan Kanya Vidyalaya at Sabarmati.
29. A special provision was made for the first time in the central budget in 1944 for the grant of scholarships for the Scheduled Castes. This facility was also extended to the Scheduled Tribes in 1948.
30. Dr. Babasaheb Ambedkar founded the People's Education Society (PES) on 8 July 1945 at Bombay. The said Society began its first college named Siddharth College at Bombay on 20 June 1946. It opened Millind MahaVidyalaya at Aurangabad on 19 June 1950.
31. The Constitution which came into force on 26 January 1950 states under its Article 29(2) that "No citizen shall be denied admission into any educational institution maintained by the State or receiving aid out of state funds on grounds only of religion, race, caste, language or any of them."

Article 15(4) states, "Nothing in this article or in clause (2) of article 29 shall prevent the state from making any special provision for the advancement of any socially and educationally backward classes of citizens or for the Scheduled Castes and the Scheduled Tribes."

When we became independent and our own Constitution was drafted, it did dwell upon the deplorable condition of Dalit and made provisions of positive discrimination to help their cause.

It was realised by the Constitution maker that Dalits needed to be brought into the mainstream nation life and their educational advancement was one of the most important ways to achieve this goal.

To achieve this end various education commissions and committees were appointed in the post-independence period. Various five years plan also reflected the same line of action. It is not that policy of positive discrimination came into being with the drafting of our Constitution. The history of positive discrimination dates back to the 19th century when for the first time, the socially and economically weaker sections were categorised and recognised. In 1885, Madras government made of provision of special facilities for students of depressed classes. In 1921, it also took initiative for higher representation of non-Brahmins in government services. This arrangement was further revised and updated in future course of action taken by the government. Other states like Mysore also took similar steps.

Apart from being socially and economically backward, Dalits were denied access to education as well, in the past. This led to their decline more than anything else. Being uneducated is as bad as being blind to the world of realities. And being unaware led to unabated discrimination with no stout resistance coming from those being discriminated. Therefore, in modern time the need arose to make the Dalits aware of their rights and fight to get them. For this, education became the highest priority. Without being educated it was unlikely that they will become conscious of their rights.

In the Constitution, the Scheduled Castes or Dalits are recognised on the basis of untouchability and are given protection and special support. Article 17 of the Constitution decrees the abolition of untouchability. Article 46 says that the state shall promote with special care the education and economic interests of the weaker sections of the people and in particular of the Scheduled

Castes. Article 29(2) prohibits discrimination in government aided educational institutions. Article 15 also prohibits discrimination on grounds of religion, race, caste, sex or place of birth. However, Article 15(4) states that notwithstanding the provisions of Article 15 and 29(2), the state may make special provisions for the advancement of Scheduled Castes.

It is believed that the first generation learners are different in many respects from the subsequent generation learners. The home environment of these two groups of children are different. In case of the subsequent generation learners there are brothers and sisters and also the parents who have already received education. These educated parents encourage their children to make greater efforts to achieve more with regard to their education. They are, for the same reason, more willing to provide them with needed facilities for better learning. Besides, they give better guidance to their children. The home environment, in this way, of the subsequent generation learners is more stimulating and facilitating. All this affects, the academic achievement and the attitudes of these children.

In contrast to the subsequent generation learners, the first generation learners come to the school without any orientation. They are, comparatively less ready and less prepared for the school life. They do not get any guidance from any one at home nor there is any stimulation for them to learn as their parents do not realize the significance of education. All this adversely affects their academic achievement and attitudes towards life and society.

But all these are assumptions, the actual position is not known. The present research is based on these assumptions which provide its rationale. It is only at the end of this study that we will get a clear picture of the status. This study will prove or disprov whether these two groups of learners are really different from one another with regard to the variables contained in the study. It is hypothesized that they are different. The study will test this hypothesis.

It cannot be denied that over the years there has been a very impressive increase in the number and spread of institutions as well as enrolment in the elementary sector of education. The good of UEE has been substantially achieved at the primary stage (Classes I-V). According to the Sixth All-India Educational Survey

(1993), 93.76 per cent of the rural population had primary schools within a walking distance of one km; 85.00 per cent of the rural population was served with the upper primary sections within a walking distance of three km. For the pre-dominantly Dalit habitations in rural areas, the corresponding figures were 91.32 per cent and 82.54 per cent respectively. The number of primary schools increased many fold. Likewise, the gross enrolment also went up. Baring the sex disparity, the participation of Dalits is now more or less in proportion to their education.

The National Policy on Education, 1986 and its Programme of Action gave unqualified priority to Universal Elementary Education and introduced many innovations. The emphasis was shifted from enrolment *per se* to enrolment as well as retention. The NPE 1986 further stressed on the removal of disparities and attainment of equalisation of educational opportunities for the Scheduled Castes, Scheduled Tribes, and other backward sections, specially girls. The POA detailed a number of strategies aimed at accelerating their rate of enrolment and retention. In 1992, some modifications were undertaken to the NPE, 1986. It placed greater stress on the education of the Scheduled Castes, Scheduled Tribes, other educationally backwrd sections and areas, minorities and physically and mentally handicapped. The central focus in the Scheduled Castes' educational development in this revised NPE, 1992, is their equalisation with non-SC population at all stages and levels of education — rural male, rural female, urban male and urban female. The Programme of Action (POA) on the new NPE, 1992 was formulated after taking into account the experience gained in the implementation of NPE, 1986 and its POA. Some of the most important programmes of action, apart from reservations and specific incentives, which have a bearing on Universal Elementary Education of the Scheduled Castes, are as follows :

It is education which decides the quality and mode of living of an individual alongwith introducing a lot of social potentialities in him. Modern education among the Scheduled Castes has been an effective source of modify their attitude, habits, manners and their mode of social living by introducing rational attitude, secular outlook, sophisticated ideas and polished manners of expression and behaviour in the wider circle of society. These changes in manners and attitudes influences the style of life to a large extent. As a consequence, the rudimentary and superstitious patterns of living, are replaced by modern materialistic mode of living among them. Changes in occupation and status leads to modify their living arrangements and patterns in the direction of modernization. The general impression derived from the empirical inference is that the scheduled castes perceive and realize that the emergence of new style of life embedded on democratic values is one of the major impact of modern education. This conclusion goes in accordance with our hypothesis that the higher the education and income of the Scheduled Castes, the greater they have receptivity and realization of modern education in mobilizing their living arrangements.

Alongwith modern education, techno industrial development and growth of democratic secular values in contemporary India have badly affected the traditional social sanctions, beliefs and customs of our society. This has enabled the Scheduled Castes to be conscious of achievement as against ascriptions and to adopt new behavioural patterns, practices and style of life. The overall changes that have occurred are the outcomes in patent and latent forms of modern education. Urban job opportunities and other such motivating factors of social mobility have completely changed their outlooks. This has also led to create wider areas of interaction with new aspirations, expectations and value orientations of material achievement rather than getting sanskritized and Hinduised on lines of traditional Hinduism.

With passage of time, the identity of every individual changes. It is the task of the social scientists to look into the problem of identity and change. It is felt that the college students of Scheduled Castes who come from unprivileged sections of the Indian society, and have been kept almost isolated from the main currents of culturl life might have social life quite different from that of the other sections. The exposure to mass media and their participation in political oriented activities are likely to break their isolation and in the process, they are likely to look for someone who may provide the frame of reference for their behaviour. Therefore, these aspects should become part of a study which is related with the exploration of the various aspects of Scheduled Castes students.

The study of changes in parental authority is another aspect which needs probing. Further, the social circles in which a student belonging to a Scheduled Caste participates helps to indicate his identification, adaptation or isolation from others. In the process of interaction with friends one is likely to experience differential treatment.

In today's world, Dalits are not as hamper as they were in earlier times as far as education is concerned. They have the assistance in the shape of reservation of seats in educational institutes, scholarships, freeships, hostel facilities and what not. Those who are able to exploit the conditions to their advantage are in some cases better placed than their higher caste counterparts.

But the problem comes in the case of rural and far-flung areas where spread of awareness is minimal and Dalits of those areas are unaware of the facilities and privileges the Government has provided for them. Mass media here is required to play a big part as are the social organisation.

Often, it is noted, people go to those areas, take photographs and collect stories of their miseries to tell and show the world the kind of life those people are leading. There work is laudable but only to a certain extent. While it is okay to make the urbanites aware of their plight, the more appreciable step would be to stay on in those areas and make those people aware of their rights so that they can make use of their rights to come up in life by acquiring first education and then economic prosperity.

One

Higher Education

Due to the hierarchical nature of Indian society with casteism and untouchability having strong hold over the minds of general people, certain sections of society have suffered a lot over the years. In order to eliminate these disadvantages, education was viewed by the Constitution makers as an instrument of social change, individual mobility, social equality for all social groups through social justice and of integration and mainstreaming. Time and again, emphasis has been laid on technical education for dalits. It is realised that the Dalits needed to be brought into the mainstream and technical knowledge is one of the ways through which they can become the part and parcel of our society. It is with this aim that various Constitutional provisions were made in the recent past.

Further to strengthen and promote the view of various education commissions and committees were appointed in the post-independence period. Various Five Year Plans also reflect the same thinking. This chapter reviews the progress in the higher education in India within the framework of preferential treatment and supportive measures for the benefit of different sectors of society.

It explains educational growth and expansion within the social context and substantiates the point that the former is closely interlinked to and interdependent on the latter. Therefore, the first section discusses the social divisions within Indian society and identifies the disadvantaged groups. The second section deals with the higher education of Scheduled Castes. The third section analyzes the reasons for the educational backwardness of this group. The fourth and concluding section tries to answer some of the fundamenal questions and discusses problem in the educational policy.

The Social Background

In this section we try to give an outline of the social setting within which the educational policies and development were undertaken. It tries to unfold the social inequalities within the society, besides revealing the multi-tiered educational system and cumulative disadvantages of those who are at the bottom of the society. The pyramidical nature of Indian society is replicated in the distribution of educational privilege.

The division of Indian society is primarily done on the basis of castes, class, religion, region and sex. Caste is the most pervasive parameter which divides Indian society, especially the Hindus who form nearly 82 per cent of the population. Other non-Hindu groups are also characterised by several features of the caste system.

By the term caste or *jati* we mean an endogamous group. By birth a person belongs to a specific class. Castes are arranged hierarchically.

Our society divides the people into clean and unclean castes on the basis of purity and pollution. Untouchables have the lowest ritual standing and economic position. They also suffer from severe social and civic disabilities. The most degrading and unclean occupations such as scavenging, sweeping, and hide and leather work are associated with them. They are also artisans such as weavers, washerman and toddy tappers. Surprisingly, though caste is determined on the basis of birth, it in turn, determines the distribution of scarce goods and resources such as income, health and education.

Since education was viewed by the makers of Constitution as an instrument of social change, social mobility, equality and integration, the political elite, social reformers and intellectuals agreed, at the advent of independence in 1947, that the disadvantaged groups had to be given access to education even if it meant giving special privileges. Hence, safeguards were provided in the Constitution to protect the rights of the Scheduled Castes, and provisions were made to enforce them through the courts of law. There are various articles in the Constitution which incorporate the view whereby preferential treatment in education to certain sections of the Indian population, as emphasized.

Positive Discrimination: Overview

The history of Positive discrimination in favour of the deprived or depressed sections dates back to the 19th century when the socially and economically disadvantaged groups were categorised and recognised. In 1885, the Madras government made a provision of special facilities for students of depressed classes and in 1921 it also took steps for higher representation of non-Brahmins in government services. In 1927 all the communities were divided into five categories and separate quotas were set aside for each.

In 1918, the Maharaja of Mysore appointed a Committee, which recommended special facilities in education and recruitment in state services to the backward communities. In 1930, the Bombay government provided special facilities for three categories of backward classes, namely, depressed classes, aboriginal and hill tribes and other backward classes.

With the Montague-Chelmsford Reforms of 1919 separate representation at the all-India level were provided to the Scheduled Castes. The Government of India Act, 1935 provided political representation to the 'depressed classes' in the Federal Legislative and Provincial Assemblies. Under the Criminal Tribes Act, 1871 the backward classes were given special protection. In 1936, the term 'depressed classes' was replaced by the term 'Scheduled Castes' to denote the untouchables and lists of these castes were notified in a schedule for various provinces.

For the first time in 1943, 8.33 per cent vacancies in government services were reserved for the Scheduled Castes. In June 1946 this was raised to 12.5 per cent to correspond with their proportion in the population. A scheme of post-matric scholarships was prepared for Scheduled Castes.

Besides being socially and economically backward, the disadvantaged sections were denied access to education as well. The history of education in India has been linked to religion. Both Hindus and Buddhists had set up formal educational institutions. The Muslim rulers followed on the footsteps and established educational institutions for imparting religious and secular instruction. With the advent of colonialism. Indian Society witnessed a mushrooming of educational institutions, imparting secular education. A majority of them were set up by various caste associations and religious organisations.

The Indian social reformers and the political leaders recognized the disadvantages of certain sections even before independence and worked for their amelioration and emphasized the need for a homogeneous and egalitarian society. The thinking is verywell reflected in the phrase 'unity in diversity'. Education was considered as a tool which would bind the nation having separate cultural , political and social identities into one single group. The special position of certain social groups and the Constitutional provisions for preferential treatment depicts this concern of the Indian political leaders. The aim of the social provisions enshrined in the Constitution is to ensure that no handicap prevents their meaningful participation in the new emerging social order and that the state helps to secure economic and political justice to its citizens.

Following are some of the provisions made to the minorities in India enjoy the guarantees of equality before the law under Article 14 of the Indian Constitution. Article 15 prohibits discrimination on grounds of religion, race, caste, sex or place of birth while Article 16 assures equality of opportunity in matters of public employment. Article 29 guarantees the rights of minorities to conserve their language, script and culture while Article 30 gives the right to establish and administer educational institutions of their choice whether based on religion or language. These include provision of adequate facilities for instruction in the mother tongue at the primary stage. However, it directs that these institutions will not impart religious instruction if they receive state funds.

In the Constitution, the Scheduled Castes are also recognised on the basis of untouchability, and are guaranteed protection and special support. Article 17 decrees the abolition of untouchability. As per Article 46, 'the state shall promote with special care the education and economic interests of the weaker sections of the people and in particular of the Scheduled Castes'. Article 29 (2) prohibits discrimination in government aided educational institutions. However, Article 15 (4) states that notwithstanding Articles 15 and 29 (2), the State may make special provisions for the advancement of the Scheduled Castes. Along with these provisions, the most important provision is the reservation of seats (15 per cent for the Scheduled Castes) in all educational institutions and jobs in organisations run by the central and state governments in accordance with their proportion in the population. This preferential treatment or compensatory/positive discrimination has come to be known as the policy of reservations and has raised controversies recently.

Besides the above stated provisions, the Constitution also provides for the appointment of a Commissioner/Special Officer for the Scheduled Castes and enjoins upon them the responsibility to submit periodic reports.

Thus independent India explicitly and clearly adopted the principle of promoting social equality through preferential treatment or positive discrimination. A series of constitutionally guaranteed provisions and rights, including the rights to social justice, formal equality and integration are formulated. These rights are also protected by statutory provisions.

To summarize, post-independent India tried its level best to bring Higher Education.

India's struggle for Independence, has clearly showed its leaders the immediate need for growth and expansion of education. After Independence in the August 1947 the idea of a literate India was clearly reflected in the Indian Constitution and there was a rapid expansion of the educational system. By 1988-89 there were 144 universities and twenty-five autonomous institutions which were granted the status of universities. The number of colleges was approximately 6,912. The total number of teachers in higher education was 54,973. The total enrollment in higher education in 1988-89 was estimated to be 3,947,922.

Thus, there has been rapid expansion in terms of enrolment number of institutions, growth rate and others, since 1951. And it is undoubted that vast sections of population have received benefit. However, survey shows that these benefits have not been equally distributed across different states and within states, between rural and urban areas, between men and women, between the Scheduled Castes and non-Scheduled Castes. In other words, the problems of uneven access, quantity, quality and relevance remain.

All the educational policies have focussed on the fulfilment of Constitutional guarantees and the identification of groups who are eligible for the state-sponsored benefits. The major emphasis has been on the provision of reservations in higher education and its implementation in order to remove disparities between the Scheduled Castes and non-Scheduled Castes. According to NPE 1986 there are four dimensions where equalisation is required, namely, rural male, rural female, urban male and urban female. It pleads for enriched environment in the tribal regions.

The 28th Report of the Commissioner for Scheduled Castes notes that,

> the most notable achievement in absolute terms has been in the field of education. The level of literacy amongst the Scheduled Castes has risen by about 45.7 per cent during the decade 1971-81 even though the gap in their literacy levels and that of the rest has also increased during the same period. The enrolment of children has also been rising at all levels. The proportion of Scheduled Castes children amongst those enrolled at the primary level more or less corresponds to their relative strength in the population. But there is a sharp decline at the middle level, particularly among the Scheduled Castes, after which, however, their position stabilises. In 1986-87 there were more than a million post-matric scholars belonging to the Scheduled Castes.

As on 30 September 1988, a total of 2,79,720 Scheduled Caste students had enrolled in higher education constituting 7.3 per cent of total enrolment respectively.

Though the number of students increased during the period of 1978-79 to 1988-89, their participation in some faculties is too small and insignificant even in 1988-89 see Table 1.1. These faculties having lower enrolment are medicine (7,170 Scheduled Castes). Another striking thing to note is that the enrolment of Scheduled Caste students has decreased from 7,553 in 1978-79 to 7,170 in 1988-89 in medical courses.

The data available for 1988-89 further indicates that the proportion of Scheduled Caste students to total enrolment in different faculties varies from 9.87 in subjects like arts and humanities to 2.91 per cent in research Table 1.2.

TABLE 1.1
ENROLLMENT OF SCHEDULED CASTE STUDENTS IN HIGHER EDUCATION (BY FACULTY—ALL LEVELS)

Subject	*Total*		*Scheduled Caste*	
	1978-79	*1988-89*	*1978-79*	*1988-89*
Arts	1,073,032	1,653,652	105,518	163,212
Science	483,359	739,752	20,711	42,215
Commerce	485,921	1,035,650	23,074	47,150
Education	67,799	91,017	3,918	6,979
Medicine	105,594	142,125	7,553	7,170
Engg./Arch	104,720	205,282	5,538	12,080
Agriculture Vet. Sc.	39,711	NA	2,379	NA
Law	168,402	NA	10,570	NA
Others	14,911	NA	797	NA
Research (All Faculties)	NA	31,386	NA	914
Total	2,558,360	3,836,976	180,058	279,720

Sources: (1) Twenty-eighth Report of the Commissioner for the Scheduled Castes and Scheduled Tribes, 1986-87, Government of India, New Delhi.
(2) Selected Educational Statistics: 1988-89, Studies in Educational Statistics No. 1, 1990, Ministry of Human Resource Development, Department of Education; Planning and Monitoring Statistics Division, Government of India, New Delhi, 1990, Table VIII, pp. 36—45.

TABLE 1.2
PROPORTION OF SCHEDULED CASTE STUDENTS IN HIGHER EDUCATION IN NUMBERS AND PERCENTAGE BY FACULTY (ALL LEVELS) 1988-89

	Scheduled Caste		*Scheduled Caste*	
	All Students	*Percentage*	*Women*	*Percentage*
Arts, Humanities and Social Sciences	163,212	9.87	35,294	2.13
Science	42,215	5.71	11,914	1.61
Commerce	47,150	4.55	6,915	0.67
Teacher's Training	6,979	7.67	2,196	2.41
Medicine	7,170	8.94	2,529	3.15
Engg./Arch.	12,080	5.88	797	0.39
Research (All Faculties)	914	2.91	182	0.60

Sources: Selected Education Statistics: 1988-89, Studies in Educational Statistics, No. 1, 1990, Ministry of Human Resource Development, Department of Education; Planning, Monitoring and Statistics Division, Government of India, New Delhi, 1990, Table VIII, pp. 36—45.

In the survey on higher education conducted by the National Commission on Teachers it was found that the increase in enrolment of Scheduled Caste students has generally been in general courses. Their proportion in professional education decreased progressively from 32.63 per cent in 1964-65 to 28.50 in 1970-71, 25.38 in 1975-76 and 17.08 in 1977-78.

Also, the proportion of Scheduled Caste students in professional courses at the postgraduate level is almost half when compared to their corresponding proportion in undergraduate level courses.

Let us now compare the enrolment of men and women within these disadvantaged groups. The enrolment of Scheduled Caste women is quite good that of all the representation of Scheduled Caste women is 0.60 per cent in research programmes. In engineering/arachitecture courses Scheduled Caste women have 0.39 per cent of the total enrolment.

Further study shows that the difference in the enrolment numbers of women in two categories, the non-Scheduled Caste and the Scheduled Caste women is very significant. For instance, there are 6,46,709 non-Scheduled Caste women in arts as compared to 35,294 from the scheduled caste category. Their numbers in medicine are 26,261 and 2,520 respectively. In general, the women of other classes are better represented in terms of numbers. Medicine is an exception where the Scheduled Caste women have the highest percentage 35.2 per cent. Though the women from weaker sections are beginning to enter commerce faculties but in the engineering and related subjects. The numbers are pathetic.

Regionwise also, there is a wide variety in terms of enrolment. As regards the Scheduled Castes, their enrolment varies from 10.4 each in Gujarat and Madhya Pradesh and 13.4 in Maharashtra to 4.2 per cent in Kerala. Similarly in the professional courses of engineering and technology and architecture the highest proportion of Scheduled Castes (between 9—10 per cent each) is in Orissa, Madhya Pradesh and Andhra Pradesh and the lowest (4.3) is in Karnataka.

Discussions of the preceeding pages clearly show that suffer from more acute handicaps. The discussion about women has to be understood in the context of class which cross-cuts gender while in the case of these weaker groups, caste overlaps with class. When class overlaps with gender and caste as in the case of Scheduled Caste then they suffer maximum disparities.

Another instance of the policy of providing equal educational opportunity to weaker sections of the society, is the access of these sections to very exclusive and prestigious institutions. For instance, certain numbers of seats are reserved for the weaker sections in the Indian Institutes of Technology, the most prestigious institutions imparting education and training in engineering and related subjects. Inspite of this the data shows a grim picture. The data on the percentage of registrants in 1979-80 and 1982-83 show that the increase in the Scheduled Caste (from 3.2 to 4.3 per cent). Moreover, the number (and therefore the percentage of seats filled) has also decreased in all the IITs during 1974-1984). For instance, the percentage of seats filled in Kharagpur was ninety-six in 1974 and forty in 1984, while it was 41 and 35 per cent respectively in Delhi IIT.

Accessing Higher Education: Problems, Issues, Strategies

The above discussion clearly shows that Scheduled Castes are most disadvantaged in higher education in our society on the basis of their enrolment.

The worst part is that this situation exists in spite of the Constitutional provisions in favour of the Scheduled Castes. It has been reiterated in every official document such as the reports of the various committees and commissions since independence that education is the major instrument of social mobility and advancement for the weaker sections. The latest policy document, namely, National Policy on Education 1986, devotes a section to the role of education in promoting equality. It underscores the twin dimensions of education, namely, removal of disparities and equalisation of educational opportunities.

The primary reason for educational backwardness relate mainly to school education. The single most common important factor at the school level is the absence of schools in areas which are accessible to girls, Muslims, Scheduled Castes.

Hence, the new policies aim at widespread establishment of schools which are approachable to the dalits. Other common problems are: poverty and lack of economic resources in the family; the utility of every extra hand for earning to make two ends meet—while young boys earn, the girls may either work or look after the household and younger siblings and release the mothers for work; lack of schooling facilities or provision of poor quality facilities (such as dilapidated buildings); single teacher schools; lack of financial help and incentives at an early age; discriminatory treatment and attitudes of teachers; indifference of parents; irrelevance of education for immediate 'productive' function instead of a deferred productive function.

The major stumbling block in the education growth of Scheduled Castes is the lack of scholarships and financial incentives at the elementary stage. Therefore, in spite of statutory quota and availability of scholarships the fellowships in higher education, very few students make it to the colleges and universities. In other words, only the well-off among them enter the portals of higher education.

This is perpetuated by the nexus between caste, adult franchise and political mobilisation, on the one hand, and reservations, on the other. Over the years it has become a tool in hands of the political elite to gain evermore concessions for their castes under the rubric of other Backward Classes. As a result, the proportion of reservations has increased to more than two-thirds in some states (for instance, seventy-eight in Madhya Pradesh, seventy-one in Andhra Pradesh, sixty-eight each in Karnataka and Tamil Nadu). The northern states are still saved from such large reservation quotas.

As a measure to curb this trend of grabbing the benefits by these minorities, the Report of the Commissioner, has underscored the need to dereserve to sift out those Scheduled Castes who have procured benefits of reservations.

Though access to higher education was limited to the minorities due to the above mentioned reasons, the same factors also pushed them into the formal educational system.

The focus towards Scheduled Caste is towards the softer non-professional subjects. Weak educational base and training as well as lack of proper counselling affect the Scheduled Castes. This is linked to poor performance at schools, of the Scheduled

Castes. Due to this special coaching facilities are provided to Scheduled Castes. Accessing professional higher education and expanding career options is, therefore, a major problem. Restructuring the educational programme to eliminate class and gender bias, review of educational content to remove traditional stereotypes; opening new subject choices and career options, are some of the important strategies which need to be implemented in the higher education of Scheduled Castes.

Till now, the problem was tackled in mainly 2 ways by giving incentives and by training and counselling. The first one provide scholarships, text books and book banks, while the other way was through encouragement to opt for science subjects through counselling, training of decision makers and administrators from among them, research-oriented women's studies centres in universities and colleges, part-time post-doctoral research associateships age relaxation for Scheduled Castes.

After the above discussion we find that the impact of various strategies is difficult to assess. The assessment of those for Scheduled Castes has been provided in the annual reports of respective Commissioners but they do not give much hope. The reservations have also been very effective. The lacunae at the implementation stage are far too many and the situation far too complex. Overall it shows that there has been a large gap between policy and practice especially because the policy pronouncements flow from the central government while the implementation is left to the state governments. This gap apart from unrealistic planning, reflects a schism in ideal and reality which, in turn, explains the extent and nature of educational disadvantage in India. There is a need for micro planning and decentralisation.

Conclusion

There are certain references which we can deduce from the above discussion. Firstly the situation relating to higher education is very complex. Secondly, that the understanding of the multi-ethnic, multi-cultural reality that is India, is imperative to understand in the growth and expansion of higher education in India. Thirdly, that the interlinkages between social context and education are inevitable but are difference in levels vary. No single factor influences the distribution of educational opportunities. Intra-group differences are as crucial as are the inter-group differences. The study of Intra-group variations show that certain sub-castes, do better than others, depending on factor like their occupation and place of residence (rural vs. urban). Therefore the benefits of higher education have remained confined to the well-off sections of all social groups under discussion.

Further gender bias seems to have a strong hold in the group, be it Scheduled Caste or non-Scheduled Castes. In comparison to the general population, the Scheduled Castes are worse off and their women are the most backward in education. The cumulative effect of the configuration of competing disadvantages has to be eliminated/reduced/constrained before women from this group can participate equally.

Various educational policy and programmes have failed to understand the hierarchical and fragmented socail reality. They are also unable to perceive the disjunction among the sectoral aims of education. For instance, how can education inculcate a parochial identity based on religion along with a pan-India identity? It is not easy to reconcile the aspirations of different groups in a culturally heterogeneous society especially when resources are scarce. It is also problematic to 'mainstream' one section, provide social justice to another and equality to those who are members of all sections of society.

The vision to envisage education as expanding its agenda into new directions to include the disadvantaged sections of society, is based on the premise that educational effort will be supplemental to an emerging egalitarian structure which, unfortunately, has not materialized in Indian Society as yet. At the same times there is disjunction between the conception of equality as social equality versus individual equality. The dilemma is how to use individual merit to promote social equality and to resolve this dilemma between the claims of equality versus merit?

The debate over the competing claims of merit or achievement vs. ascriptive criteria and of hierarchy and equality are unlikely to be resolved unless the inherent contradictions and the disjunctions are eliminated through a process restructuring of the educational discourse and construction of a new approach to educational policy which takes an integrated view of the ground reality and encompasses the multiple goals of social justice, equality and mainstreaming in an overall framework.

Technical Education for Dalits

The development of education in the Indian sub-continent has a most significant phenomenon. With a long history of its back, its development had been through numerous phases. Whereas efforts were made to promote social sciences, it was also seen that technical education should also receive its due share.

Time and again, emphasis has been laid on technical education for dalits. The idea was that they should be given technical knowledge so that they could be part and parcel of our society.

Indeed the usefulness of technical education is unlimited. It produces good engineers and technocrats in civil, mechanical, marine, electrical, aeronautical as well as computer. But it so happens that it has become difficult for dalits to compete with caste-students whose family background is otherwise far better. Enquiry committees on prominent technical institutions revealed that the dalit students failed to get admission in the engineering colleges for having low gradation in the marks sheets.

So to encourage and promote their interest in the academic world a flexible quota ranging from 25 per cent onward has been fixed in several regional and All India Technical Institutions.

This step in deep has given them much academic boost. It has been felt that this kind of decision out various levels has proved academically viable and numerous students have been awarded Bachelors and Masters Degrees in various subjects of engineering. After coming out of these institutions, these dalit students both boys and girls are doing fairly well.

Indeed without the policy of reservation, these dalit students could not have the proper road to academic attainmetns. And once they get admission, a sense of responsibility dawns on them, and day in and day out, they work hard to build up their career by burning the mid night oil. Thus these young dalit engineers and technocrats have shown their skill and valuable experience in various walks of life. It may be defence of India or a private concern or a government department, their work has been greatly applanded and appreciated.

This policy of the State Governments and all India level has brought about much valuable dividends and it is hoped that in a few years, we would be able to cash a better crop which would be more useful at national and international level.

Two

The Background

From the ancient period of the Aryans society, in India the scheduled castes have been the last on the hierarchical ladder of the society's structure. They have suffered from distinct social, economic and educational disabilities. It was mainly due to the Caste system which has a unique position in Hindu Society. It influences people's selection of a profession and many other aspects of life in India. A man's dignity as a human being is also related to the caste to which he belongs. The British regime also favoured the socially advanced classes which got the advantage of education and employment opportunities. But, gradually, times changed and awakening came. And hence, after the attainment of Independence in the year 1947 the Constituent Assembly provided statutory safeguards in the Constitution for the people of the scheduled castes, the scheduled tribes and other depressed classes by defining them as socially and educationally backward classes. Article 46 of the Indian Constitution lays down a directive principle of the state policy which provides that "The state shall promote with special care the educational and economic interests of the people and, in particular, of the scheduled castes and scheduled tribes, and shall protect them from social injustices and all forms of exploitation."

India's National Policy on Education (1986) stated "In our national perception education is essentially for all. This is fundamental to our all-round development, material and spiritual" (A special consideration was made for the education of the scheduled castes). The 20-Point programme of Rajeev Gandhi's Government (No. 11) has also reiterated the importance of "Justice to scheduled castes and scheduled tribes". This programme mainly focussed on the constitutional provisions and laws for the scheduled castes and scheduled tribes. The programme also mentioned that to improve educational standards of the scheduled castes special coaching programmes need to be organized. Besides, this, the constitutional provisions and laws for the scheduled castes provide for ensuring possession of land alotted to scheduled caste people, revitalising land allotment programmes, organising and assisting special coaching programmes to improve educational standards, eradicating scavenging and rehabilitating the "Safai Karmacharis" through special programmes, providing better direction and adquate funds for the special component programmes, pursuing programmes for the fuller integration of scheduled castes with the rest of the society and ensuring the rehabilitation of tribals displaced from their habitat. The primary aim of these efforts to eradicate the hindrances that stood in the way of the uplift and education of the scheduled caste people. Guided by constitutional provisions the Government of India has made provisions for scholarships, reservation of seats in educational institutions and relaxation of age for admission to various courses and relaxation of qualifications for different types of government services. Inspite of all these it was felt that these efforts are not sufficient to achieve the objectives, as is reflected in the following statement made in the Challenge of Education: A Poilicy Perspective.

> One very significant issue which has to be discussed here pertains to the specifically oriented educational efforts essential for reducing those disabilities of scheduled caste and scheduled tribe students which cannot be removed only by the provision for reservation. It has to be recognized that the majority of scheduled castes and scheduled tribes students are first generation learners and these as well as others who may not fall in this category, often, suffer from the after effects of early childhood malnutrition, a sense of social inadequacy, unsuitable work habits and lack of self-confidence in realizing their academic potentials. These factors, often, militate against their adjustment in the streams of higher education and professional work and their performance vis-a-vis others in a competitive situation. This leads to psychological strain and tension vis-a-vis their peers. While some programmes for enhancing the competence of scheduled caste and scheduled tribe students

have been initiated, appropriate steps are still to be taken to ensure that young people from these backgrounds get fully integrated with the others.

Since 1951, government has extended special support and facilities to the scheduled caste students in the field of education. But, all sections of the scheduled caste population have not been in a position to utilize them. Consequently this has led to the formation of a two classes among the scheduled castes (i) one who have utilized these facilities, and (ii) others who have not utilized these facilities. Those scheduled castes are developing and growing educationally who have utilized facilities provided by the Government of India. In fact their children are subsequent generation learners. On the other hand those who have failed to utilize these facilities and are still suffering from many kinds of socio-economic barriers. Presently, there seem to be clear-cut two groups of students even in the population of the scheduled caste people—one consisting of the students whose parents have already received the benefit of special facilities and Government's support with the result that they are educated and are well settled in jobs of various kinds. But obvious, the children of these scheduled castes have more facilities, a richer home environment and better parental guidance available in the family while on the other hand are the children of those scheduled castes who are not educated and not employed in jobs as they have not utilized the facilities made available by the Government. These two groups of school-going children have been called as subsequent generation learners and first generation learners respectively. Presently upliftment of the first generation learners in the focus of the socieity, specially so that they may also be able to derive complete advantage from the schemes started by the Government of India. In the present context understanding of the first generation learners of the scheduled castes seems to be of great importance as the emphasis in our new Education Policy of 1986, so far education is concerned, is on equalization of scheduled castes and scheduled tribes population with the non-scheduled caste population at all stages and levels of education. For achieving this objective of equalization, special attention has to be paid to this group of first generation learners of the scheduled castes. Probably, they are facing some kind of problems related to their school learning and school adjustment. If this is found to be true, efforts need to be made to eradicate them in order to lift them up to the level of other children, subsequent generation learners of the scheduled castes and the children of the non-scheduled castes. Due to this it is imperative to understand more fully the first generation learner children of the scheduled castes, with regard to their academic achievement, adjustment, studies etc., in comparison to the subsequent learners of the scheduled castes, and this is what this study is all about.

In this study 'scheduled castes means those castes which have been included in the list prepared and published by the Government of India'. According to this list scheduled castes have been classified into 66 categories. These are given in the Table 1.1, Appendix-A.

The scheduled castes, accordingly means such castes races or tribes parts or groups within such castes, races or tribes as are deemed under Article 341 to be the scheduled castes for the purpose of the Constitution of India. A list of the scheduled castes had been published under the President's Order of 1950 after consultation with the Government of the States. According to caste system, scheduled castes mean the castes put into a scheduled. Each caste is sub-divided into many sub-castes which in their turn form a hierarchy within the caste. Thus, the whole caste system is very intricate structure which consists of a large number of social groups or innumerable strata each indicative of a certain status and function. Each sub-caste is generally an endogamous group spread over one linguistic region.

According to a census, almost every sixth Indian belongs to the scheduled castes. If we add the scheduled tribes, every fourth or fifth Indian falls in this category. The combined population of scheduled castes and scheduled tribes of India is larger than the population of England or Germany and equal to the population of Japan or Indonesia. The scheduled castes of U.P. form a major group. An account of dominant scheduled castes and their distributions as given by Uttar Pradesh Government is presented in Table 1 which shows position of different castes among the scheduled castes. This special tabulation and distribution of the scheduled castes was presented with a view to reserve seats in the legislative assembly for the election since 1951, and till a period of ten years. In order to upgrade the social and economic conditions of these castes, the U.P. Government has liberalised the policy of providing scholarships to the children of these castes up to class X. Earlier they were granted to those students whose guardians earned up to Rs. 500 per month. Under the new policy the income limit has been raised to Rs. 750 per month. For the students studying in higher secondary classes this limit has been raised up to Rs. 1,500 from Rs. 750. Medical and Engineering students will get other aids in addition to the scholarship.

TABLE 2.1
MAJOR DISTRIBUTION OF SCHEDULED CASTES IN UTTAR PRADESH

Sl. No.	*Dominant Scheduled Castes*	*Population*	*Percentage of Scheduled Castes*
1.	The Chamar, Dhusia Jhusia and Jatava	86,93,327	56.5
2.	The Pasi and Tarmali	22,21,131	14.4
3.	The Dhobi	8,88,446	5.8
4.	The Kori	7,10,241	4.6
5.	The Balmikie	5,58,389	3.06
6.	The Shilpkar	4,65,870	3.03
7.	The Khutik	3,05,326	2.0
8.	The Dhanuk	2,24,055	1.5

The Planning Commission, through National Five Year Plans, had also been proposing schemes for the development of scheduled castes children. To narrow down the wide disparities that exist with regard to their socio-economic and educational conditions extra facilities and special schemes are provided to them.

Scheduled Castes have remained socially, economically and educationally backward since the begining of caste startification of Indian society. The constitutional safeguards are provided to the scheduled castes by article 15 and 16 which say that "the state shall not discriminate against any citizen on grounds only of religion, race, caste, sex, place of birth or any of them and there shall be equality of opportunity for all citizens in matters of public employment of appointment to any office under the State.

The Indian Constitution and the Scheduled Castes

Mahatma Gandhi and Dr. B.R. Ambedkar were the greatest champions of the Scheduled Castes, Scheduled Tribes and Other weaker sections of the society. It was due to their effrts that many commissions and committees were appointed to study the conditions of the backward classes. In January 1979 a Commission headed by B.P. Mandal was formed. The first Backward Class Panel of Kaka Kalelkar had identified 2399 communities as backward, the criterion for determining backwardness being the caste.

To promote the educational and economic interests of the Scheduled Castes and Scheduled Tribes 15 per cent and 7.5 per cent seats are reserved for Scheduled Castes and Scheduled Tribes respectively in educational institutions. Such reservations are permitted under Article 15(4) and Article 46 of the Constitution for admission to educational institutions. The Article 16(4) and 335 as well as Article 46 provide for the reservation of seats for the Scheduled Castes and Scheduled Tribes in all kinds of services.

The Union Government has advised the States to adopt economic backwardness as the criterion in place of the caste. The criterion for backwardness adopted by the Mandal Commission though not known publicly, states that 50 per cent of the population falls under the backward category. The interests of this half of the population are to be safeguarded.

Section 4 of Article 15 states "Nothing in this Article shall prevent the states from making any provisions for the advancement of any socially and educationally backward classes of citizens of the scheduled castes and the scheduled tribes." Many articles of the Constitution mentions special provision for the promotion of educational and economic interests of the Scheduled Castes and Scheduled Tribes and Other weaker sections of the society.

Towards Equalisation of Educational Opportunities

One of the primary objectives of education as per our constitution is to provide equal opportunities for all. Inequalities of educational opportunities arise from the following conditions:

1. Non-existence of schools.
2. Poverty.

3. High standards of schools.
4. Home environment of a family.
5. Wide disparity of educational development between the backward classes and the advanced classes.

Society as a whole, needs to identify factors which tend to create various forms of inequalities among people and to adopt measures either to eliminate them altogether or at least reduce them to the minimum. For the early solution of the problem of educational expansion for backward classes the Education Commission has recommended continuance of existing programmes. Their case was examined in detail by the Commission on Scheduled Castes and Scheduled Tribes under the Chairmanship of U.N. Dhebar. Various Seminars are organised by Planning Commission, NCERT and others to discuss ways and means of equalising educational opportunities for Scheduled Castes and Scheduled Tribes.

Origin of the Problem

Since the beginning of caste startification of Indian society, the Scheduled Castes were considered untouchables and were discarded majority in every sphere of life. Though, times are changing but the first generation learners are still suffering from social, economic and educational problems. The problems of their being educationally backward is a comprehensive one involving many factors. It is the most baffling national problem posing a great challenge to the leaders, rulers and the people of India. There seems to be a great need to improve the first generation learners in all respects. But, education being the key factor, this has to be given priority. The intensity of the efforts depend on the extent of the disparity which exists between the first generation learners and the subsequent generation learners of the Scheduled Castes. The present study had its origin in this background.

A major difference between the first generation and subsequent generation learners of the scheduled castes is the level of learning. But, level of learning or academic achievement may be found related to several personality traits such as adjustment, attitudes and many others problems currently being faced by these children. If children make good adjustments and have desirable attitudes and are free from problems, they may achieve more. All these personality traits are considered as variable by us and hence, are selected for study and comparison among the scheduled caste first generation and subsequent generation learners. If it is found that there are significant differences on these variables between them, suggestion can be made to minimize them so that first generation learners are brought, in course of time, at par with the subsequent generation learners of the Scheduled Caste children.

Research on education of the Scheduled Caste children had been emphasized by the NCERT in 1975. In 1982-83 it issued a list of 30 specific problems related to the education of the Scheduled Castes and Scheduled Tribes. The *Challenge of Education* and the *National Policy on Education*, 1986 have, for the first time, hinted upon the importance and study of the first generation learners. *The Programme of Action* of the *National Policy of Education* has, in every chapter, referred to the need for taking special care of the education of the scheduled caste children. On page 3 while saying the ECCE (early child care and child education) in the first instance, will be directed to the most under-privileged groups enumerated under the para adds that "special attention should be given to Scheduled Castes and Scheduled Tribes in all these defined categories".

It is not only the Scheduled Caste first generation learners, rather the first generation learners in all castes from a special group and pose a problem for the leaders of the nation. This fact was well recognised by the authors of the *Challenge of Education* who said "It seems essential to juxtapose the scenerio of the education system against the internal dynamics of a society in which 64 per cent of the population is illiterate and large percentage of students are first generation learners. It is necessary that greater attention should be paid to the education and development of the first generation learners irrespective of the caste. Without that it will not be possible to move the country into the twenty-first century on two legs. It is, primarily the first generation learners who turn out to be the largest number of drop-outs at all leves of education, contributing, thus a large share to wastage in education. This may be more so in case of the first generation learners of the Scheduled Castes. The all India literacy rate of Scheduled Castes is 21.38 as against 41.20 of non-Scheduled Castes. The literacy rate of Scheduled Caste women is 10.93 as against 29.43 of the non-scheduled castes women. These are the figures which have been quoted in the *Programme of Action*. The problem may be more serious in case of the Scheduled Caste first generation learners boys and girls both. This situation calls for systematic efforts on studying and helping the scheduled caste first generation learners.

The new Education Policy (1986) focuses on the equalization of the scheduled caste with the non-Scheduled Caste population at all stages and levels of education. It is stated that cent per cent enrolment of Scheduled Caste children in the age group of 6—11 (classes I-V) ensuring their retention leading to satisfactory completion of the primary stage of education has to be achieved by 1990. It further says that at least 75 per cent of the children in the group 11—14 (classes VI—VIII) will have to be enrolled and retained in school leading to satisfactory completion of class VIII. Various steps have been suggested to be taken in the *Programme of Action* to achieve these objectives. But, before the objectives can be met a thorough study needs to be undertaken. Thus the origin of the present study.

The study aims at bringing out the differences, if at all they exist, on achievement, attitudes, adjustment and problems between the first and subsequent generation learners of the Scheduled Castes. The study hypothesizes that for several reasons differences on these variables between them do exist, since the first generation learners are going to the schools for the first time in the history of their parenthood and since their home-environment lacks oriented to education of the children, also that they may be facing many kinds of problems in the schools leading to their poor achievement, poor adjustment and less positive attitudes. The study is based on comparative nature. The first generation learners of the Scheduled Castes have been compared in the foregoing respects with the subsequent generation learners of the scheduled castes.

Significance of the Problem

The Natural Policy on Education says that there should be "constant micro planning and verification to ensure that the enrolment, retention and successful completion of courses by SC

(Scheduled Caste) students do not fall at any stage, and provision of remedial courses to improve their prospects for further education and employment." Hence it is imperative to pay special attention to the problems of the first generation learners of the Scheduled Castes. Since these children are comparatively more disadvantaged as pointed out earlier, the changes of their dropping out at any stage of education are more in comparison to the subsequent generation learners. Similarly risk of non-completion of courses is also comparatively higher in their case. Hence, specific efforts need to be made. But, before the specific efforts to be made are identified, it is necessary to point out the areas or aspects of life in which such efforts have got to be made. The present study is an attempt in this direction which seeks to study the problems which are being faced by the first generation learners of the scheduled castes. Having known these, efforts can be made to remove or, at least, minimize them. More relevant "remedial courses to improve their prospects for further education and employment" as incorporated in the foregoing *National Policy on Education* recommendation may be designed in view of the results obtained through this study. Further this study is significant also as it draws attention of the planners more specifically towards the more disadvantaged group of students, the first generation learners within the scheduled castes. Presently very little is known about this group of students. This study will verify and bring out the facts and it will yield useful information about the first generation learners of the scheduled castes.

Rationale and Assumptions

It is believed that the first generation learners are different in many respects from the subsequent generation learners. The home environment of these two groups of children are different. In case of the subsequent generation learners there are brothers and sisters and also the parents who have already received education. These educated parents encourage their children to make greater efforts to achieve more with regard to their education. They are, for the same reason, more willing to provide them with needed facilities for better learning. Besides, they give better guidance to their children. The home environment, in this way, of the subsequent generation learners is more stimulating and facilitating. All this affects the academic achievement and the attitudes of these children.

In contrast to the subsequent generation learners, the first generation learners come to the school without any orientation. They are, comparatively, less ready and less prepared for the school life. They do not get any guidance from any one at home nor there is any stimulation for them to learn as their parents do not realize the significane of education. All this adversely affects their academic achievement and attitudes towards life and society.

But all these are assumptions, the actual position is not known. The present research is based on these assumptions which provide its rationale. It is only at the end of this study that we will get a clear picture of the status. This study will prove or disprove whether these two groups of learners are really different from one another with regard to the variables contained in the study. It is hypothesized that they are different. The study will test this hypothesis.

Objectives of the Study

The following are the main objectives of the study under consideration—

(1) To study and compare the enrolment of the first and subsequent generation learners belonging to the scheduled caste population.

(2) To study and compare the achievement of the first and subsequent generation learners.

(3) To study and compare the adjustment of the first and subsequent generation learners.

(4) To study and compare the attitudes of the first and subsequent generation learners towards—

(a) school.

(b) teachers.

(c) education.

(d) society.

(5) To study and compare the first and subsequent generation learners in terms of problems related to—

(a) health and physical development.

(b) finances, living conditions and employment.
(c) social and recreational activities.
(d) social psychological relations.
(e) personal psychological relations.
(f) courtship, sex and marriage.
(g) home and faculty.
(h) morals and religion.
(i) adjustment to school work.
(j) future, vocational and educational.
(k) curriculum and teaching procedure.

Further, the study also aims at comparing areawise least prominent and most prominent problems of first generation as well as the subsequent/second generation learners, along with.

Analysing the most acute problems faced by both generations of learners.

Hypotheses

The following nullhypotheses were formulated for proving the above mentioned objectives:

(1) There is no significant difference between the enrolment of the first and subsequent generation learners belonging to the scheduled caste population.

(2) There is no significant difference between the achievement of the first and subsequent generation learners.

(3) There is no significant difference between the adjustment of first and subsequent generation learners.

(4) There is no significant differences between the first and subsequent generation learners with respect to their attitudes towards.

(a) school.
(b) teachers.
(c) education.
(d) society.

(5) There is no significant difference between the first and subsequent generation learners in terms of facing the problems related to—

(a) health and physical development.

(b) finances, living conditions and employment.
(c) social and recreational activities.
(d) social psychological relations.
(e) personal psychological relations.
(f) courtship, sex and marriage.
(g) home and faculty.
(h) morals and religion.
(i) adjustment to school work.
(j) the future, vocational and educational.
(k) curriculum and teaching procedure.

Further, it is hypothesised that there is no significant difference between the areawise least prominent and most prominent problems of first and subsequent generation learners.

Also, there is no significant difference between the most acute problems of first and subsequent generation learners.

Definition of Technical Terms

The term used in this study have the following meanings:

1. First Generation Learners

It refers to those students who of their family members have come for education for the first time in schools and their parents have no formal education at all or they have studied up to only class X. The justification of fixing the limit of being uneducated up to class X is that on the basis of his personal experience the researcher feels that even the X class level education does not have any impact on the quality of life and home environment of these families. Even having studied up to class X these people live the same kind of life as they were living. Significant difference between them and the uneducated is not found. Hence, the first generation learners have been defined as the learners belonging to the parents who are uneducated or have received education only up to class X.

2. Subsequent Generation Learners

These are learners who belong to the parents who have received formal education up to any class beyond class X. The subsequent generation include second, third, fourth generations etc.

Delimitations

The study has been confined to the higher secondary schools of Meerut region. The first and subsequent generation male learners of scheduled castes drawn from class XI of randomly selected higher secondary schools of Meerut region form the basis of this research.

Three

Issues and Problems

In order to bring equality in the society and uplift the condition of the downtrodden sections of the society, post independent era saw the mushrooming of educational institutions. The school system is supposed to offer the Harijan children an opportunity, on equal terms with others, to gain knowledge and enable them to rise in social and economic status. It allows them to learn and develop together with other caste children, to see experiment and imbibe values of higher communities. Hence in short education can be conceived as a great human experiment in community interaction, a process of continuous learning. An act of dropping out, therefore, signifies an end of a potentially fruitful adventure. School drop-out implies withdrawal from a system which was very essential for one's development. So, the dilemma is why do Harijan children drop-out from the school if the latter has the potency to deliver them goods? This chapter attempts to answer this question. It is observed that generally the explanations offered in reply to this question are too simplistic or evasive in nature with an implicit assumption that the actual situation does not admit of any complexities. This is really not the case, as we shall soon see.

To find out the reasons underlying the school drop-out of Harijan children, a direct question was asked to the parents. "Why did your child stop going to school?"

The most significant variable relataing to drop-out is the incapacity of parents to meet the educational needs of the child (86 out of 300 cases). These include expenses for books, exercise notebooks, slates, pencils, etc. On enquiry it was found that though the Harijan Welfare Office in the region or the offices of the Basic education were supplying. These items at irregular intervals but these supplies were limited to a few schools and were inadequate in quantity Harijans parents were, therefore, justified in claiming that no assistance or help was rendered to their children in this respect (all the 300 parents replied that they received no help whatsoever from educational authorities). Further, due to their poor financial conditions, they were unable to spend money towards these items. As long as they could, they helped the child as per their capacity. Continued lack of books and other materials was stated to the cause of child's declining involvement in school studies. Teachers on their part kept on pushing the students. The child was, in most cases, helpless, and so were his parents. This resulted in school drop-out of some Harijan children.

Another variable contributing to school drop-out was the direct monetary liability on the part of Harijan parents. Nearly 80 per cent of Harijan parents were required to pay between Rs. 2 and Rs. 15 per annum towards fees. Besides, there were various ways through which school used to extract money from these parents. There was game fees charged to the students which was reportedly nominal, i.e., 10 N.P. per month per student. Other channels of money collection were popularly known as 'Pass Karahi'; 'Centre Kharcha' and 'TC Expenses'. It was reported by some parents that the school children had to pay 'pass Karahi' ranging between Rs. 2 to Rs. 10 which meant payments for promoting the child to higher class. Some parents even alleged that when this payment was not made their children were detained in the same class by declaring them as failure cases. Another monetary diability was the contribution realized from children of Class V appearing for the Zilla Parishad Examination. As this examination was usually conducted at the Junior High School premises, it was reported that payments ranging between Rs. 1 and Rs. 3 were collected from children to defray hospitality expenses on the examiners. Some-times even tea and other hospitality arrangements during the inspection of a school were made reportedly at the cost of the school children. Finally, 'TC Expenses' relates to the payment demanded from the parents by the teaching staff to issue transfer certificate (TC) to the outgoing child. As the inter-school mobility was not very high in the villages, this demand affected primarily those students who desired to join the Senior Basic School after passing the examination in Class V.

TABLE 3.1
DROP-OUT CAUSES INDICATED BY HARIJAN/PARENTS

Reasons	*Rasra Block (N=150)*	*Ranipur Block (N=150)*	*Total (N=350)*	*%*
1. Domestic work including the care of infants	25	45	70	(11.1)
2. For placing the child in gainful employment	26	21	47	(7.5)
3. Sickness/death in the family	25	36	61	(9.8)
4. Prolonged illness of the child	8	8	16	(2.6)
5. Distance, location and other incongenial aspects of the school	11	18	29	(4.7)
6. Ill-treatment/Unhelpful attitude of school teachers	40	31	71	(11.4)
7. Ill-treatment/dominance by schoolmates	12	12	24	(3.9)
8. Unproductive school experiences, bad habits and traits in the child	14	22	36	(5.8)
9. Lack of monetary support books, copies and other educational aids	48	38	86	(13.8)
10. Lack of interest in studies	37	40	77	(12.4)
11. Inability to meet physical needs of the child	30	30	60	(9.6)
12. Cultural factors: beliefs and values	14	27	41	(6.6)
13. Any others	3	2	5	(0.8)
Total No. of responses	293	330	623	(100.0)

When the teachers were asked to justify the above allegations, most of them tried hard to defend their school against such charges and at the same time pointed an accusing finger at other schools. A few teachers, however, confessed that their meagre salary did not permit them to spend lavishly on those conducting school inspection or examination. Whatever may be the reason the fact that the poor parents are being coerced to make gratifications is in itself a most disturbing phenomenon. Children of other castes were equally affected such unofficial demands, but as some of their parents were probably better off, they could to comply with these. Till the times these Harijan parents, poor as they were could continue to pay to the school teachers they did. But as their financial helplessness grew, they were constrained to drop the child from the school. Nearly one out of every three Harijan children was out of school due to lack of financial support and educational material (86 responses against Item-ix.)

Third crucial reason for drop-out seems to be the lack of child's interest in studies (77 out of 300 cases). Harijan parents felt that as the child grew, he became less and less punctual in his school attendance and home assignments, grew careless about examination and felt more secure at home than in school. He also showed signs of mental irritation whenever asked about school activities. Some parents bemoaned that their child stubbornly refuse to study at home. Few parents could not understand the reasons behind such a sweeping change in the child from a peaceful and well-adjusted to a disturbed and aggressive behaviour. While in other cases, the teachers themselves reported the undesirable developments in the child to the parents and advised them to pay closer attention. Sometimes, the parents went to the school to request the teacher to help the child in studies. But efforts such as these proved infructuous.

Another heart rending factor was the unhelpful attitude of the teachers and illtreatment meted out by them to the Harijan students that forced as many as 71 of them (23 per cent of the total sample) to leave the school. Articulate parents gave a brief account of how their children were ill-treated, harassed and discriminated against. Parents majority complained about the incidence of beating. A Harijan child was beaten up by the teachers for various reasons, may be simply because the child could not fulfil their demands of 'Fee; 'Pass Karahi'; Dodnations '(Chanda)', etc. In some cases, the Harijan child got scared of his teacher after witnessing the way the other children were handled in the class-room. Teacher's unhelpful attitude was further reflected in Scholding, use of indecent language and wilful neglect of the child's interest. In some cases, it was also reported that the Harijan child was asked to sit away from other students. More humiliating were the assignments were the child was made to carry the teacher's persosnal luggage, doing their domestic work and even rendering free help in agricultural operations. At some places, it was reported that Harijan child were not permitted to touch the blackboard, chalk or a book handled by the teacher. It is an irony that teachers whose hands should shape the personality of the child in a constructive manner, should practice such subtle forms of exploitation and harassment.

"But this happened and happens every day." said one Harijan parent agitatedly waving his hands in the air. He added:

> "When my child casually reported these happenings in the school. I hardly believed them to be true. I went to school and saw with my own eyes that Harijan children were accommodated in the rearmost part of the class, huddled together on a shabby may (which later I came to know was brought by one of the Harijan boys from home). All of these children (they were nine in total), were looking alike in dress and in everything. Why this separation? Why this isolation on caste lines? How my child and other children can learn better human values in this atmosphere? He will grow and die in this world in the same degraded manner as I would and as my parents and grand-parents did. Education is force and nothing less than a force in the hands of these fanatic teachers".

He was fuming with anger when he ended his arguments. This emotional outcome, was not his prejudice or bias? It was the truth. There are innumerable instance which affirm to this. And hence, the parents saw no justification in coercing the child to remain in the school.

Along with this discriminatory, debasing treatment meted out by the teachers was the highhanded, arrogant and aggressive attitudes of school mates mostly belonging to the upper castes. Though the distance are rare but it is not an ignorable matter. A probing on this fact revealed that in some schools, the most pampered and arrogant caste-Hindu children harassed the Harijan child, particularly the new entrants, by pinching, hitting or pulling his hair. They used to hid his slate, book and pencil. At the height of mischief, they used to break the slate or tear the book to pieces. In a few cases, the children of upper castes used to form a group (should we call it a gang) of their own and beat the Harijan child, bruise his arm or leg. Nearly one out of every 10 Harijan children was a victim of such boyish banditry. It is difficult to make a categorical statement for want of sufficient evidence, but we cannot dismiss this alarming fact.

The fourth factor for dropout is the pressure of domestic work on these tiny shoulders. It causes of the drop-out of 70 children (23 per cent of the total). The job of taking care of infants and younger siblings poses a barrier in his way of schooling. Since both the parents went out for work and remained out for uncertain hours, it fell to the lot of the unfortunate schooling child to wind up his studies in order to take care of the young ones. Condition of the Harijan girls was more indefensible as they were the first to be asked to leave the school should there arise any need or eventuality at home.

It would not be inappropriate to mention that some parents, albeit a minority, were selfish and short-sighted. They used the services of the child for domestic work and were guided by the immediate, short range benefits. Cattle-grazing, sheep care, grass cutting and collection of firewood were the jobs some parents trusted on their children at the expense of their school education. Inspite of the fact that most of them were living from hand-to-mouth yet they strived hard to educate their children. Being agricultural labourers, they were unable to take the little child along with them. Nor could they leave him alone, unprotected. Similarly poverty taught them to be cautions of their little possessions like a pair of bullocks, sheep or goat which needed shepherding. In dearth of alternative arrangements they were constrained to use the services of the school-going child and the final outcome was that they dropped out.

Another reason cited by 47 families who discontinued the education of their child was in order to employ him in some gainful activity. He was placed into such minor occupations as assistance to farm labourers in sowing, weeding operations, selling firewood or basketware in the market, shepherding for others, domestic work for land-owning castes, casual work at brick kilns etc. Economic hardships compelled these parents to employ gainfully their younger sons and even daughters. At least one out of every 10 Harijan children in our study was condemned to adulthood tasks before his teens. (See Item ii).

Though, it is difficult to establish a direct relationship between living conditions and the status of health, yet through various research studies one can easily guess that they could not have been healthy. Poor working and living conditions, financial worries including heavy indebtedness, recurring drought situation entailing hunger and starvation; all contributed negatively to their physical well-being. Added to these were, in some cases atleast, the practice of liquor consumption, narcotic addiction etc. In most cases, illness in the family is a perpetual phenomenon. Due to lack of money many of them could not avail proper medical help and they tried indigenous herbal medicines which often failed to bring early relief. Unfortunately of the prolonged illness is of the bread-winner, then the entire household economy goes out of gear which further aggravats their plight. Schooling of the boys as well as girls, came to a halt as soon as the head of the family was bedridden. They were required to attend to the ailing and, luck and age permitting, compensate for the loss of earnings through engagements in gainful activity. Dath of the householder was a devastating mishap which directly affected the schooling of the child. Every two out of 10 Harijan children were forced to leave their studies on the grounds of illness or death in the family. In 16 cases, prolonged illness of the school-going child led to his drop-out.

Another significant reason responsible for drop-out relates to the inability of Harijan parents to comply with the physical needs and requirements of the child. Regular breakfast or meals depending upon the school timings, a pair of clothes and possibly a pair of shoes. Though the last item, i.e., footwear was often dispensed with and the Harijan children were accustomed to attend school bare-footed. The most important issue was clothing. When at home, the children could carry on in rags. But in school, when other children came dressed in better clothes, it was indeed humiliating for the poor Harijan child to sit alongwith them. Though at some places, particularly in the Harijan special schools, even the rags could scrape through; but then there were the teachers who scolded the child for inadequate clothing and sent them back home for proper dress. Besides for some families their economic level kept them restrained from providing certain level of cleanliness and hygiene in respect of their children. This was a source of great mental conflict within the child. Though some parents did realised these but either they were too helpless or insensitive to resolve these. Their helplessness is reflected in some cases where the families lived on borrowed food or cooked herbs and plants. Sending a child to school in the morning was often-times a nightmare because the child had nothing to eat at home. Being hungry or half-starved he was hardly able to concentrate on his studies in the class-room. Though many school teachers and they are aware of this pitiable state and they did extend a helping hand sometime, but they could not afford to feed them regularly. Some Harijan parents, on the other hand, felt compelled to ignore the physical needs of their child on account of severe poverty conditions. The end result was the discontinuation of the child's studies which could not claim a priority in a situation where hunger and starvation reigned supreme.

In some cases, cultural values and beliefs among the Harijan community came in the way of the proper growth of children. There was a near-unanimity among them on one issue that higher education to girls of their community was totally undesirable. There was strong feeling that the girls should not be educated beyond junior basic level. One of the parents remarked—

> "What she must know in the school is how to read and write. After all she is somebody else's property. She will be married and sent away from this house. If she knows by way of schooling enough to write a letter to us from her new home, that will be the sufficient achievement on her part."

According to them, higher education would lead their daughter astray, expose them to upper-caste fads and fashions, enthuse them to mix freely with children of the opposite sex and would ultimately bring a bad name to their family and community. Hence, there was no need to teach them beyond junior basic level.

There are families were superstitions and beliefs of the elders were responsible for the stoppage of the boy's education. Recurring fever of the school-going child, any major accident inflicting physical injuries and such other events were interpreted as bad omens resulting from his schooling. They put in thus: "Education is harmful to him. It will not do him any good. Even his father had suffered a similar accident in his school days and had left his studies." Such credulous, superstitious ideas haunted many a Harijan families. Though it is sounds unbelievable, yet these beliefs and values disrupted the educational career of 41 cases in our sample. (See Item xii).

The study shows that in 36 cases, unproductive school experiences were accountable for their drop-out. The Harijan parents explained that the child was learning bad habits, acquiring undesirable behaviour patterns like telling balatant lies, absconding from school and playing truants, gambling and smoking. Finding no other solution, they thought it wise to stop his schooling altogether. In a few cases, there were complaints from the school techers about the Harijan child being violent in the class-room quarrelling with others and coming to blows with them.

Though relatively unimportant, factors such as distance and location of school also contributed to drop-out incidence in a few cases. Apart from physical distance which was two to three kms. there were other obstacles like absence of walkable pathways, existence of nullah or drain-pits or similar obstacles which made the schoolward movement of a very young child extremely difficult and sometimes insecure. Due to lack of concrete roads, during rainy days it was a feat to reach school. Added to this was the appalling physical condition of school buildings, their roots leaking from all sides. Drenched and shivering, the children used to face all these odds. Some school buildings had developed deep cracks in the walls and the supporting pillars were thoroughly unsafe. Heavy rains could easily bring down the entire edifice within moments. Some parents were very much worried about their children's schooling in such ramshackle buildings. Briefly therefore, nearly one out of every 10 Harijan children dropped out of the school because of its distance and location which made its accessibility less easy and also because of its dilapidated physical structure.

The forgoing analysis gives a very clear picture that the problem of school drop-out among Harijan children is a complex one, having multiple reason behind it. We need to integrate the items to draw a coherent picture. There are 13 items in Table 3.1 detailing drop-out reasons. If we exclude the last category of a miscellaneous nature, we get 618 responses against 12 items by 295 respondents i.e., Harijan parents. We may classify these responses into five broad categories as shown in Table 3.2.

TABLE 3.2
MAJOR CATEGORIES OF DROP-OUT CAUSES
(based on the responses of Harijan Parents)

Major Category	*Inclusive Sub-categories and Responses*	*Total No. of Responses*	*%*
1. Poverty and Economic Hardships	(a) Child's gainful employment (47) (b) Lack of basic educational equipments (86) (c) Non-provision of physical Needs (60) (d) Engagement in domestic work (70)	263	42.6
2. School and School-related Factors	(e) Distance, location etc. (29) (f) Behaviour of the school teachers (71) (g) Behaviour of school-mates (24) (h) Unproductive school impact (36)	160	25.9
3. Domestic Existencies	(i) Sickness/death in family (61) (j) Prolonged illness of the child (16)	77	12.5
4. Individual Deficiency	(k) Lack of interest in studies (77)	77	12.5
5. Cultural Factors	(l) Beliefs, values, community reactions (41)	41	6.5
	Grand Total of Responses	618	100.0

After categoriatism, it clearly depicts that the first and foremost reason for the drop-out incidence among the Harijan children is the poverty and its associated factors. The next contributory force to reckon with is the existing inadequacies of the school system. Punitive, unhelpful and impersonal attitudes of the school teachers as well as the aggressive and unfriendly acts of the school inmates seem to have created a credibility gap between the Harijan students and the school system. The last three categories are independent in themselves and relate to family or personal issues like sickness and death, declining interest of the child in studies and superstitious beliefs and values against the continuity of school education. On the whole, the economic backwardness of the Harijan families and unreceptive and discourteous atmosphere in the school constitute two major barriers that lie at the root of the drop-out problem among Harijan children.

Information available in peer literature relates to the drop-out reasons as indicated by the children themselves. Lack of educational equipments such as books, copies etc., is a most dominating reasons. Around one-fourth of the children (45 out of 198) have stated that they left studies due to lack of interest. It is worth nothing that the children, unlike their parents, made no reference to cultural factors. On the whole, there is substantial agreement between children, i.e., drop-out cases and their parents, regarding the causes that underlie the drop-out incidence.

TABLE 3.3
DROP-OUT CAUSES INDICATED BY CHILDREN

Reasons	*Rasra Block (N=108)*	*Ranipur Block (N=90)*	*Total (N=198)*	*%*
1. Domestic work including infant care	10	18	28	(9.9)
2. For placement in some gainful employment	9	6	15	(5.3)
3. Sickness/death in the family	21	22	43	(15.3)
4. Prolonged illness of the child	1	3	4	(1.4)
5. Distance, location and other incongenial aspects of the school	6	4	10	(3.6)
6. Ill-treatment/unhelpful attitude of school teachers or school mates	26	18	44	(15.7)
7. Lack of books, copies and uniform	49	22	71	(25.3)
8. Lack of interest in studies	21	24	45	(16.0)
9. Physical needs not met	7	4	11	(3.9)
10. Any others	3	7	10	(3.6)
Total No. of responses	153	128	281	(100.0)

Note: *Out of 300 drop-out children, 102 children (42 from Rasra and 60 from Ranipur Block) were not available/suitable, for interviews. Responses shown in this table are from 198 cases only.

Further for the reasons behind school drop-outs are summarised into broad categories as shown in Table 3.4 Analysis of response categories reveals boldly that economic hardships seem to play a major role in augmenting drop-out situation. In this case, questions were mainly asked to village leaders, teachers and also few parents.

TABLE 3.4
A COMPOSITE DATA IN RESPECT OF MAJOR CATEGORIES OF DROP-OUT CAUSES INDICATED BY HARIJAN PARENTS*, VILLAGE LEADERS AND SCHOOL TEACHERS

*Major Categories***	*Response Percentage*		
	Parents (N=300)	*Village Leaders (N=60)*	*School Teachers (N=40)*
1. Poverty and Economic hardships	47.8	51.6	53.6
2. School and School related factors	13.7	12.0	0.7
3. Domestic Exigencies	0.9	0.5	8.4
4. Individual Deficiencies	24.0	24.4	16.1
5. Cultural Community Factors	13.6	11.5	11.2
Total No. of Responses	(766) 100%	(209) 100%	(143) 100%

* Responses recorded in this table refer to a different question relating to general causes contributing to drop-out problem in a Harijan Community.

** Categories listed here include, in addition to sub-categories (See Table 3.2) mentioned earlier, the following:

Item I : Lack of facilities at home.
Item IV : Parental apathy and indifference.
Item V : Unhealthy caste and community influences

Next in importance is the factor that relates to the apathy and indifference of Harijan parents and child's lack of interest in studies. This time, even the parents came out strongly against the negataive attitudes of the Harijan family towards education of their children. But this time too, the school teachers maintained a discreet silence over the inadequacies and deficiencies of the school system (only 0.7 per cent response). But, village leaders and parents spared no words in criticising the inhibitive and discriminatory aspects of the school system. Almost with similar intensity, both these groups have condemned the unhealthy, crippling and regressive caste and community practices like early marriage, liquor addiction, family feuds over petty issues, indebtedness on account of avoidable expenditure on rituals and ceremonies and blind faith in superstitions. They united believed that all these add up negatively to the educational interests of the Harijan Child. Domestic exigencies, which accounted for the drop-out of at least one-fourth of our sample (77 cases), find the rearmost place in the general assessment of the parents, teachers and village leaders.

To summarise the factors responsible for drop-out among the Harijan children covered in our study, we may say that economic backwardness of Harijans is a dominant factor underlying drop-out incidence. Other factors of varying significance can be listed as incongenial school atmosphere, domestic exigencies, lack of involvement on the part of parents as well as children in the school activities, and unfavourable influences of caste and community.

Either singularly or in combination these factors seems to generate an atmosphere in which the schooling of the Harijan child becomes an impossibility. Apathy of parents or vagrancy of the child may be the result of poverty conditions. Whatever may be the reasons, dropping out of the school is a complex event encompassing various tends and hence at becomes imperative to study the situation in its totality. Evidence that we have here amply proves the point.

To begin we need to have information on the age at which the Harijan child drops-out from the school system so as to formulate suitable preventive programmes for such cases. Data obtained in this respect (Table 3.5) suggests that over 72 per cent of drop-out cases (217 out of 300) were below 10 years of age. Of these 217 cases, 100 belonged to the age-group 9-10 years. In other words, one out of every three drop-outs (100 out of 300) belonged to the age group 9-10 years. The mean age for the total sample stood at 9.3 years (9.4 years for Rastra block and 9.2 years for Ranipur block). This indicates that the moment the children from the Harijan community reach a critical age of 8-9, or 10 years they withdrawn from the school system. At this stage and onwards the usefulness of children for domestic help and outside activities becomes intensive. The Harijan families begin to view their children as working assets.

TABLE 3.5
AGE FACTOR IN HARIJAN CHILDREN DROP-OUT RATE SCHOOL SYSTEM

Drop-out age	*Rasra Block*	*Ranipur Block*	*Total*	*(%)*
Below 7 years	15	9	24	(8.0)
7 years	27	12	39	(13.0)
8 years	21	33	54	(18.0)
9 years	22	29	51	(17.0)
10 years	18	31	49	(16.3)
11 years	15	19	34	(11.3)
12 years	14	9	23	(7.6)
13 years and above	18	8	26	(8.8)
Total	150	150	300	(100.0)

The second aspect which draws our attention is, who in the family generally takes the decision about dropping the child from the school?" The study reveals a very unexpected (Table 3.6). Though, in nearly seven out of ten cases (69.3 per cent) the decision is reported to have been taken by the father, mother or other elderly person from the child's family, it is really strange that in 30 per cent of cases, the drop-out child himself was the sole arbiter. In other words, three out of every 10 children who dropped out of the school, were doing so on their own initiative.

TABLE 3.6
QUESTION : WHO IN YOUR FAMILY TOOK THE DECISION OF NOT SENDING YOUR CHILD TO SCHOOL? (PARENT'S VERSION)

Response	*Rasra Block*	*Ranipur Block*	*Total*	*(%)*
Fataher	60	69	129	(43.0)
Mother	35	32	67	(22.3)
Child himself	45	47	92	(30.7)
Other Rélatives	10	2	12	(4.0)
Total	150	150	300	(100.0)

Here two explanations can be cited for this unusual trend. First, the parents who were questioned might have shifted the onus of drop-out decision to their child to conveniently escape from the moral responsibility alongwith presenting a positive picture about themselves. A second explanation could be that the answers are representative of a true position: parents were unwilling or indecided but the child was bent upon withdrawing from the school system. The second explanation seems more plausible. The Harijan child did not find school education a very rewarding experience due to ill-treatment of teachers, unsociability of schoolmates and some incongenial aspects of school itself. Besides, due to the lack of books copies and other educational aids along with physical needs made him loose his interest in studies. These are sharp indications of child's disenchantment with school education. It may, therefore, be possible that the child himself opted against the continuity of school studies. Broadly speaking, however, the child's parents have taken decision in dropping him out of the school.

TABLE 3.7
MAIN CONSIDERATION BEHIND THE DROP-OUT DECISION

	Main Consideration	*No. of Respondents*	
1.	Relief from school expenses	80	(38.5)
2.	Physical help from the child	39	(18.7)
3.	Cultural factors, beliefs and attitudes	32	(15.4)
4.	Unhealthy school experiences	30	(14.4)
5.	Economic help from the child	27	(13.0)
	Total	208*	(100.0)

* This figure excludes 92 cases wherein the respondents have treated the child as a decision-maker in drop-out situation.

The next question which follows is "Why did the Harijan parents decide to drop their child from school? What was the main consideration behind their decision?" Answers to this question are recorded in Table 3.7. Only 208 respondents have replied to the question as they were directly responsible for taking a decision in the matter. Once again the data highlights the economic inapacity of Harijan families as the main reason behind the decision of parents. We notice that in nearly 50 per cent of cases (146 out of 300), the Harijan parents decided to keep the child at home due to their financial inability, pressure of domestic work (which frequently emanantes from economic hardships) and urgency of some economic support through the employment of the child. Further 62 out of 208 respondents (over 20 per cent in a total sample of 300) decided to stop school education of their child on account of their beliefs and attitudes (which favoured less education) and unpleasant school experiences of the child. By and large, the economic helplessness, traditional thinking and unproductive school experiences were the three main considerations which acted as a driving force in drop-out situations.

Moreover, we need to find out whether the issue of school drop-out of a Harijan child was treated as an insignificant, trivial matter in his family or whether it created some flutter, some argumentative situation with exchange of views between father and mother or between parents and other elderly persons in the family. In 135 families drop-out became a serious subject of discussion the issue was debated in these families, some members supporting and some opposing the decision on various considerations. It is indicative of awareness and involvement of family members in the child's educational prospects. It is, however, unfortunate that in 55 per cent of cases, there was no such anxiety or curiosity and the matter was allowed to be settled unilaterally by the father, mother or a child. In these cases evidently no concern was shown about the future of the child's education.

To a question: Further when the parents were asked "What did you/your wife feel when your child stopped going to school? 196 fathers, and 204 mothers were reported to have felt unhappy. Surprisingly, a somewhat different position obtains in regard to a drop-out child. According to the parents estimate, nearly 40 per cent of children felt 'happy', over 10 per cent indifferent and around 50 per cent 'unhappy' immediately after drop-out. Table 3.8 suggests this though, at is sad to see that quite a large number drop-out cases had no sense of grief over the loss of school education but we have no justification in this regard. Were they too young and immature to evaluate their prospects? Did they consider a drop-out an opportunity to escape from frustrating and humiliating experiences in school and at home? We have no answers to these questions. Anyhow, it would be sufficient to conclude that a majority of parents and a fairly large number of drop-outs themselves felt anguished and disheartened for the loss following the discontinuation of school studies.

TABLE 3.8
FEELINGS OF THE FATHER, MOTHER AND THE CHILD (DROP-OUT CAUSE) IMMEDIATELY AFTER DROP-OUT: (PARENT'S VERSION)

What did they feel?	*Father (%)*	*Mother (%)*	*Drop-out Child (%)*
Happy	51 (18.9)	66 (22.8)	116 (38.7)
Indifferent	22 (8.2)	19 (6.6)	37 (12.3)
Unhappy	196 (72.9)	204 (70.6)	147 (49.0)
Total	269 (100.0)	289 (100.0)	300 (100.0)

If we consider feelings of happiness, indifference and unhappiness as equivalent to positive, neutral and negative reactions to drop-out incidence, we obtain the following position Table 3.9. In all, 266 families in whose cases the reactions of all the three persons were available, are distributed within two polar limits of extremely positive and extremely negative reactions towards drop-out situation. The result is clear enough to suggst that 62 families had a positive or favourable reaction; only 9 families seemed to be neutral while a large majority of 195 families (nearly two-third of the total sample) were negatively disposed towards drop-out. This further demonstrates that a large number of families have acted under compulsions of social and economic reality, disregarding their personal preferences and volitions.

Though the data shows that a large number of children were happy over loss of education but it was parents who gave the insight of the child's mind. When asked whether the child (drop-out case) had expressed his or her desire to rejoin the studies, 115 have answered the questions in the affirmative. In other words, as per parents reports, at least one out of every three drop-out children, had openly expressed their willingness to restart their chequered career. Of these cases, 62 belonged to Rasra while 53 came from Ranipur Block. When a somewhat similar question was asked to children themselves, 72 out of 198 cases (36 per cent) gave positive replies stating that they strongly felt like continuing their studies.

This data directly points towards the child's positive frame of mind in respect of school education. A further proof in this respect can be had from the school teachers. When asked, "Do you think that the Harijan children who dropped out were unwilling to discontinue their studies?", 23 out of 40 school teachers replied 'most of them', four 'some of them' and 13 a 'few of them'. In short majority opined that most of the drop-out cases were in fact favourably disposed towards school education and had shown willingness for its continuation.

TABLE 3.9

FAMILY REACTIONS TO DROP-OUT INCIDENCE*

Reaction Range	*No. of Families*	*(%)*
Extremely positive	34	(12.8)
Moderately	28	(10.5)
Average/Neutral	9	(3.4)
Moderately Negative	104	(39.1)
Extremely Negative	91	(34.2)
Total	266	(100.0)

*Note: It is a composite table based on the addition of scores assigned to each scale. Family includes father, mother and a drop-out case and the reaction evaluation is made by the respondent. For father and mother, a three point scale was given assigning scores as follows:
Happy-1; Indifferent-2; Unhappy-3.
For the child, a five-point scale was designed with the following values:
Very Happy-1; Happy-2; Indifferent-3; Unhappy-4; Very Unhappy-5.
The computation was done in two stages. First, the child's score was recorded by assigning values as under:
1 to 1 or 2; 2 to 3; and 3 to 4 or 5.
Secondly, individual scores of father, mother and child were combined with a result that the total score range varied between 3 and 9.

As we see that unwillingness to discontinue the studies was the general view, we feel that forceful discontinuation must have led to some behavioural changes among them. This assumption proved to be correct in 86 cases (nearly 29 per cent) where these children showed specific changes in their behaviour and dealings with their parents and other family members, friends and neighbours. Their behaviour immediately after drop-out alternated between over aggressiveness and passive, negative withdrawal. As one sensitive mother put it thus:

> "The day after his schooling was discontinued; he started cold-shouldering every one in the family, including his youngest sister. He roamed about in the neighbourhood listlessly and ignored even our slightest demand. He used to come home twice in the day, to take afternoon meals and spent the night. If I tried to penetrate into his thoughts, he would burst out saying all were keen to tie him to the job on land and waste his life toiling. The temperament of his lasted for over six months."

Similar instances were quoted by countless others. Weeping and crying; shrinking work; spoiling food and breakiang dishes; abusing parents; avoiding friends and relatives; these and many other behavioural postures were adopted by those children who felt seriously jolted by their separation from school.

Taking the child out of school not only affects the child but it may affect the surrounding as well. For instance, the drop-out of an elder brother might affect the studies of the younger one. It might set an unhealthy precedent in the neighbourhood. If a drop-out child is sociable and has leadership qualities, other neighbouring children who felt secure and happy under his stewardship might soon follow his example. Hence, it is necessary to view the drop-out problem in a wider perspective. It may lead to undesirable trends in the family or locality. Our survey shows that Table 3.10 in 15 per cent of cases, the parents have reported that the other school-going children in the family were badly affected, either they stepped into his shoes or started comparing their own performance with that of a drop-out case. This led to quarrels and unpleasant feelings within the family. Another 17 per cent of cases talked about its impact over the locality. Not only the children in the neighbourhood started neglecting their studies but some even stopped going to school. Out of every 10 drop out cases, three were reported to be positively responsible for adverse effects on school going children in the family or locality. These facts got to prove that impact of drop outs registers itself not only in the family but it also extends to the neighbourhood.

The drop-out child himself suffered a great deal in terms of learning on account of the absence of any opportunity to practise things at home. While at school, he could read and write, try his hand in drawing and painting, take part in cultural activities and above all play and make friends. Further, dropping out means putting a stop at his mental growth. It reduced the chances of developing his facilities in other spheres of life. The data in this respect gives clear indications of how the drop-out affected the Harijan children Table 3.11. When in school, the child besides reading and writing used to partaicipate in cultural actives, games, painting etc. but it was observed that out of 300 drop-out cases, over 57 per cent (172 cases) of them totally abandoned the practice of any of the school subjects or activities. In other words, only four out of ten drop out children practised at home what they earlier learnt at school. Even under the category of 'games and sports' there were only 16 children reported to be actively associated with it. In the pre-drop-out situation, the corresponding figure was as high as 159. A comparatively higher number of children seemed to be retaining their knowledge of reading and writing. In general, the children who dropped out seemed to show little concern or involvement in the subjects or activities they learnt at school and which stimulated them most during the school career. Hence, it was not only a loss to drop-out cases but to the school administration as well which invested so much resources for imparting education.

TABLE 3.10
QUESTION: DID THE SCHOOL DROP-OUT OF YOUR CHILD ADVERSELY AFFECT THE EDUCATION OF OTHER CHILD/ CHILDREN OF YOUR FAMILYY IN THE LOCALITY?

Reply	*No. of Respondents*	*(%)*
Yes, family children affected	45	(15.0)
Yes, locality children affected	51	(17.0)
No none was affected	204	(68.0)
Total	300	(100.0)

Now, it is time to study the daily routing of a drop-out child? In which activities, did the drop-out child engage himself/herself? Data in this matter is recorded in Table 3.12. For purposes of comparison, the routine activities performed by the Harijan child during his school career has also been recorded. To begin, the number of children who extended their help in household and other activities has increased from 256 to 289 after their drop-out.

Secondly, the number of children in some activities for which data has not changed. The activities are: cattle or sheep grazing, household work, looking after younger children etc. After drop-out, more children have taken to farm labour, grass cutting, help in the studies of younger children and independent jobs for earning a livelihood and income supplementation.

TABLE 3.11
SHOWING DROP-OUT IMPACT ON LEARNING AREAS/ SUBJECTS

Subjects/Areas	*No. of children practising subjects at home after drop-out*	*Percentage of children practising the subjects after drop-out (%)*
Reading and writing	77 (199)	38.7
Games and Sports	16 (159)	10.1
Arithmetic/Minor calculations	28 (110)	25.5
Singing/dancing etc.	12 (49)	24.5
Drawing/Painting	4 (45)	8.9
Clay modelling/Craft/Needle work	12 (42)	28.6

(Figures in bracket refer to No. of children reported to have learnt the subjects/activities during the course of schooling).

TABLE 3.12
TYPE OF WORK IN WHICH THE HARIJAN CHILD WAS ENGAGED BEFORE AND AFTER DROP-OUT

Type of work activity	*After drop-out (1) (N=289)*	*Before drop-out (2) (N-256)*	*Proportionate difference of (1) over (2) (%)*
Farm labour	55	34	+ 61.8
Grass cutting	137	108	+ 26.9
Household work	141	144	– 2.1
Cattle/sheep grazing	124	126	– 1.6
Looking after younger children	65	67	– 3.0
Help in the studies of younger children	22	16	+ 37.5
Independent employment	83	16	+ 418.8
Any others	29	14	+ 107.7

(Out of 300 children, eight in Rasra and three in Ranipur block did not offer any help in domestic or other duties after drop-out. Corresponding figures in pre-drop-out situation was 44).

On the whole, after drop-out, there has been a five fold increase in the number of children doing independent jobs like domestic work in the families of higher castes, work at construction sites, casual jobs like house repairing or processing at brick kilns, pulling of cycle-rickshaw etc. Inspite of their young age and less physical strength, they were engaged in independent employment. This finding testifies to the earlier evidence that the economic backwardness of Harijan families contributed a major hurdle in the advancement of their younger generation.

If we recall at this juncture the parent's statement on drop-out reasons Table 3.1 we would notice that only in 47 cases, did gainful employment constitute one of the factors in drop-out incidence. Later, we were told that only in 27 cases, the employment of the child remained a primary consideration Table 3.6. In practice however, this number rose to 83 and this signifies the shaky status of the Harijan's household economy. It also is one of the reasons of the child getting drifted away once he left school. Domestic work which claimed only a part of their time during school career, could now absorb most of their time. Whether willing or not, the Harijan child had to support the household in its daily chores, inside or outside. It was, as it were their inescapable destiny.

When in school, the Harijan child treated his school as a major interest and played at best a supportive role in the household affairs. But after drop-out, he had to devote the major part of his time and energy in attending to domestic assignments as well as to unsteady and strenuous outside employment which had poor remunerative prospects Table 3.13.

TABLE 3.13
TIME DEVOTED BY CHILDREN TO HOUSEHOLD WORK AND OTHER ACTIVITIES EVERY DAY

Daily work labours	*After Drop-out (1)*	*%*	*Before Drop-out (2)*	*%*
1-2 hours	9	(3.1)	154	(60.1)
3-4 hours	27	(9.3)	66	(25.8)
5-6 hours	83	(28.7)	34	(13.3)
7-8 hours	94	(32.5)	1	(0.4)
8 hours or more	76	(26.4)	1	(0.4)
	289	(100.0)	256	(100.0)

Upon the termination of contacts with the school, their potentialities remain undeveloped, talents unexplored and their energy diffused over the wide assortment of uncreative jobs. Circumstances such as these are bound to stultify the achievement motive of the individual. How else can we explain the data in Table 3.14, showing the level of aspirations of 198 drop-out cases.

Out of every 10 drop-out children, one child seemed to have no aspiration at all, about three preferred to remain as housewives (all girls' cases) or farm labourers. One wanted factory work or some skilled job, three wanted to join any unskilled job category and the remaining two wanted to start their business or take up white-collar occupations like teaching, clerical assistance etc. In short, because of an extremely low level of education, their aspirations have got become limited.

Even those students who had left studies few years back, when interviewed expressed their desire to rejoin their studies out of 198 children , 65 replied in affirmative. In other words, three out of every 10 drop-out children were conscious even at this stage (with a comfortable gap of two to eight years) that they should educate themselves to improve their social and economic position. But it was sad to find that economic compulsions would not permit most of them to devote sufficient time for educational activities, even if they succeeded in re-admitting themselves.

TABLE 3.14

POSITIONS ASPIRED TO BY THE DROP-OUT CASES: NO. OF CHILDREN

Aspirational Level	*Rasra Block*	*Ranipur Block*	*Total (%)*
No aspiration at all	18	5	23 (11.0)
Housewife	19	8	27 (13.6)
Farm Labourer	2	27	29 (14.6)
Factory worker	6	3	9 (4.6)
Businessman trader	12	11	23 (11.6)
Unskilled worker	39	27	66 (33.3)
Skilled worker	4	7	11 (5.6)
White-collar occupation	8	2	10 (5.1)
Total	108	90	198 (100.0)

Before we conclude let's have a glimpse as the present activities (till the time of this study) performed by these drop-out students. We learn from parents that out of 300 children, 133 are unemployed but assisting them in household work and other activities while 167 are working independently in some gainful activities. In other words, nearly 56 per cent of the drop-out cases are providing much needed economic support to their families. If we look into the present age of the drop-out cases, we find that out of 300 children, 62 per cent of them (186 cases) are below 14 years of age while remaining 38 per cent are above that age, only seven cases are above 21 years. Since the employed children constitute 56 per cent of our total sample, it is more than obvious that quite a large number of children below 14 years of age are in independent employment, a fact that underscores the economic contributions of child labour in the Harijan families. Harijan households are constrained to use child-power for livelihood.

The discussions in preceding pages have thrown sufficient light on the causes underlying drop-out and the consequences emanating from it. Still, we are uncertain about the influence of child's family in his educational efforts, the extent of contribution of school system and the nature of community influences. Each of these has some part to play in the child's itinerary from home to school and back. Further research is needed to decipher the educational problems of the Harijan children.

Four

Universal Elementary Education

The Constitution of our country envisages universal provision of educational facilities for both primary and upper primary stages. There is a directive under Article 45 to provide free and compulsory education to all children up to the age of 14. The Article 45 presupposes that the goal of achieving universalisation of elementary education should have been realized by 1960, i.e., within ten years of the commencement of the Constitution. This target date was first revised to 1970, then to 1976, 1988 and 1990. The National Policy on Education (NPE), 1986 fixed revised time targets for achieving universal and free education up to the age of 11 by 1990 and up to the age of 14 by 1995. This was further revised by NPE 1992, which proposed to provide free and compulsory education of satisfactory quality to all children up to 14 years of age before AD 2000. The new thrust in elementary education emphasizes three aspects: (1) universal access and enrolment; (2) universal retention of children up to 14 years of age, and (3) a substantial improvement in the quality of education to enable children to achieve essential level of learning.

To achieve this mammoth task of universal education in the age group 6-14 it has been divided into three phases which is to be pursued simultaneously.

(1) The first phase is universal provision of schools which aims at establishing primary and middle schools within easy access from the home of every child.

(2) The second phase is that of universal enrolment. Although the total enrolment in elementary education in the country has increased from 223 lakh in classes I-VIII in 1950-51 to around 905 lakh in 1970-80, 1,360.3 lakh in 1991-92, and 1,570.5 lakh in 1995-96 but achievement has not been so commendable when we

compare it with the figures of population growth on the one hand and by the problem of drop-outs and stagnation on the other. The proportion of enrolment of Scheduled Caste and Scheduled Tribe children is very less as compared to their population, except in case of primary education where the enrolment ratios are comparable to the general enrolment. Again, the number of non-attending children is not equitably distributed between the different States and Union Territories. This is the least in the educationally advanced States like Kerala, Tamil Nadu, Maharashtra and Gujarat. But it forms a very large proportion of the total number of non-attending children in the educationally less advanced States like Uttar Pradesh, Madhya Pradesh, Rajasthan and Orissa.

(3) The third phase is that of universal retention as the drop-outs are still high. According to the Ministry of Human Resource Development estimates in 1995-96, 61 out of 100 children enrolled in Grade I in primary schools seem to reach Grade V and 42 reach Grade VIII. There appears to have been some improvement in the level of retention because according to an estimate made in 1986, of every 100 children that entered Class I, only 49 reached Class V and only 31 reached Class VIII, the corresponding figures for the Scheduled Caste children being 44 and 26 respectively. We need to curb the drop-out rates and need to ensure that every child enrolled in Class I remains in school till he or she completes the Upper Primary School or reached the age of 14. That is the reason why the Revised NPE, 1992, has given the highest priority to solving the problem of children dropping out of schools and to ensuring children's retention at schools. This effort will be fully coordinated with the network of non-formal education.

This chapter concentrates on the study of: (1) Existing schooling facilities — the number of Primary and Upper Primary Schools and the Primary and Upper Primary Schools within various distance slabs, both in general habitations and in predominantly Scheduled Caste habitations; (2) Enrolment of children in primary sections and upper primary sections and the hiatus between the rural and urban areas, between the boys and girls in relation to the general students vis-a-vis the Scheduled Caste students; (3) Drop-outs and stagnation in the primary sections and upper primary sections for the general students as well as the Scheduled Caste students; and lastly, (4) Resources for elementary education, in order to have a comprehensive idea about the position of Scheduled Caste students in the matter of Universal Elementary Education (UEE) in relation to the general students.

Educational Facilities at Different School Stages

In order to achieve the objective of UEE, the most important prerequisite towards the achievement of universal elementary education, henceforth, UEE is the establishment of both primary and upper primary schools in all places for all children, rural and urban, throughout the country. Annexure Table VII shows the educational facilities and enrolment at different school stages in various plan periods, from 1946-47 to 1995-96.

Primary Schools

Though Annexure Table VII indicates that the number of primary schools almost trebled in the first twenty years of independence (from 1.35 lakh in 1946-47 to 3.87 lakhs in 1965-66), it considerably slackened during the next thirty years, when it increased by 50 per cent only, the overall increase during these 50 years being four times (from 1.35 lakh in 1946-47 to 5.90 lakhs in 1995). The number of primary schools registered an increase of 321 per cent during the period 1950-51 to 1995-96 (from 1.84 lakh to 5.90 lakhs). But when we compare it with our population figures which increased from 36.1 crore to 93.42 crore during the same period, i.e., an increase of 262 per cent, then the increase in the number of primary schools does not appear to be at all impressive. Further, many of these schools have no infrastructural and teaching facilities. The Fifth All-India Survey 1986, gave a dismal picture 0.4 per cent of the primary schools had no teacher, 28.90 per cent had only a single teacher and another 31.86 per cent had only two teachers (the corresponding figures for the rural areas being 0.46 per cent, 31.45 per cent and 34.07 per cent respectively), and 7.52 per cent of the primary schools were functioning in open spaces, 0.49 per cent in tents, 5.53 per cent in thatched huts and 13.92 per cent in *kachcha* buildings and the remaining 72.54 per cent in *pucca*/party *pucca* buildings, including one-room ones.

Added to this, only 26.18 per cent of the primary schools had library facilities, 55.41 per cent had adequate supply of chalks and 71.84 per cent had adequate supply of dusters, 16.74 per cent had both almirahs and trunks/boxes, 15.78 per cent only almirahs and another 36.14 per cent had only trunks/boxes, while 31.34 per cent had neither almirahs nor boxes/trunks for keeping records, 54.50 per cent did not have any mats/furniture for students, 41.75 per cent had no playground facilities and 38.17 per cent schools could not provide either a chair or a table for the teachers. These figures does not leave much to our imagination to understand the condition of these schools. A study, initiated in 1989 and conducted in 23 States covering over 60,000 pupils by the National Council of Educational Research and Training (NCERT), the findings of which were released in 1995, has expressed concern over the declining levels in primary schools. There is a deterioration in achievement as the child moves to higher classes. The study revealed that differences between the aggregate achievement of boys and girls did not have the same direction. Differences in favour of boys were noted in Rajasthan, Tripura, Uttar Pradesh and West Bengal, while the reverse was true in Meghalaya, Punjab, Sikkim and Delhi. No differences were noted in Kerala, Tamil Nadu and Jammu & Kashmir. Inadequate knowledge of the teachers about their teaching subjects was another finding. Their educational qualifications was shocking. The study showed that more than four per cent of the teachers were non-Matriculates, while 17 per cent were graduates, the rest having obtained schooling between Classes X and XII. Another, study conducted jointly by the Indian Statistical Institute (ISI) and the State Council of Educational Research and Training (SCERT) in 1991-93 in 882 Government and non-Government primary schools covering 11,406 students studying in Class IV in 17 districts of West Bengal revealed the dismal standard of learning. 16 per cent of the students could not read at all, while 56 per cent could with difficulty read from the textbooks. Only 20 per cent of the students could achieve the minimum standard fixed at 48 marks for Bengali and 50 for Arithmetic. Looking at how the progress of primary education works, an analyst rightly wonders whether the expansion of educational facilities was meant for educating children or for providing teaching jobs to educated young people.

Presently, the environment of the schools, particularly those in rural areas—such as the quality of teachers, furniture and educational equipment—is so depressing and unattractive that it does not have the power to hold the children in such schools. Social justice demands that all the schools, including those in rural areas, should be compatiable to, if not better than, the best schools in the country, so that the children are not deprived of proper educational facilities in these schools. Lack of much initiative in this direction has now led to a unique situation were primary schools, even in urban areas are getting closed for dearth of students and at the same time a long queue of students seeking admission in well-run Government schools, as seen. The plight not only of the children who are denied the opportunity of proper schooling facilities in a 'standard' school, but also of their parents can well be imagined. It has been suggested that the Government should declare all poorly equipped schools as 'Educationally Priority Areas' and bring them to the level of best schools in the country. Though the task is vast but the Government cannot ignore this responsibility, if equality of opportunity to all the children of this country, irrespective of caste, creed, sex, religion or social background, is to be assured. It is good that this point has been taken note of by the revised NPE, 1992, which pledges to give due emphasis on substantial improvement in the quality of education to enable all children to achieve essential levels of learning.

Upper Primary Stage

The number of Upper Primary Schools and the number of Primary Schools need to be in perfect synchronization. Each and every child after completing his schooling in the primary section should get a chance to continue his education in the Upper Primary School. Though there has been a 21-fold increase in the number of Upper Primary Schools in the 50 years since Independence (from 8,294 in 1946-47 to 1,71,216 in 1995-96), as Annexure Table VII indicates, and a 14-fold increase during the period 1950-51 to 1995-96, the number of Upper Primary Schools is inadequate enough to meet the demands of children, even after taking into account the fact that only one out of every two children enrolled in Class I in the primary section goes for education in the Upper

Primary School. The inadequate number of Upper Primary Schools, is also directly responsible for the heavy drop-out rates and thus, a vicious chain reaction sets in.

Here again, it has been envisaged that the infrastructure at the Upper Primary stage will be expanded in order to increase enrolment at that stage. Further, the norm of providing an upper primary school within three km walking distance has now been relaxed and the new ratio between primary and upper primary school is 2:1. It has been decided to upgrade every second primary school to the upper primary level during the Eighth Plan period. It is, however, primarily the responsibility of the State Governments to observe this norm of school-mapping.

Till 1976, education was largely the responsibility of States, the Central Government being only concerned with certain areas like coordination and determination of standards in technical and higher education, etc. In 1976, through a constitutional amendment, education became the joint responsibility of the Centre and the State. Henceforth various schemes were started by Centre to supplement the efforts of States for achieving the target of UEE. Operation Blackboard was started in 1987-88 to provide every primary schools in the country with an acceptable level of physical facilities and basic amenities and a second teacher in single-teacher schools. This programme has been expanded to cover upper primary schools and to provide three teachers in every primary school. Provision had been made in the budget for 1994-95 to provide under Operation Blackboard a third teacher in primary schools with enrolment of more than 100 children.

It is estimated that by AD 2000, the increase in student population would require an additional 11 lakhs classrooms to be built in the next seven years. This also calls for increasing the number of teachers from the present 27 lakhs to 45 lakhs, based on the teacher-pupil ratio of 1:40. This is an uphill task and can only be implemented if ther is an political will.

Primary Schools and Upper Primary Schools within Various Distance Slabs

Another pre-requisite for achieving the objectives of UEE, is that a primary school/upper primary school be provided within a convenient walking distance from the homes of every child.

Primary Schools

Annexure Table VIII gives the habitation and population, of both general and Scheduled Caste, in rural areas according to primary schooling facilities available within various distance slabs as revealed dby the All-India Educational Surveys conducted by the NCERT during the period 1957-93.

All Habitations: the first Survey (31 March, 1957) revealed that 59.75 per cent of the rural population had primary sections within habitations of residence, while 83.09 per cent had primary sections either in their habitations or at a walking distance of one mile (1.6 km). Hence it was estimated that 99.03 per cent of the rural population could be served with schooling facilities at the primary stage.

According to the Second Survey (31 March, 1965), out of the 9,82,251 rural habitations identified, 3,73,086 (37.98 per cent) accounting for 71.48 per cent of the rural population had primary sections within their own habitations and 8,56,816 (87.23 per cent) habitations were served by primary sections either within them or within a walking distance of one mile meeting the needs of 94.96 per cent of the rural population.

The Third Survey conducted on 31 December, 1973 revealed that out of 9,53,734 rural habitations identified, 4,22,766 (44.33 per cent) habitations had primary sections within them, while 7,20,809 (75.59 per cent) enjoyed the facilities either within the habitations themselves or within a walking distance of one km. The figures show that the needs of 76.12 per cent and 90.34 per cent of the rural population were met. However, 9.90 per cent of the habitations covering a population of 3.42 per cent was not served even up to two kms.

The Fourth Survey which was conducted on 30 September, 1978 identified a total number of 9,64,664 rural habitations, among which 4,51,457 (46.80 per cent) had primary sections within them, while a total of 7,73,998 (80.24 per cent) habitations were served either through primary sections within them or within a walking distance of one km. In terms of population, while those who were served by primary sections in the habitations of residence came up to 78.53 per cent, 92.82 per cent of the rural population had these facilities either within their own habitations or within a distance of one km. But, 6.84 per cent of the habitations covering a population of 2.15 per cent was not served even up to two kms.

In the Fifth Survey (30 September, 1986) the total number of 9,81,864 rural habitations in the country with a population of 5,93,560,310 were identified. Out of these habitations, 5,02,343 (51.16 per cent) had primary sections within them, while 3,20,834 (32.68 per cent) had this facility outside them up to a distance of one km. In short, as many as 8,23,177 (83.84 per cent) habitations could be considered to be served according to the above criteria. Others were served by the facilities for primary schooling at greater distances. The survey revealed that there were still 52,543 (5.35 per cent) habitations that did not have primary sections even upto a distance of two kms.

To summarise 80.38 per cent of the rural population was served by primary sections in the habitation of their residence and 14.07 per cent of the rural population had this facility at varying distances up to one km. On the whole, 94.45 per cent of the rural population had a primary section either within their own habitation or within a walking distance of one km. A small fraction (1.49 per cent) of the rural population was not served even up to a distance of two km.

The Sixth Survey (30 September, 1993) revealed that out of 10,60,612 rural habitations identified, 5,28,051 (49.79 per cent) habitations had primary sections within them, while 8,84,089 (83.36 per cent) enjoyed the facilities either within the habitations themselves, or within a walking distance of one km.

The figures shows that the needs of 77.81 per cent and 93.76 per cent of the rural population were met, respectively. However, 5.92 per cent of the habitations covering a population of 2.00 per cent was not served even up to two kms.

In short, as per the second, third, fourth, fifth and sixth surveys 87.23 per cent, 75.59 per cent, 80.24 per cent, 83.84 per cent and 83.36 per cent respectively of the habitations in the rural areas had primary sections either within the habitations or within a walking distance of one km (1.6 km in the case of the Second Survey) thereby, covering 94.96 per cent, 90.34 per cent, 92.82 per cent, 94.45 per cent and 93.76 per cent of the rural population respectively. In terms of distance, a sizeable number of habitations were having primary sections at a distance of more than one km and 5.92 per cent of them covering 2.00 per cent of the population were having primary sections not even within a distance of two kms at the time of the Sixth All-India Educational Survey in 1993.

It was during the 4th All-India Educational Survey that the data on availability of the schooling facilities in habitations predominantly populated by Scheduled Castes (i.e., the habitations in which the Scheduled Caste population constitutes 50 per cent or more) were collected for the first time. It was found that out of 9,64,664 rural habitations, 69,038 (7.1 per cent) were predominantly populated by the Scheduled Castes with a population of 2,32,19,446. The data further revealed that more than 80 per cent (80.91 per cent to be exact) of these habitations were concentrated in population slabs below 500, and, in fact, 49.69 per cent of such habitations were in the population slabs below 200. Of these habitations, 21,799 (31.58 per cent) habitations had primary sections in them and 53,823 (77.96 per cent) were served by primary sections either in the habitation of residence or within a walking distance of one km. Also, the habitations which did not have primary sections up to a distance of two kms. comprised of 4,311 (6.24 per cent) . In terms of population, 62.40 per cent population in these habitations was served by primary sections in the habitation of residence and 88.94 per cent was served either in the habitation of residence or within a distance of one km. 2.74 per cent of the population was not served up to two km.

According to the Fifth Survey there were 77,780 habitations predominantly populated by the Scheduled Castes with a population of 3,17,85,596. Out of these 29,297 habitations (37.67 per cent) had primary sections within the habitation of residence while another 34,166 habitations (43.92 per cent) had primary sections within a walking distance of one km, covering a population of 66.31 per cent and 24.83 per cent respectively. Inspite of all this, there were still 4,230 (5.44 per cent) habitations covering a population of 7,23,415 (2.28 per cent) that did not have primary sections even up to a distance of two kms.

During the Sixth Survey which was conducted on 30 September, 1993 a total number of 1,20,517 habitations predominantly populated by the Scheduled Castes with a population of 5,39,93,578 were identified. Of them, 44,629 (37.03 per cent) habitations had primary sections within the habitations, while another 54.559 (45.27 per cent) habitations had primary sections within a walking distance of one km covering a population of 64.27 per cent and 27.05 per cent respectively. Again, there were 6,638 habitations (5.51 per cent) covering a population oof 13,30,644 (2.46 per cent) that did not have primary sections even up to a distance of two kms.

A comparative chart of statistics relating to the Sixth Survey, as in Annexure Table VIII, shows that the Scheduled Caste habitations are comparatively worse than the other habitations. Though, for the category 'between 0.1 to 1.0 km', the Scheduled Caste habitations are in a better position, a near-parity situation exists in respect of the category 'beyond 2 km' In regard to population served by the primary sections within a certain distance, the Scheduled Caste population is comparatively worse than the other population in both the categories 'upto 1.0 km' and 'beyond 2 km', but is comparatively better placed in 'between 0.1 to 1.0 km' and 'between 1.0 km and 2.0 kms' categories.

Upper Primary Schools

The growth of schooling facilities at the upper primary stage since the First Survey, both in regard to other habitations and predominantly Scheduled Caste habitations is depicted in Table 3.1. During the First and Second All-India Educational Surveys, conducted in the years 1957 and 1965 respectively, a distance of three miles or five km. (approximately) was considered to be a convenient walking distance for children in Classes VI to VIII, i.e., upper primary stage. Later the distance limit was brought down to three kms ever since the Third All-India Educational Survey in 1973.

General Habitations: All the six All-India Educational Surveys conducted so far reveal that the percentage of habitations served by an upper primary school or section within the walking distance of five kms increased from 50.34 in 1957 to 90.28 in 1993. But looking at the revised distance criterion of three km, the percentage dropped to 76.15 in 1993. Though the recorded growth could be considered encouraging, but it shows that the goal of providing upper primary schooling facilities within a distance of three kms, is a far cry.

TABLE 4.1
SCHOOLING FACILITIES AT UPPER PRIMARY STAGE IN RURAL HABITATIONS WITHIN VARIOUS DISTANCE SLABS

		Percentage of Habitation served within			*Percentage of Population served within*			*Source*
All-India Survey	*Year in which conducted*	*The Habitation*	*Distance 3 km*	*Distance 5 km*	*The Habitation*	*Distance 3 km*	*Distance 5 km*	
(a) General Population								
First	1957	3.13		50.34				a
Second	1965	7.07		72.39	25.45		82.20	b
Third	1973	8.69	58.26	78.43	28.86	71.97	86.91	c
Fourth	1978	10.74	66.86	85.52	33.47	78.83	92.09	d
Fifth	1986	13.13	74.00	89.84	36.85	83.98		e
Sixth	1993	13.87	76.15	90.28	37.02	85.00	94.70	f
(b) Scheduled Caste Population								
Fourth	1978	3.59		88.4	12.92	74.14	91.28	g
Fifth	1986		74.43			79.38		h
Sixth	1993	6.5	77.64	91.77	18.50	82.54	94.06	i

Sources: a — p. 41 of Fifth All-India Educational Survey, 1986, Vol. I.
b — p. 53 of Fourth All-India Educational Survey, 1978.
c — p. 33 of Third All-India Educational Survey, 1973.
d — p. 54 of Fourth All-India Educational Survey, 1978.
e — p. 41 of Fifth All-India Educational Survey, 1986, Vol. I.
f — p. 41 of Sixth All-India Educational Survey, 1993, Vol. I.
g — pp. 63-64 and p. 197 of Fourth All-India Educational Survey, 1978.
h — p. 44 of Fifth All-India Educational Survey, 1986, Vol. I.
i — p. 42 of Sixth All-India Educational Survey, 1993, Vol. I.

There is a similar growth of percentage of the population served by a school at the upper primary stage within a walking distance of three km. From 71.97 per cent in 1973, it has moved up to 85.00 per cent in 1993. Though the data showing an increase in the availability of the facility in 17.89 per cent of the habitations does not apparently look to be spectacular. However, if we consider the difficult terrain in some States, and the existence of a very large number of extremely small habitations, it is no mean achievement.

Predominantly Scheduled Caste Habitations: Table 4.1 shows that among the habitations predominantly inhabited by the Scheduled Castes during the Fourth Survey, only 3.59 per cent

(2,479) habitations were served by middle sections in them catering to 12.92 per cent of population of these habitations. Only 8,011 (11.6 per cent) habitations accounting for 8.72 per cent of the population were not served by a middle section within five kms. The data showed a very happy state of affair. About three-fourths (74.14 per cent) of the population was served within a distance of three kms and 91.28 per cent of the population within a distance of five kms, which compared favourably with the 92.09 per cent in case of the general population.

During the Sixty Survey, 77.64 per cent of the total number of habitations predominantly populated by those belonging to the Scheduled Castes had a school at the upper primary stage within a walking distance of three kms. The percentage of the population served with an upper primary section in case of the Scheduled Caste habitations was 82.54 as against 85.00 for the general habitations, due to the fact that the habitations predomiddnantly populated by those belonging to the Scheduled Castes were smaller in size than those of the general population.

Enrolment

Primary Section

Table 4.2 gives the enrolment of children in primary sections (Classes I-V) since 1946-47 along with the corresponding figure of enrolment of the Scheduled Caste children as also their growth percentage.

General Population: Since 1946-47, the enrolment of children in the primary section has increased manifold. In the first 20 years it increased there was a five times increase to the first 20 years, followed by nearly doubled increase in the next 30 years. Overall the increase being eleven times during the period 1946-47 to 1995-96 (from 96 lakh to 1,097 lakh). But this growth is marred by manifold increase in the population of India and hence, all children could not be put through the primary schooling, even within 50 years of Independence.

The enrolment of girls has also increased. Girls constituted 36.20 per cent of the total enrolment in 1965, 37.67 per cent in 1973, 38.27 per cent in 1978 and 40.81 per cent in 1986, as shown in Table 4.3.

The Report of the Sixty Survey (1993) has not been published till now. The Annual Report of the Department of Education, Ministry of Human Resource Development for the year 1996-97, however, indicates that in 1995-96, girls constituted 43.17 per cent of the total enrolment in primary sections (473 lakh out of 1,097 lakh). Thus, the girls' enrolment showed a steady rise throughout this 30-year period. In 1965, girls constituted a little over one-third of the total enrolment and in 1995, they constituted more than two-fifths of the total enrolment. Inspite of this growth, it has not yet touched 50 per cent. According to the Ministry of Human Resource Development Report, the States/UTs of Sikkim (48.63 per cent), Kerala (48.68 per cent), Pondicherry (48.58 per cent) Goa (47.97 per cent) Nagaland (47.89 per cent), Daman & Diu (47.82 per cent), Andaman & Nicobar Islands (47.80 per cent), Meghalaya (47.75 per cent), West Bengal (47.59 per cent), Mizoram (47.35 per cent), Maharashtra (47.30 per cent), Punjab (47.28 per cent) and Manipur (47.00 per cent) were slowly approaching the target of 50 per cent of girls' enrolment.

TABLE 4.2
ENROLMENT OF CHILDREN IN PRIMARY SECTIONS, 1946-95

Period	*Enrolment of all children*	*Growth Percent-age*	*Source*	*Enrolment of SC children*	*Growth Percent-age of SC Children*	*SC Enrol-ment as % of Total Enrolment*	*Source*
1946-47	9,647,317		a				
1951-52	16,288,960	68.84	a				
1956-57	23,922,567	46.86	a				
1961-62	29,474,377	23.21	a				
1965	48,834,588	65.68	a				
1973	61,255,290	25.43	a	8,077,567		13.19	b
1978	68,602,224	11.99	a	10,106,897	25.12	14.73	c
1986	85,913,478	25.23	a	14,704,908	45.49	17.12	d
1995	109,734,292	27.73	e	18,537,423	26.06	16.89	f

Sources: a — Annexure Table VII.
b — p. 30 of Third All-India Educational Survey, 1973.
c — p. 51 of Fourth All-India Educational Survey, 1978.
d — p. 39 of Fifth All-India Educational Survey, 1986, Vol. I.
e — p. 261 of Annual Report, 1996-97, PART-1, Department of Education, Ministry of Human Resource Development.
f — p. 263, *Ibid.*

TABLE 4.3
ENROLMENT OF GIRLS IN PRIMARY SECTION

Survey	*Period*	*Rural*	*Urban*	*Total*	*Source*
Second	1965	34.26	43.20	36.20	a
Third	1973	35.79	44.05	37.67	b
Fourth	1978	36.18	44.75	38.27	c
Fifth	1986	39.48	45.16	40.81	d

Sources: a — pp. 3-4 of Second All-India Educational Survey, 1965.
b — p. 28 of Third All-India Educational Survey, 1973.
c — pp. 46-47 of Fourth All-India Educational Survey, 1978.
d — p. 36 of Fifth All-India Educational Survey, 1986, Vol. I.

There has been a steady increase on enrolment of girls in both rural and urban areas. In the rural areas the increase has been 34.26 per cent in 1965 to 39.48 per cent in 1986. In urban areas, the increase from 43.20 per cent to 45.16 per cent during the same period, as Table 3.3 indicates, the percentage of girls' enrolment was comparatively lower in rural areas (39.48 per cent) than in urban areas (45.16 per cent) even in 1986. A better position is expected to be revealed by the Sixth Survey (1993).

Scheduled Castes: As Table 3.2 reveals, the overall enrolment in Class I to V saw an increase of 11.99 per cent from 612.55 lakhs to 686.02 lakhs between 1973 and 1987 but during the same period, the Scheduled Caste enrolment increased from 80.77 lakhs to 101.06 lakhs accounting for an increase of 25.12 per cent. The overall enrolment in Classes I to V increased from 686.02 lakhs to 859.13 lakhs between 1978 and 1986, registering an increase of 25.23 per cent, the corresponding increase in case of the Scheduled Caste children being 45.49 per cent. The overall enrolment in Classes I to V increased from 859.13 lakhs to 1097.34 lakhs between 1986 and 1995 accounting for an increase of 27.73 per cent, the corresponding increase in case of the Scheduled Castes being 26.06 per cent. The increase in enrolment of the Scheduled Caste children during the 22-year period (1973-95) was 119.49 per cent as against a corresponding increase of 79.21 per cent in the total enrolment. This increased enrolment of the Scheduled Caste children in the primary sections has been reflected in the Scheduled Caste literacy rates, which increased by 75 per cent during the decade 1981-91.

In all, there were 1,85,37,423 Scheduled Caste students in Classes I-V and they constituted 16.89 per cent of the total enrolment in these classes during the year 1995, which was marginally higher than their share in the total population of 16.73 per cent in the 1991 census. The corresponding percentages at the time of the Fifth Survey (1986), Fourth Survey (1978) and Third Survey (1973) were 17.12, 14.73 and 13.19 respectively.

The Scheduled Caste enrolment in rural areas show a negative trend, the percentage of enrolment in rural areas declined in 1986 compared to 1978. Further, while the percentage of the Scheduled Caste boys' enrolment not only in rural areas but in urban as well decreased, the percentage of the Scheduled Caste girls' enrolment showed an imaprovement in both rural and urban areas in 1986 compared to 1978, as would be evident from the Table 4.4

TABLE 4.4
GENERAL VS SCHEDULED CASTE ENROLMENT IN PRIMARY SCHOOLS OF GIRLS AND BOY

	General enrolment				*Scheduled Caste enrolment*			
	Boys	*Girls*	*Total*	*Source*	*Boys*	*Girls*	*Total*	*Source*
Fourth Survey (1978)								
Rural	63.82	36.18	75.70		67.31	32.69	79.70	
Urban	55.25	44.75	24.30		59.07	40.93	20.30	
Total	61.73	38.27		a	65.64	34.36		b
Fifth Survey (1986)								
Rural	60.52	39.48	76.59		62.81	37.19	78.76	
Urban	54.84	45.16	23.41		56.40	43.60	21.24	
Total	59.19	48.81		c	61.45	38.55		d

Sources: a — pp. 46-47 of the Fourth All-India Educational Survey, 1978.
b — p. 51, *Ibid.*
c — p. 36 of the Fifth-All India Educational Survey, 1986, Vol. I.
d — p. 39, *ibid.*

Earlier, in 1978, the proportion of boys attending schools was more than the girls. Of the total Scheduled Caste enrolment, 65.64 per cent were boys and 34.36 per cent were girls. For the rural areas, the corresponding percentages for boys and girls were 67.31 and 32.69. In the urban areas, girls constituted 40.93 per cent of the Scheduled Caste enrolment.

1986 data shows that the gap between the boys and girls had reduced. Of the total enrolment of children belonging to the Scheduled Caste in 1986, 61.45 per cent were boys and 38.55 per cent were girls. Girls' enrolment in rural areas (37.19 per cent) was lower than that in urban areas (43.60 per cent).

In 1995, out of the total Scheduled Caste enrolment of 18,537,423, 7,601,593 (41 per cent) were girls whereas it was 43.17 per cent for the general girl students, i.e., a difference of 2.17 percentage point. In 1986, it was 2.26 percentage points (40.81 per cent and 38.55 per cent) and in 1978, it was 3.91 percentage points (38.27 per cent and 34.36 per cent). Thus, overall not only the gap between Scheduled Caste boys and Scheduled Caste girls but also between Scheduled Caste girls and General girls has considerably narrowed down over the years. This shows a positive trend.

Upper Primary Stage

Table 3.5 gives the details of the enrolment of children in upper primary sections since 1946-47 along with the corresponding figure of enrolment of Scheduled Caste children.

General Population: Between 1946-47 to 1995, the enrolment of children in Classes VI to VIII has increased 36 times (from 11.30 lakh in 1946-47 to 410.14 lakh in 1995). As compared to the nine-fold increase in the enrolment of children in the primary sections during the same period, the progress in the enrolment of children in the upper primary sections appear to be satisfactory. At the time of the Second Survey (1965), only 30.15 per cent of children of the age group 11-13 were in Classes VI-VIII, which marginally improved to 33.15 per cent during the Third Survey (1973), and to 36.92 per cent during the Fourth Survey (1978). In 1985-86, 56.63 per cent children of the age group 11-14 were in Classes VI-VIII, which increased to 67.6 per cent in 1995-96.

The overall annual increase in enrolment at the upper primary stage between the Third and the Fourth Surveys was found to be 4.96 per cent, while that was 6.48 per cent between the Fourth and the Fifth Surveys. Interestingly, in both the periods, the rate of increase in enrolment has been more in rural areas than in urban areas. Yet, it will be seen from Table 3.6 that rural areas are still lagging behind the urban areas in the matter of achievement of enrolment at the upper primary stage.

TABLE 4.5
ENROLMENT OF CHILDREN IN UPPER PRIMARY SECTIONS, 1946-47.

Period	*Enrolment of all children*	*Growth Percent-age*	*Source*	*Enrolment of SC children*	*Growth Percent-age of SC Children*	*SC Enrol-ment as %age of Total Enrolment*	*Source*
1946-47	1,129,955		a				
1951-52	1,880,726	67.69	a				
1956-57	4,392,223	133.42	a				
1961-62	12,136,018	176.31	a				
1965	10,244,621	–15.59	a				
1973	14,387,748	40.44	a	1,218,728		8.74	b
1978	17,958,477	24.82	a	2,012,412	65.12	11.21	b
1986	27,272,336	51.69	a	4,006,855	99.11	14.69	b
1995	41,014,136	50.39	c	5,853,823	46.10	14.27	d

Sources: a — Annexure Table VII.
b — pp. 50-51 of Fifth All-India Educational Survey, 1986, Vol. I.
c — p. 261 of Annual Report, 1996-97, Ministry of Human Resource Development, Department of Education.
d — p. 263, *Ibid.*

TABLE 4.6
ENROLMENT OF GIRLS AND BOYS AT UPPER PRIMARY STAGE IN RURAL AND URBAN AREAS

Survey	*Area*	*Environment in Classes VI-VIII*				
		Boys	*Percentage to Total*	*Girls*	*Percentage To Total*	*Total*
	R	6517388	73.36	2366171	26.64	8883559 (60.5)
Third	U	3319758	60.31	2184431	39.69	5504189 (39.5)
(1973)	T	9837146	68.37	4550602	31.63	14387748
	R	7910325	72.18	3049879	27.82	10960204 (61.0)
Fourth	U	4175944	59.67	2822329	40.33	6998273 (39.0)
(1978)	T	12086269	67.30	5872208	32.70	17958477
	R	12089291	68.19	5640427	31.81	17729718 (65.0)
Fifth	U	5551065	58.17	3991553	41.83	9542618 (35.0)
(1986)	T	17640356	64.70	9631980	35.30	27272336

Source: p. 49 of the Fifth All-India Educational Survey, 1986, Vol. I.
R — Rural; U — Urban.

According to the Fifth Survey, the total enrolment at the upper primary stage was 27,272,336 out of which 65.0 per cent belonged to rural areas. This depicts a good improvement as compared to the 60.5 per cent of the Third Survey and 61.0 per cent of the Fourth Survey. However, when compared to the child population, the enrolment was considerably lower in rural areas.

Like the earlier Surveys, the Fifth Survey revealed a huge gap in the enrolment between boys and girls at the upper primary stage. This is particularly so in rural areas in many States. Though there is a slight increase from 32.70 in the Fourth Survey and 31.63 in the Third Survey, to 35.30 in the Fifth Survey, but the overall position of girls' enrolment has not changed much in rural areas. In rural areas, the percentage of girls' enrolment has increased from 26.64 in the Third Survey to 31.81 in the Fifth Survey.

The position as revealed in the Sixth Survey (1993) has not yet been made known. But the Department of Education, Ministry of Human Resource Development, Annual Report for the year 1996-97 indicates that in 1995, out of the total enrolment of 4,10,14,136 students, 1,60,42,890 (39.12 per cent) were girls. During the 22 year period (1973-95) the enrolment of girls in the primary sections increased by 8.50 (from 37.67 per cent to 43.17 per cent) percentage points, whereas it increased by 7.49 (from 31.63 per cent to 39.12 per cent) percentage points in the upper primary sections. So, it can be said that the increase in the enrolment of girls students in the upper primary sections was commensurate with that of the primary sections.

Scheduled Castes: The enrolment of children belonging to the Scheduled Caste population at the upper primary stage was 58,53,823 in 1995 which is an increase of 380.32 per cent from the period 1973-95. In short, it is an average increase of 17.27 per cent per annum between the period 1973 and 1995. Though it was 4.9 per cent growth as compared to general population but still the Scheduled Caste students constituted only 14.27 per cent of the total enrolment in Classes VI-VIII during 1995, which was much below their share in the total population.

Table 4.7 presents the actual enrolment of both boys and girls belonging to the Scheduled Caste population in Classes VI-VIII in rural and urban areas.

Enrolment belonging to the Scheduled Caste students in rural areas, has gone up from 65.9 per cent and 65.3 per cent of the Fourth and Third Surveys respectively to 68.2 per cent in the Fifth Survey.

TABLE 4.7
ENROLMENT OF THE SCHEDULED CASTE STUDENTS AT UPPER PRIMARY STAGE IN RURAL AND URBAN AREAS

Survey	*Rural*	*Urban*	*Total*	*Boys*	*Girls*	*Total*
Third (1973)	796,115 (65.32)	422,613 (34.68)	1,12,8728	923,623 (75.79)	295,105 (24.21)	1,218,728
Fourth (1978)	1,327,159 (65.95)	685,253 (34.05)	2,012,412	1,492,745 (74.18)	519,667 (25.82)	2,012,412
Fifth (1986)	2,732,141 (68.19)	1,274,714 (31.81)	4,006,855	2,759,724 (68.88)	1,247,131 (31.12)	4,006,855

Source: pp. 50-51 of the Fifth All-India Educational Survey, 1986, Vol. I.

As regards the enrolment of girls belonging to the Scheduled Caste population, the Fifth Survey found 31.12 per cent girls in Classes VI-VIII as compared to 25.82 per cent in the Fourth Survey and 24.21 of the Third Survey. Though the overall increase in enrolment of girls between the Third and Fifth Surveys (1973-86) was considerably more than the increase in enrolment of the Scheduled Caste students during the same period — 412.29 per cent as against 328.77 per cent — it was still lower than the enrolment of the general girls. The gap between these two categories had, however, narrowed down during this period.

In 1995, out of the total Scheduled Caste enrolment of 58,53,823 students in the middle sections, 21,52,901 (36.78 per cent) were girls, which indicates that the gap between the enrolment of boys and girls had narrowed down over the years — from 24.21 per cent in 1973 to 36.78 per cent in 1995. The main reason for the low rate of increase in Scheduled Caste girls' education is the disappointing performance in the State of Rajasthan, Uttar Pradesh, Bihar and Madhya Pradesh, wherein the percentage of girls was the lowest during the year 1995, viz., 20.20, 20.82, 25.25 and 28.91 respectively. The States where the percentage of enrolment of girls belonging to the Scheduled Caste was the highest were Pondicherry (50.19 per cent), Tripura (49.76 per cent), Kerala (48.58 per cent), West Bengal (47.96 per cent) and Manipur (47.18 per cent).

Enrolment Ratio

Let us look at this problem from another angle, i.e., the through the angle of enrolment ratios of students belonging to all communities vis-a-vis the Scheduled Castes. The enrolment ratio is calculated as follows:

$$\frac{\text{Enrolment of SC students on roll}}{\text{Population of SC in the corresponding age group}} \times 100$$

The enrolment ratio of the Scheduled Caste students at Primary Stage increased from 82.2 per cent 1980-81 to 84.8 per cent in 1986-87, 102.2 per cent in 1990-91 and 111.91 per cent in 1995-96. Similarly, the corresponding enrolment at Middle Stage increased from 29.1 per cent in 1980-81 to 40.0 in 1986-87, 47.7 per cent in 1990-91 and 61.33 per cent in 1995-96. The details of the increase in gross enrolment ratios are given in Table 3.8.

The state-wise enrolment ratios of general students and SC students at primary stage and upper primary stage in 1995-96 are given in Tables 3.9 and 3.10 respectively and that of SC girls in relation to general students and general girls.

TABLE 4.8

ENROLMENT RATIO OF SCHEDULED CASTE AND TOTAL ENROLMENT RATIO DURING 1980-96

Class		*1980-81*	*1986-87*	*1990-91*	*1995-96*
(a) Total Enrolment					
Classes I-V	Girls	69.9	79.21	85.97	93.3
	Total	84.6	95.96	101.03	104.3
Classes VI-VIII	Girls	31.1	38.95	46.13	54.9
	Total	44.2	53.14	60.11	67.6
(b) Scheduled Caste Enrolment					
Class I-V	Girls	57.8	64.8	80.6	95.12
	Total	82.2	84.8	102.2	111.91
Classes VI-VIII	Girls	16.2	26.5	33.3	46.77
	Total	29.1	40.0	47.7	61.33
Source		a	b	b	c

*Relates to non-SC/ST students.

Sources: a State-wise Information on Education of Scheduled Castes and Scheduled Tribes, Ministry of Education, 1985, p.4.

b Programme of Action, 1992, Ministry of Human Resource Development of Education, p. 35.

c Annual Report, 1996-97, Ministry of Human Resource Development, Departament of Education, pp. 262 and p. 264.

TABLE 4.9
ENROLMENT RATIO OF GENERAL STUDENTS AND SCHEDULED CASTE STUDENTS IN CLASSES I-V IN 1995-96

Sl. No.	*States/UTs*	*General*			*Scheduled Caste*		
		Boys	*Girls*	*Total*	*Boys*	*Girls*	*Total*
1.	Andhra Pradesh	99.6	89.9	94.9	140.68	121.73	131.4
2.	Arunachal Pradesh	115.5	103.9	110.0	25.33	27.50	26.2
3.	Assam	133.4	124.0	128.8	257.62	239.07	248.5
4.	Bihar	93.0	55.4	75.1	102.04	51.39	77.8
5.	Goa	90.6	100.5	95.1	105.31	116.77	110.4
6.	Gujarat	158.3	106.8	131.41	213.43	155.06	182.9
7.	Haryana	86.4	84.8	85.6	108.12	105.84	107
8.	Himachal Pradesh	108.4	113.7	110.8	115.15	115.75	115.4
9.	Jammu & Kashmir	88.6	72.2	81.2	96.14	83.43	90.6
10.	Karnataka	131.1	123.5	127.4	158.59	137.96	148.5
11.	Kerala	98.4	95.4	96.9	107.64	102.45	105
12.	Madhya Pradesh	112.9	88.9	101.4	129.68	93.68	112.2
13.	Maharashtra	125.5	120.2	122.9	268.31	257.96	263.3
14.	Manipur	93.1	100.3	96.4	153.65	179.19	165
15.	Meghalaya	105.3	125.4	114.4	-	-	-
16.	Mizoram	112.6	124.8	118.1	-	-	-
17.	Nagaland	120.6	135.5	127.3	-	-	-
18.	Orissa	113.4	78.2	95.6	152.85	95.29	123.7
19.	Punjab	92.4	90.7	91.5	134.77	129.98	132.4
20.	Rajasthan	129.3	75.3	103.4	121.53	48.62	86.5
21.	Sikkim	104.2	118.4	110.6	103.75	114.00	108.4
22.	Tamil Nadu	159.3	145.6	152.6	176.76	154.02	165.6
23.	Tripura	122.7	124.4	123.5	147.05	144.14	145.7
24.	Uttar Pradesh	104.3	72.0	89.1	88.94	42.05	68.8
25.	West Bengal	128.6	122.3	125.5	129.79	116.93	123.5
26.	A & N Islands	76.6	69.2	72.9	-	-	-
27.	Chandigarh	36.4	40.4	38.2	82.85	92.93	87.3
28.	D & N Haveli	121.0	102.7	112.7	74.67	87.00	79.6
29.	Daman & Diu	93.0	88.6	90.8	-	-	-
30.	Delhi	67.7	77.8	72.1	83.49	91.76	87
31.	Lakshadweep	125.3	125.3	125.3	-	-	-
32.	Pondicherry	117.2	133.3	124.5	141.29	170.18	154.4
	India	114.5	93.3	104.3	127.56	95.12	111.91

Source: Annual Report, 1996-97, Ministry of Human Resource Development, Department of Education, pp. 262, 264.

TABLE 4.10
ENROLMENT RATIO OF GENERAL STUDENTS AND SCHEDULED CASTE STUDENTS IN CLASS VI-VIII IN 1995-96

Sl. No.	States/UTs	General			Scheduled Caste		
		Boys	Girls	Total	Boys	Girls	Total
1.	Andhra Pradesh	57.3	41.8	49.7	67.03	42.63	55.82
2.	Arunachal Pradesh	61.3	45.2	53.3	21	13	17
3.	Assam	91.6	65.9	79.1	190.13	161.51	176.16
4.	Bihar	47.5	21.9	35.3	38.2	14.03	26.62
5.	Goa	95.1	84.1	89.6	69.5	55.33	62.79
6.	Gujarat	81.1	61.5	71.6	117.32	76	97.32
7.	Haryana	70.9	56.7	64.2	65.81	47.85	57.36
8.	Himachal Pradesh	112.7	90.5	101.8	90.14	63.06	76.80
9.	Jammu & Kashmir	73.3	46.8	60.5	80.24	59.68	70.34
10.	Karnataka	78.1	66.8	72.6	81.78	57.60	70.04
11.	Kerala	105.1	101.5	103.3	118.31	114.56	116.46
12.	Madhya Pradesh	91.6	43.3	68.4	80.98	35.62	59.19
13.	Maharashtra	92.4	77.2	85.0	180.15	137.47	159.53
14.	Manipur	69.4	63.2	66.4	93.64	92	92.86
15.	Meghalaya	51.6	45.5	48.6	-	-	-
16.	Mizoram	67.3	67.7	67.5	-	-	-
17.	Nagaland	52.5	51.2	51.9	-	-	-
18.	Orissa	73.0	39.8	56.2	71.82	43.17	57.29
19.	Punjab	74.0	65.0	69.7	79.75	64.83	72.65
20.	Rajasthan	79.9	32.0	56.9	78.13	21.44	50.93
21.	Sikkim	50.5	50.8	50.7	50.83	43.17	47.00
22.	Tamil Nadu	118.2	99.5	109.1	111.26	84.74	98.34
23.	Tripura	66.8	57.0	62.0	63.43	66.69	65.01
24.	Uttar Pradesh	72.3	34.9	54.7	53.34	15.82	35.70
25.	West Bengal	102.8	91.5	97.2	72.03	69.00	70.59
26.	A & N Islands	73.5	68.6	71.1	-	-	-
27.	Chandigarh	36.4	34.9	35.6	68.33	59.02	68.83
28.	D & N Haveli	59.2	40.8	50.6	99	93	96.00
29.	Daman & Diu	92.5	84.7	83.7	-	-	-
30.	Delhi	71.1	67.3	69.3	72.66	68.66	70.83
31.	Lakshadweep	112.0	81.2	96.6	-	-	-
32.	Pondicherry	113.0	109.6	111.3	147.36	154.87	151.03
	India	79.5	54.9	67.6	74.88	46.77	61.33

Source: Annual Report, 1996-97, Ministry of Human Resource Development, Department of Education, pp. 262, 264.

Primary Stage

Data shows that the enrolment ratio of the Scheduled Caste students and the enrolment ratio of Scheduled Caste girls has both crossed the total enrolments. Further, it would appear from Table 3.9 that the enrolment ratios of total Scheduled Caste students and of Scheduled Caste boys and Scheduled Caste girls exceeded that of general total students and of general boys and girls in 19 States/UTs — Andhra Pradesh, Assam, Goa, Gujarat, Haryana, Himachal Pradesh, Jammu & Kashmir, Karnataka, Kerala, Madhya Pradesh, Maharashtra, Manipur, Orissa, Punjab, Tamil Nadu, Tripura, Chandigarh, Delhi and Pondicherry. The enrolment ratios were lower than that of general students on all the three counts in six States/UTs — Arunachal Pradesh, Rajasthan, Sikkim, Uttar Pradesh, Dadra and Nagar Haveli, and West Bengal (except boys). In the State of Bihar, though the enrolment ratios of total SC students and of SC boys were higher than that of the general students, it was lower in respect of girls.

An interesting fact was that the enrolment ratios not only of Scheduled Caste boys but also of Scheduled Caste girls were 110 per cent or more in many States. It has even crossed 200 per cent in the three States (Assam, Gujarat and Maharashtra) in relation to Scheduled Caste boys and in two States (Assam and Maharashtra) in relation to girls. But for the poor performance of Rajasthan and Uttar Pradesh, the two populous States, the All-India enrolment ratio of Scheduled Caste children would have been even higher.

Upper Primary Stage

As compared to the primary stage, the enrolment ratio of Scheduled Caste student at the upper primary stage was much lower than the corresponding enrolment ratio for students belonging to all communities. In case of Scheduled Caste girls, though the enrolment ratio has nearly trebled during the period 1980-95, it was much lower than the corresponding general enrolment ratio for girls. Inspite of this comparative data, Table 3.10 shows that in 11 States/UTs, the enrolment ratio of SC students was higher than that of the general students in respect of all the three categories. These are: Andhra Pradesh, Assam, Gujarat, Jammu and Kashmir, Kerala, Maharashtra, Manipur, Chandigarh,

Dadra & Nagar Haveli, Delhi and Pondicherry. The enrolment ratio of Scheduled Caste children was higher than that of the general students in respect of total enrolment and either of boys/girls in three states — Orissa (except boys), Punjab (except girls), and Tripura (except boys). So many States/UTs — 14-registering an increase in enrolment ratio in the middle section is really an achievement. A little more attention to the educationally backward States of Bihar, Rajasthan, Madhya Pradesh and Uttar Pradesh would have changed the overall position not only of Scheduled Caste children but also of general students.

Wastage - Drop-outs and Stagnation

Till, universal retention of children in schools is ensured UEE would remain an elusive goal. The ideal situation in the field of education will be achieved when a child enrolled in Class I leaves the school only after completing his or her education in Class VIII within the stipulated period. As the 'Programme of Action 1986' put it crisply, enrolment by itself is of no importance if children do not continue beyond one year, many of them not seeing the school for more than a few days.

The term 'wastage' encompasses both the 'drop-outs' and 'repetition'. Whereas 'drop-out' refers to the premature withdrawal of pupils from the educational cycle at a particular stage of instruction, 'repetition', 'retardation' or 'stagnation' refers to the continuance of pupils in the same grade for more than one academic year on account of unsatisfactory progress. While drop-outs directly constitute wastage, repetition adds to it by lengthening the effective duration of the course.

Studies reveal that Drop-out and stagnation are higher among the Scheduled Caste students as compared to the students of other communities due to various socio-economic reasons. When a student drops out in the middle of his or her educational career, the entire investment on education goes waste. In case of repetition, the educational development of the students gets impaired. To combat the stagnation problem, the Ministry of Education has suggested to the States "to introduce the ungraded system and 'non-detention' policy so that every child shall complete one class in each year and will be promoted to the next higher grade till he or she completes class VIII, but with adequate safeguards by way of periodic assessment and evaluation on a continuing basis". This policy of non-detention at the primary stage is retained in the Revised National Policy on Education, 1992 as well, making evaluation as disaggregated as feasible. A flexible scheme of Continuous Comprehensive Evaluation (CCE) at the elementary stage has been evolved so as to make the evalaution process an integral part of teaching and learning at this stage. These evaluation will be reported in the form of grades on a comprehensive proforma.

From the decline in the number of children enrolled in different classes from I-V and VI-VIII, one can evaluate the intensity of wastage.

Primary Stage

The distribution of enrolment in Classes I-V as revealed in the Educational Survey is given in Table 4.11.

Though the retention rates have consistently shown signs of improvement during the period 1965-86 till it is much below the required level.

TABLE 4.11

DISTRIBUTION OF ENROLMENT FROM CLASSES I TO V

Class	*2nd Survey*	*3rd Survey*		*4th Survey*		*5th Survey*	
	General	*General*	*SC*	*General*	*SC*	*General*	*SC*
Class I	37.77	34.93	39.79	31.42	34.91	28.97	29.91
Class II	20.89	22.67	23.17	22.91	23.33	21.25	21.84
Class III	16.80	17.73	16.70	18.55	18.10	19.07	19.22
Class IV	13.67	13.72	11.80	14.87	13.48	16.40	15.90
Class V	10.87	10.95	8.54	12.25	10.18	14.31	13.13
Source	a	b	c	d	e	f	g
Retention rate in class V	28.78	31.35	21.46	39.00	29.16	49.40	43.90

Sources: a — p. 31 of the Second All-India Educational Survey, 1965.
b — p. 29 of the Third All-India Educational Survey, 1973.
c — p. 30, *ibid.*
d — p. 40 of the Fourth All-India Educational Survey, 1978.
e — p. 51, *Ibid.*
f — p. 38 of the Fifth All-India Educational Survey, 1986.
g — p. 39 of *Ibid.*

The retention rate of the Scheduled Caste children was much less compared to the general children. It is, however, expected that the retention rates of both the general students and the Scheduled Caste students would improve further during the Sixth Survey (1993).

Upper Primary Stage

The retention rates at the upper primary stage are, however, comparatively better as Table 3.12 will indicate.

TABLE 4.12
RETENTION RATES AT THE UPPER PRIMARY STAGE

Class	*2nd Survey*	*3rd Survey*		*4th Survey*		*5th Survey*	
	General	*General*	*SC*	*General*	*SC*	*General*	*SC*
Class VI	39.93	40.12	40.54	39.40	40.48	38.51	38.67
Class VII	32.59	32.77	32.54	32.92	32.94	32.70	32.94
Class VIII	27.48	27.11	26.92	27.68	26.58	28.79	28.39
Source	a	b	c	d	e	f	g
Retention rate in Class VIII	68.82	67.57	66.40	70.25	65.66	74.77	73.42

Sources: a — p. 47 of the Second All-India Educational Survey, 1965.
b — p. 44 of the Third All-India Educational Survey, 1973.
c — pp. 328-33, *Ibid.*
d — p. 71 of the Fourth All-India Educational Survey, 1978.
e — pp. 884-87, *Ibid.*
f — p. 48 of the Fifth All-India Educational Survey, 1986, Vol. I.
g — pp. 1072-73, *Ibid.*

The improvement in retention rates was, however, less spectacular when compared with that at the primary stage; the increase was only 8.65 per cent during the period 1965-86. An important trend at upper primary stage is that the retention rates of both the general students and the Scheduled Caste students have reached near parity by 1986. The same trend is likely to be maintained in the Sixth Survey (1993) as well.

Drop-outs

One can get a better idea of the wastage from the drop-out rates in different classes from Table 4.13.

TABLE 4.13
DROP-OUT RATES IN 1988-89

Classes	*Scheduled Caste*			*General*		
	Male	*Female*	*Total*	*Male*	*Female*	*Total*
I-V	47.24	53.39	49.62	46.74	49.69	47.93
I-VIII	64.37	73.60	67.78	59.38	68.31	65.40
I-X	76.52	85.62	79.88	72.68	79.46	75.36

Source: Education for All, The Indian Scene, Ministry of HRD, p. 119.

Drop-out rate is calculated as follows:

Drop-out rate from Classes I to V for the year 1988-89=

$$\frac{\text{No. of students enrolled in Class V in 1988-89}}{\text{No. of students enrolled in Class I in 1984-85}} \times 100$$

Drop-out rate from Classes I to VIII for the year 1988-89 =

$$\frac{\text{No. of students enrolled in Class VIII in 1988-89}}{\text{No. of students enrolled in Class I in 1981-82}} \times 100$$

The ratio does not take into account repeaters and children who enter the system after Class I.

The above analysis shows that the drop-out rates of all the three stages of education in 1988-89 are higher among the Scheduled Caste students than the general students and it is still higher among the Scheduled Caste girl students when compared with that of the general girl students and the Scheduled Caste boy students.

The yearwise break-up-of drop-out rates among all communities and the Scheduled Castes for both the primary stage and the upper primary stage for the years 1980-81 to 1988-89 is given in Table 4.14 shows that the drop-out rates among the students belonging to all communities in the primary section as well as in the upper primary section declined over the years during this 8-year period, though an upward swing was noticed in 1986-87 in the primary section and in 1983-84 in the upper primary section.

Interestingly the overall improvement in the drop-out rates in both the primary section and the upper primary section was, however, higher than that of the students belonging to all communities. It is 11.13 percentage points improvement in the primary section and 9.06 percentage points in the upper primary section for scheduled castes as against 10.54 percentage points and 8.63 percentage points respectively, in regard to students belonging to all communities during the 8-year period.

TABLE 4.14
DROP-OUT RATES : 1980-81 TO 1988-89

Period	*Scheduled Caste*		*All Communities*	
	Primary	*Upper Primary*	*Primary*	*Upper Primary*
1980-81	60.16	76.84	75.66	86.71
1981-82	59.21	74.76	74.00	84.99
1982-83	60.27	72.44	72.44	83.35
1983-84	57.84	72.36	70.63	83.74
1984-85	55.40	72.16	69.40	82.86
1985-86	52.53	72.50	65.56	81.86
1986-87	50.79	69.15	66.12	80.19
1987-88	51.38	68.81	65.21	80.01
1988-89	49.62	67.78	64.53	78.08

Source: Education for All, The Indian Scene, Ministry of Human Resource Development, Deparatment of Education, 1993, p. 117.

These were 39.37 drop-outs at primary stage and 57.77 for Classes I-VIII during the year 1995-96. Though no separate figures for the Scheduled Caste students are available, it is quite likely that the drop-out rates have declined in their case as well. The latest information for the Scheduled Castes is available for the year 1989-90, which indicates that the drop-out rates have decreased marginally to 49.03 at primary stage and to 67.62 at upper primary stage. The Statewise break-up is given in Table 4.15.

Table 4.15 shows that there is a great variation from state to state in terms of the drop-out rates of the Scheduled Caste students. These were less than the All-India drop-out rates at the primary stage in 16 States/UTs, viz., Goa, Gujarat, Haryana, Himachal Pradesh, Jammu and Kashmir, Kerala, Madhya Pradesh, Maharashtra, Meghalaya, Punjab, Tamil Nadu, Uttar Pradesh, Chandigarh, Dadra and Nagar Haveli, Delhi and Pondicherry, while these were higher than the All-India average in the remaining ten States of Andhra Pradesh, Assam, Bihar, Karnataka, Manipur, Orissa, Rajasthan, Sikkim, Tripura, and West Bengal for all the three categories of students — boys, girls and total.

TABLE 4.15
STATE-WISE BREAK UP OF DROP-OUT RATES OF SCHEDULED CASTES
1989-90

Sl. No.	States/UTs	Primary Stage			Middle Stage		
		Boys	*Girls*	*Total*	*Boys*	*Girls*	*Total*
1.	Andhra Pradesh*	60.53	65.83	62.80	77.41	85.44	80.85
2.	Arunachal Pradesh	-	-	-	-	-	-
3.	Assam	46.88	55.89	50.80	64.91	63.47	64.30
4.	Bihar	67.69	73.50	69.33	83.37	89.79	85.04
5.	Goa	39.27	32.06	36.02	55.52	65.68	60.28
6.	Gujarat	24.95	45.55	34.13	50.40	70.34	59.11
7.	Haryana	33.90	43.18	38.00	59.19	75.36	65.71
8.	Himachal Pradesh	36.29	36.50	36.39	32.27	41.88	36.44
9.	Jammu & Kashmir	39.27	30.39	35.84	50.11	52.73	51.10
10.	Karnataka	51.05	59.59	54.90	62.11	73.77	67.08
11.	Kerala	0	1.78	0.50	19.04	15.60	17.37
12.	Madhya Pradesh	36.31	52.37	42.41	62.34	79.40	67.78
13.	Maharashtra	38.54	51.58	44.60	52.90	69.77	60.54
14.	Manipur	79.86	82.21	81.03	84.89	86.07	85.48
15.	Meghalaya	33.13	41.88	37.46	27.86	51.85	39.64
16.	Mizoram	-	-	-	-	-	-
17.	Nagaland	-	-	-	-	-	-
18.	Orissa*	55.16	59.22	56.77	75.97	83.19	78.76
19.	Punjab	36.53	41.59	38.79	63.36	70.56	66.52
20.	Rajasthan	60.42	74.37	63.89	69.53	83.53	72.18
21.	Sikkim	70.00	67.85	69.04	84.96	83.67	84.37
22.	Tamil Nadu	22.56	29.68	25.92	51.04	53.14	51.97
23.	Tripura	58.21	63.09	60.47	75.87	81.84	78.60
24.	Uttar Pradesh	32.89	51.69	38.86	57.92	69.52	60.87
25.	West Bengal*	58.54	66.71	61.92	74.18	84.88	79.02
26.	A & N Islands	-	-	-	-	-	-
27.	Chandigarh	0	0	0	0	0	0
28.	D & N Haveli	18.60	36.96	28.09	0	0	0
29.	Daman & Diu	-	-	-	-	-	-
30.	Delhi	33.74	35.74	34.63	47.68	58.61	52.79
31.	Lakshadweep	-	-	-	-	-	-
32.	Pondicherry	0	0	0	0	11.96	5.45
	India	45.93	53.74	49.03	64.29	73.10	67.62

* Relates to 1988-89; @ Included in Goa

Source: Educational Development of Scheduled Castes and Scheduled Tribes, Status and Programmes, Ministry of Human Resources Development, Department of Education, 1995, p. 32.

More or less the same picture emerged in the drop-out rates at the Middle stage. These were lower than the All-India average for all the three categories of students in 14 States/UTs, namely, Goa, Gujarat, Himachal Pradesh, Jammu & Kashmir, Kerala, Maharashtra, Meghalaya, Punjab, Tamil Nadu, Uttar Pradesh, Chandigarh, Dadra and Nagar Haveli, Delhi and Pondicherry and were lower for only two categories of students in three States—Assam (except boys), Haryana (except girls) and Karnataka (except girls). All these States/UTs except Assam and Karnataka registered the same trend at the primary stage. In the remaining nine States of Andhra Pradesh, Bihar, Manipur, Orissa, Rajasthan, Sikkim, Tripura, West Bengal and Madhya Pradesh (except boys), the drop-out rates were higher than the All-India average. All these States except Madhya Pradesh showed the same trend at the primary stage. Thus, while Assam and Karnataka had improved their position at the middle stage, Madhya Pradesh could not retain its position. Further, the data shows that Orissa, Bihar, West Bengal, Sikkim, Tripura and Manipur, and partly Assam have failed to tackle the problem of drop-outs among the Scheduled Caste students in an effective manner.

From the above, we can say that unless effective ways and means are devised and drastically minimizing the staggering proportions of drop-outs the constitutional objective of imparting free and compulsory elementary education to all children, including those belonging to the Scheduled Castes, up to the age of 14 will remain an unattainable one.

Resources for Education

To achieve the objective of universalisation of elementary education; liquidating illiteracy, equality of access to educational opportunities to all sections throughout the country; enhancing the social relevance, quality and functional effectiveness of educational programmes; generating knowledge and developing technologies in scientific fields crucial to self-sustaining economic development and creating a critical consciousness of the values and imperatives of national survival, we need to make adequate investments in education.

Education is funded largely by the Central and State

Government in which, elementary education is funded almost wholly by the Government.

After the inception of planning in 1950-51, spending on education as a proportion of GNP increased steadily from about 1.2 per cent to about 3.9 per cent in 1989-90, while expenditure on elementary education increased from 0.48 per cent of GNP in 1950-51 to 1.72 per cent in 1989-90, as will be evident from Table 4.16.

TABLE 4.16
PUBLIC EXPENDITURE ON EDUCATION AS A SHARE OF GNP (PERCENTAGE)

Year	*Total*	*Primary*	*Upper Primary*	*Elementary*
1950-51	1.2	0.40	0.08	0.48
1960-61	2.5	0.45	0.31	0.76
1970-71	3.1	0.65	0.47	1.12
1980-81	3.1	0.71	0.48	1.19
1989-90	3.9			1.72

Source: Education for All, The Indian Scene, Ministry of HRD, p. 77.

While the increase was significant but the availability of resources was inadequate due to financial constraints and competing priorities.

The Kothari Commission on Education (1966) had first put forth the view that public expenditure on education should be six per cent of the GNP. This view has been reiterated time and again and the NPE, 1992 had proclaimed that from the Eighth Plan onwards the outlay on education would uniformly exceed six per cent of the National Income. Though all the Five-Year Plans had stressed the importance of education but in the matter of allocation of resources it has received a backseat. The Plan outlay for education which was 7.2 per cent in the First Five-Year Plan, declined to 2.6 per cent in the Sixth Five-Year Plan. This declining trend was arrested in the Seventh outlay. In the Eighth Five-Year Plan 4.9 per cent of the plan-resources were allocated to education. But during the first three years of the plan, education received only 3.5 to 3.9 per cent of the total plan resources. Hence there is a urgent need to significantly step up the plan resources for education in order to keep up to its goal. As a matter of fact, it is now being increasingly felt that 8 to 10 (or higher) per cent of the national income would be needed for the educational system to fulfil the government's stated goal of education for all by AD 2000.

Table 4.17, gives an intra-sectoral analysis of the plan expenditure on education during the different plan periods. It brought out two distinct trends. In the first phase, expansion of higher and technical education received a higher inter se priority. Two things happened by the end of the first phase, one, there was a realisation that the network of higher and technical institutions was sufficient to meet the anticipated manpower needs. Secondly, elementary education came to be perceived as a minimum need.

There was lot of argumentive discussions on the policy of laying greater stress on the expansion of higher education at the cost of elementary education-stating that the rates of social return from secondary and general higher education are considerably less than those from primary and middle school education. Studies have also been made in the United States which establish beyond doubt that the rate of return from college education is lower than that from elementary and secondary education. Finally, there was a plea for allocation of funds for the improvement of the quality of primary education. As a result, there was a marked jump upward in public expenditure on elementary education, as would be evident from Table 4.18.

It would be seen that during the 1980s alone, the public expenditure on elementary education increased by 4.5 times, from Rs. 15,373 million at the beginning of the decade to Rs. 68,883 million in 1989-90. Elementary education began to receive a higher proportion of plan allocation on education. This trend which received appreciable boost after NPE, 1986 has become still more pronounced during the Eighth Plan. While the expenditure on education accounted for 4.2 per cent of the GNP in 1992-93, the share of elementary education in total public expenditure on education is about 45 to 46 per cent.

With the launching of centrally sponsored schemes to promote non-formal education and improve the quality of elementary education, the Central Government's share in plan expenditure on elementary education has increased considerably. From a mere 9.7 per cent of the total plan expenditure on elementary education in 1984-85, it increased almost four-fold to 37.1 per cent in 1987-88, but again decreased to 28 per cent in 1991-92.

TABLE 4.17
PLAN EXPENDITURE ON DIFFERENT SECTORS OF EDUCATION (PERCENTAGE)

Sector	1st Plan Expdt. 1951-56	2nd Plan Expdt. 1956-61	3rd Plan Expdt. 1961-66	Plan Holiday Expdt. 1966-69	4th Plan Expdt. 1969-74	5th Plan Expdt. 1974-79	6th Plan Expdt. 1980-85	7th Plan Expdt. 1985-90	Annual Plan Outlay 1990-92	8th Plan Outlay 1992-97
Elementary education	56	35	34	24	30	35	33	37	37	47
	(850)	(950)	(2010)	(750)	(2390)	(3170)	(8360)	(28490)	(17290)	(92010)
Secondary education	13	19	18	16	18	17	21	24	22	18
	(200)	(510)	(1030)	(530)	(1400)	(1560)	(5300)	(18320)	(10530)	(34980)
Adult education						9	6	9	9	
							(2240)	(4700)	(4160)	(18480)
Higher education	9	18	15	24	25	22	22	16	12	8
	(140)	(480)	(870)	(770)	(1950)	(2050)	(5590)	(12010)	(5880)	(15160)
Others	9	10	12	11	14	4	4	3	2	4
	(140)	(300)	(730)	(370)	(1060)	(1060)	(1080)	(1980)	(1180)	(7510)
Technical education	13	18	21	25	13	12	11	14	17	14
	(200)	(490)	(1250)	(810)	(1060)	(1070)	(2730)	(10830)	(8230)	(27860)
Total	100	100	100	100	100	100	100	100	100	100
	(1530)	(2730)	(5890)	(3230)	(7860)	(9120)	(25300)	(76330)	(47270)	(196000)

Note: Figures in parenthesis in millions of rupees.
Source: Education for All, The Indian Scene, MHRD, 1993, p. 121.

As early as 1986, the Indian Education Commission had articulated the need for according priority to elementary education. Again, in 1929, the Hartog Committee, after making an indepth study of primary education, observed that the Government of India should serve as a centre of educational information for the whole of India and should be constitutionally enabled to make good such financial deficiencies in the interests of India as a whole.

TABLE 4.18
PLAN AND NON-PLAN EXPENDITURE ON ELEMENTARY EDUCATION IN INDIA

(Rs. in 10 million at current prices)

Year	*Plan*	*Expenditure Non-Plan*	*Total*	*Share in Total Expenditure on Education*
1980-81	91.0	1446.3	1537.3	45.6
	(5.9)	(94.1)	(100)	
1981-82	103.4	1557.3	1660.7	43.8
	(6.2)	(93.8)	(100)	
1982-83	158.9	2013.2	2172.1	45.6
	(7.3)	(92.7)	(100)	
1983-84	218.8	2256.5	2475.3	45.4
	(8.8)	(91.2)	(100)	
1984-85	263.5	2591.4	2854.9	44.9
	(9.2)	(90.8)	(100)	
1985-86	266.7	3181.6	3448.3	46.2
	(7.7)	(92.3)	(100)	
1986-87	346.2	3535.5	3881.7	45.9
	(8.9)	(91.1)	(100)	
1987-88	572.9	4283.8	4856.7	46.6
	(11.8)	(88.2)	(100)	
1988-89	714.0	4825.8	5539.8	44.6
	(12.9)	(87.1)	(100)	
1989-90	966.1	5922.2	6888.3	45.8
(14.0)	(86.0)	(100)		
1990-91(R)	907.4	6917.2	7824.6	45.2
	(11.6)	(88.4)	(100)	
1991-92(B)	963.3	7050.9	8014.2	43.8
	(12.0)	(88.0)	(100.0)	
Rate of growth	23.92%	15.49%	16.12%	

Source: Education for All, The Indian Scene, MHRD, 1993, p. 122.

The expenditure on elementary education received a boost, ironically not under the nation's own constitutional obligation, but under the pressure of International Bodies. A number of foreign-aided programmes have been designed to address certain facets of universal elementary education, like the Mahila Samakhya (a Dutch assisted Programme in the States of Gujarat, Karnatgaka, Andhra Pradesh and U.P.); Andhra Pradesh Primary Education Project (fully supported by the Overseas Development Administration); Siksha Marmi Project Lok Jumbish in Rajasthan; (supported by the Swedish International Development Authority); Bihar Education Project (supported by the UNICEF); U.P. Basic Education Project (funded by World Bank) and District Primary Education Programme (DPEP)supported by a multitude of international organizations in a number of States. A large part of the expenditure of these projects is fully reimbursed by external aid organizations and the remaining part is met by the States. According to an estimate, the expected flow of external funding for elementary education during the Eighth Five-Year Plan (1992-97) for all these projects would be Rs. 24,517.9 million out of the total outlay of Rs. 29,262.9 million. Though with the help of this external funding-the goal of UEE has got a great impetus but it also makes apparent that the growth in public expenditure on elementary education is largely a 'borrowed growth'. There may be a setback in the inflow of foreign funds due to the economic sanctions imposed by the US, Japan and Germany in the wake of the Pokhran explosion.

Challenge Ahead

Irrespective of the source of funds, it cannot be denied that over the years there has been a very impressive increase in the number and spread of institutions as well as enrolment in the elementary sector of education. The good of UEE has been substantially achieved at the primary stage (Classes I-V). According to the Sixth All-India Educational Survey (1993), 93.76 per cent of the rural population had primary schools within a walking distance of one km; 85.00 per cent of the rural population was served with the upper primary sections within a walking distance of three km. For the pre-dominantly Scheduled Caste habitations in rural areas, the corresponding figures were 91.32 per cent and 82.54 per cent respectively. The number of primary schools increased from 1.84

lakh in 1951-52 to 5.90 lakh in 1995-96. Similarly, the number of upper primary schools went up to 1.71 lakh in 1995-96 as compared to 12,124 in 1951-52. The gross enrolment of 6-11 age group increased from 42.6 per cent in 1950-51 to 104.3 per cent in 1995-96. Likewise, the gross enrolment of 11-14 age group increased from 12.7 per cent in 1950-51 to 67.6 per cent in 1995-96. For the Scheduled Caste children the enrolment ratio in primary stage was 111.91 per cent and in upper primary stage 61.33 per cent in 1995-96. Except a little of sex disparity — the participation of the Scheduled Castes is now more or less in proportion to their share in population at the primary stage.

However, the drop-out rates continue to be very high. It was 47.93 per cent in Classes I-V and 65.40 per cent in Classes I-VIII in 1988-89 compared to 49.62 per cent and 67.78 per cent respectively for the Scheduled Caste students. Wastage in education among the SC students is primarily due to various socio-economic reasons. Highlighting the fact that children from these communities are generally first generation learners, the Working Group on Development and Welfare of Scheduled Castes during the Eighth Five-Year Plan commented that it is to be recognized and accepted that economic development of the Scheduled Castes in isolation is not a solution to their problems and educational development as an integrated part of their comprehensive development package has to be properly monitored.

The National Policy on Education, 1986 and its Programme of Action gave unqualified priority to Universal Elementary Education and introduced many innovations. The emphasis was shifted from enrolment *per se* to enrolment as well as retention. The NPE 1986 further stressed on the removal of disparities and attainment of equalisation of educational opportunities for the Scheduled Castes, Scheduled Tribes and other backward sections, specially girls. The POA detailed a number of strategies aimed at accelerating their rate of enrolment and retention. In 1992, some modifications were undertaken to the NPE, 1986. It placed greater stress on the education of the Scheduled Castes, Scheduled Tribes, other educationally backward sections and areas, minorities and physically and mentally handicapped. The central focus in the Scheduled Castes' educational development in this revised NPE, 1992, is their equalisation with non-SC population at all stages and levels of education — rural male, rural female, urban male and urban female. The Programme of Action (POA) on the new NPE, 1992 was formulated after taking into account the experience gained in the implementation of NPE, 1986 and its POA. Some of the important programmes of action, apart from reservations and specific incentives, which have a bearing on Universal Elementary Education of the Scheduled Castes, are as follows:

1. In opening primary and upper primary schools priority would be given to the needs of the Scheduled Caste habitations and hamlets. As far as possible, pre-primary section will be an integral part of such schools.
2. For the Scheduled Caste children access and enrolment will be assured primarily in the formal school. Incase of inability to attend the formal school, provision for non-formal and distance education centres will be made to ensure universal access and enrolment.
3. It will be the responsibility of the teachers along with voluntary agencies to organize drives at the beginning of every academic session to enrol all school-age children, specially girls, belonging to the Scheduled Castes, Scheduled Tribes and Other Backward sections. To motivate the parents and children for studies, traditional and folk media should be used.
4. Adequate incentives will be provided for the children of the Scheduled Castes, Scheduled Tribes and Other Backward sections in the form of scholarships, uniforms, textbooks, stationery and mid-day meals.
5. Operation Blackboard shall cover with a period of two years all schools in tribal areas and 'Harijan Bastis' irrespective of the date on which the school was set up.
6. The indigent families among the Scheduled Castes/ Scheduled Tribes will be given incentives to send their children, particularly girls, to schools.
7. It will be ensured that Minimum Level of Learning (MLL) already set-up for primary schools will be achieved and that the necessary standards of three rupees are acquired by all children in the Scheduled Caste and Scheduled Tribe communities. Effective methodologies for measurement of MLL will be implemented.

8. In case of unavailability of teachers in the Scheduled Caste and Scheduled Tribe localities, crash programmes for giving suitable training to eligible persons from Scheduled Castes and Scheduled Tribes will be started. The eligible amongst them will be appointed as teachers in the schools.
9. A chain of pace-setting institutions from primary to higher secondary will be established in areas of the Scheduled Caste and Scheduled Tribe concentration for providing quality education to talented learners as well as for upgrading their achievement levels of comparatively slow learners in these communities.

Under the UEE, alongwith the other segments of population the SC population also enjoyed the fruits of the narrow government efforts. It would however not be proper to assume that all the Scheduled Castes in a State/UT have attained the same standard in elementary education or that all the regions in a State have progressed uniformly in Universal Elementary Education. Though, the castewise disparities in the matter of educational facilities or achievements among the Scheduled Castes in elementary education have not been discussed here but it is quite likely that similar disparaities exist between one Scheduled Caste community and another, and between one region and another in the matter of UEE as well. Though the POA, 1992 talks of 'participating planning' to formulate familywise and childwise design of action to ensure that every child attends school, and completes the elementary education until the age of 14 years, but unfortunately, not much study on this aspect of the problem in the matter of realization of UEE has been conducted.

The need of the time is to identify the Scheduled Caste communities as also the areas which have been denied the fruits of UEE so that, corrective and remedial measures can be taken to rectify the imbalances and the disparities, so as to improve their prospects for further education. Unless this is done, some Scheduled Caste communities will continue to remain educationally backward as they are now, and the UEE in its totality will remain an elusive goal.

Five

A Prerequisite for Mobilisation

This chapter analyses the emerging patterns, forms and trends of social, occupational and generational mobility among the scheduled castes of Varanasi. To substantiate the above analysis emphasis is given to study the impact of education in creating and motivating the mobilization process in the social status, occupational structure, life style, habits, social structure and social relations of the scheduled castes. The combined effect of all these facators lead to the evolution of new value orientations, ideas, beliefs and behaviour patterns leading finally to intergenerational upward mobility.

The term mobility refers to 'moving up and down' of individuals from their positions in class, caste and power structure. Inter generational trends form an important part of this process of going up and coming down. Thus social mobility in the present context refers to two things:

(i) the variation in social origin and positions of the members of scheduled castes, and

(ii) the way in which socio political opportunities available to them are utilized by them according to their various social characteristics.

The concept of change is embeded in the phenomenon of social mobility. The earlier social mobility studies have mainly shown the departure from traditional caste based occupation. A 1954 Survey of Poona showed that the traditional relationship, between caste and occupation had considerably changed, Brahmins were example, found in all grades of occupation except in unskilled manual work (Ghurye, 1961 : 273-76). In the last few decades, a number of studies and artaicles on social mobility in India have been published. In the works of Milton Singer, Singer and Gohn,

Silverberg and Beteille the focus has been mainly on caste, class and mobility. The studies show that social mobility is not just a new phenomenon in India. Brown notes that shifting has been constant in class composition and caste hierarchy. The studies made by Stein, Orans and Rowe uphold the same view. Lynch observes that the Jatavs (a sub caste of Chamar) of Agra city by receiving modern education and utilizing democratic facilities, special provisions of reservations, improved their social and economic position, entered various secular occupations, government jobs and politics, claimed the status of Kshatriya. All this was an outcome of constant upward mobility.

It is with reference to modern education among the scheduled castes in Varanasi city that an attempt is made, to analyse social mobility. During the last decades modern education in India has been one of the powerful instruments of social change and mobility in the caste structured society. It has created a special socio-political consciousness among the educated scheduled castes by setting new avenues and strategies of social stratification and social ranking in modern India. The impetus for social mobility was given by the provision of "protective discrimination" or special reservations for education, job and political participation . 'Protective discrimination' acts as a ladder for the down trodden section of society by setting them on platforms equal to the higher caste Hindus in social, political, economic and cultural spheres of society. Social mobility in turn, brings mobility among them in occupational sphere as well for example, when scheduled caste agricultural labourer grows to become a factory worker, living style also changes. Similar is the case when a scheduled caste family moves from a smali house in a isolated part of a town to a larger house in the better colonised part of the town. In short, the term mobility is used here to mean movement from one social stratum, position or caste to another involving consolidation of various elements of new social position, including occupation, income, style of life, habits, manners, change in caste names and nomenclature, types of houses, participation in socio-political organization, friendship circle, etc.

(a) *Upward social mobility*: Mobility can be categoriesed into various types: most commonly observed among the Scheduled Castes. It requires learning of a new skill and better culture, thereby, achieving higher statuses in social hierarchy. For example, to be born in the family of an unskilled labourer and to grow to a position of an administrator or government functionary, or a teacher in society. This trend is commonly among the scheduled castes in Varanasi. The studies of Rao, Rowe and Lynch support the idea in this connection.

(b) *Downward Social Mobility* is less observed than upward mobility and especially in case of the scheduled castes in matters of status and occupation it is not fisible as they have been in the bottom of the caste hierarchy in terms of their traditional origin. Hence, in their case mobility has to be upwards most of the time. Downward mobility comes to the people who do not strive to keep up with the standard of living, e.g., when a youth of the improved scheduled caste family performs poorly in the college and ends up with an average job in adulthood, he gets separated from his associates when they proceed forward. He does not rise in the social hierarchy and is unable to change his life style.

(c) *Vertical Mobility* is that in which the scheduled castes move upward by getting modern education, new techniques, skill and adopting the ritual and manners of higher status or caste groups, changing their caste names, nomenclature, and occupation, and maintain the higher position.

(d) *Horizontal mobility* happens within the same generation or occupational cadre proceeding from inferior to rather superior position. The study of "individual mobility" in social position among the scheduled castes has been considered in this context.

(e) *Spatial mobility* is very frequent among the scheduled castes. It refers to "intragenerational mobility" which is outcome of migration or shifting of places. It may happen as a result of migration from rural to urban community or social improvement of individuals of scheduled castes within the same family. And hence, it provides chances for change in culture. In this regard some of the scholars of social change and mobility have discussed about the units of mobility in the form of *"individual"*, *"familial"*, *"group"* and *"corporate mobility"*. The mobility study of these units can be subsumed under the above patterns. Modern education, and means of mass communication have facilitated the "corporate mobility" in modern India society, while "family mobility" was more a phenomenon of medieval period in India.

Now, that we are aware of the types of mobility, we need to analyse the significance of modern education with respect to mobility in social position, the inter generational mobility, the mobility in living arrangement, and finally mobility in occuaption and attitude.

Since Sanskritization and westernization have their limited scope and is applied in cultural context assuming caste as a cultural phenomenon, we have employed here Priedl's theory of "Lagging emulation" under the Mertonion frame-work of Reference Group which appears to be logically more adequate and critically useful in the present context of the study of scheduled castes. It is an accepted fact the processes of social change and mobility are continuously on going. It is felt that the "Savarnas" or the higher caste Hindus themselves have vacated the spot and have gone up to the higher hill. In such a situation the question is, who will then be the reference model or model for imitation of the scheduled castes.

Though, the models of limitation may even be their caste fellowmen of elevated social standing but still, it delimits the wider scope of mobility in practical sense for the scheduled castes in modern educational, technical and industrial context. Hence, for the present study the theory of Lagging Emulation serves a useful purpose as it Widens the scope and opens out the choice for the prevailing trends, patterns and forms of social mobility among them in an urban setting. In the past, the theory of sanskritization, has been useful to a considerable extent in the present context there are several objections and difficulties in its application and reliance. The difficulties faced are as follows:

(i) Caste has been hypothesized as an "adaptive structure" through which its members relate and re-relate themselves to the members of other caste in terms of potentialities provided to them by the socio-political environment. Therefore, Sanskritization has no scope and logic to furnish explanation because it explains mobility in ritual and cultural context.

(ii) The concept of individual mobility cannot be fully understood with the theory of Sanskritization as it refers to mobility of a caste within the caste structure. The mobility in this regard implies upward mobility within the caste hierarchy by a whole caste or its larger segment.

(iii) In today's fast changing modern Indian society, the means available to scheduled castes for upward mobility are no longer limited to sanskritization, throgh the end may remain the same, i.e., higher social status. In such a critical social situation the theory of "Lagging emulation" under the frame of imitative reference group serves a useful purpose in analysing the social mobility among the scheduled castes.

Mobility in Social Position

Higher education itself is a prestige indicator in India. With higher modern education several privileges are endowed to them by the government thereby helping them to improve their social position. The study reveals that education has played major role in improving the social status. It awakens status consciousness among the individuals and changes their attitude to life and society. In this light it is found that majoirty of the respondents of each educational category have even minded opinion about education in improving the social status. In terms of income it is traced out that the higher the income, the greater they realize the importance of education in social improvement.

Mobility in Occupations

Till recent past, the selection of occupation in Indian Society was by and large governed by the caste norms and traditions. The children had to adopt the occupation of their father, sanctioned by the caste. It was more true in case of the scheduled castes. The higher occupations, the remunerative and sophisticated jobs were the monopoly of the higher castes and well to do sections of society. Besides due to lack of higher education, the scheduled and other downtrodden castes could not enter higher occupations. But now with the abolition of untouchability, caste disabilities and the provision for "protective discrimination", they are getting in occupations of their liking and moving up in the social hierarchy. Though, several studies have been conducted inthe sphere of occupational mobility, but studies reflecting the attitude and aspirations of the scheduled castes towards occupational mobility are very few. Hence, there is a need for intensive analysis.

Gradually with the growth of modern education and the democratic privileges, the traditional relationship between caste and occupation has considerably changed. the special reservations provided to the scheduled castes and other weaker sections of society have been a major incentive for them to shift their attachment from traditional caste based occupations to modern secular occupations attainable on the basis of educational achievements, personal efficiency and ability irrespective of the caste discriminations. The recent survey of scheduled castes show that a vast majority of them perceive the paramount role of education in occupational mobility.They realize that education is instrumental in creating changes, new occupational aspirations and choices in the scheduled caste community. The highly educated scheduled castes in Indian society are very much conscious of social status. As a consequence, there is a relative reluctance towards their traditional callings. They regard them as. hurdle in their social and economic uplift. Their general awareness has led them to aspire for more prestigious, power oriented and economically remunerative jobs through which they can equate with the position of the higher castes in Indian social structure.

The scheduled castes job aspirants are majority in favour of salaried official occupations and the administrative jobs in government departments. The research conducted ffound that the higher the education and income among the scheduled castes, the greater is their choice for administrative and professional jobs such as office executives, civil servants, doctors, engineers and law officers. In short, more the urban growth of scheduled castes, the greater they have aspirations for administrative jobs.

Mobility in Living Arrangements

Again, it is education which decides the quality and mode of living of an individual alongwith introducing a lot of social potentialities in him. Modern education among the Scheduled Castes has been an effective source to modify their attitude, habits, manners and their mode of social living by introducing rational attitude, secular outlook, sophisticated ideas and polished manners of expression and behaviour in the wider circle of society. These changes in manners and attitudes influences the style of life to a large extent. As a consequence, the rudimentary and superstitious patterns of living, are replaced by modern materialistic mode of living among them. Changes in occupation and status leads to modify their living arrangements and patterns in the direction of modernization.

The general impression derived from the empirical inference is that the scheduled castes perceive and realize that the emergence of new style of life embedded on democratic values is one of the major impact of modern education. This conclusion goes in accordance with our hypothesis that the higher the education and income of the scheduled castes, the greater they have receptivity and realization of modern education in mobilizing their living arrangements.

Alongwith modern education, techno industrial development and growth of democratic secular values in contemporary India have badly affected the traditional social sanctions, beliefs and customs of our society. This has enabled the scheduled castes to be conscious of achievement as against ascriptions and to adopt new behavioural patterns, practaices and style of life. The overall changes that have occurred are the outcomes in patent and latent forms of modern education. Urban job opportunities and other such motivating factors of social mobility have completely changed their outlooks. This has also led to create wider areas of interaction with new aspirations, expectations and value orientations of material achievement rather than getting sanskritized and Hinduised on lines of traditional Hinduism.

The upward trend of aspirations and motivataions among scheduled castes confirm the validity of our hypotheses *viz.*, (i) 'the more the growth of motivative potentialities provided by socio-political milieu to a caste, the greater its members develop adoptability to relate themselves with the members of other castes', and (ii) 'the higher the growth of status consciousness through education and democratic secularism, the greater there is reluctance to sanskritization and Hinduisation among the scheduled castes'. Further, the upward movement of schedule castes functionaires acts as a motivating factor and has a positive 'demonstration effect' on all the other people of their caste. Being the last in the ladder of the traditional Hindu Society scheduled castes were made to bear several social, cultural, economical, religious and educational disabilities, and therefore it still appears to the educated so called untouchables as a *veritable chamber of horrors* along with its disgusting doctrine of Karma and irrational sanctions of ascribed status. These are to be scheduled castes the instruments which have multilated, blasted and blighted their life.

In the wake of modernization, the higher caste Hindus too have left their traditional norms and culture and therefore, the traditional model of higher caste Hindus does not seem to be very attractive and appreciative of the educated scheduled castes. No scheduled castes in contemporary society are willing to observe vegetarianism or teetotalism and such other restrictions as they perceive these as mythical, mystical and full of nonsense. On the contrary, they join more and more non-vegetarian dinner parties, club, and restaurants which they perceive as better place of social equality. After discussing the role of education in bringing mobilityy among the scheduled castes, it is time to discuss some of the contemporary changes occuring in social contacts and patterns of behaviour of the scheduled castes. Modern education has, no doubt, created tremendous changes in the habits, attitudes, aspirations, sentiments and patterns of behaviour of the backward classes in general and of scheduled castes and scheduled tribes in particular. In order to further improve their socio-cultural status, the scheduled castes have resorted to Sanskritization and Westernization at the same time, adopting things as per their liking and availability. But at the individual level they try to emulate the practices, ideology and life patterns of the "elite sections" of any caste or cultural background who live under urban influence with secular values.

In this case strategy of adoption given to them by modern education. By receiving modern education and democratic facilities the scheduled castes are constantly striving to stand in "equality competition" with the higher castes. The consequence is a continuous change in their social and cultural life. Earlier, our analysis has shown that the higher the education and urban interplay of the scheduled castes with the higher castes and outer world, the greater they realize the importance of education in enabling them to adopt the manners and behaviour patterns of higher castes. The realization of the significance of education in modification of behaviour, attitudes and sentiments is sharper among the urban dwellers. The two variables viz., education and urban living positively affect each other. Further, education has also opened up new avenues of economic opportunities in industrial and urban areas. Having perceived the healthy and desirous outcomes of modern education and political support from the government, they find it more convenient to migrate to cities and towns where they enter into secular jobs, settle down there and create new friendship circle, new neighbourhood with a sharp consciousness to brush aside the age-ridden stigma of their traditional sub-caste names and nomenclature. In addition, the urbo-industrial social milieu provides them new chances to move up higher on the material platform of society in the wave of contemporary changes. It was found during the survey that to do away with the age old stigma of their sub-caste names and titles a bulk of the scheduled caste functionaries have eagerly adopted new names and sub-caste titles of higher castes as well as secular titles which do not have caste connotations or caste smell such as 'Bhaskar', 'Shastri', 'Sonkar', 'Rastrapal', 'Batsyana', 'Bisharad' and so on. It appears that higher education and income have imprignated their minds with choices for putting on new sub-caste names and titles. Those who have an ordinary education and income, occupying an average middle or lower middle class of jobs in government and outside have adopted the sub-caste names and titles such as 'Singh', 'Gupta', 'Prasad', etc., while those who have attained higher technical and vocational education, and hence have become government bureaucrats, administrators, doctors, engineers and lawyers have adopted more secular titles such as 'Bhaskar', 'Shastri', 'Bisharad', 'Rastrapal' and so on which do not give any caste connotation. It is many steps beyond Sanskritization. The socio-economic mobility have changed their basic conception of hereditary status and traditional orthodoxy of Hinduism by drifting them towards new value orientations and motivations in contemporary social structure. They have encouraged, enlarged and enriched their social, political, economic and cultural capacities to uplift their status in the social hierarchy and are actively playing in the arena of social contest to equate themselves with the higher castes. There is an inherent tendency of 'emulation solidarity content' among them in the existing situation. Equipped with present socio-economic and political potentialities they have developed a tendency to defy the sheat of traditional Hinduism.

Inter-Generational Mobility

Since independence, the Government of India has enforced the implementation of 'Ptotective Discrimination' for scheduled castes, scheduled tribes and other backward classes to improve their socio-economic and cultural standard of life by providing them special facilities in the field of education, government jobs and political participations. This has led to the enormous growth of integenerational mobility and changes among these backward classes specially in terms of their uplift in socio-economic status and cultural conditions. The Sixth Five-Year Plan (1980-85) was a land mark in this direction. Another commendable effort from the government towards the socio-economic development of the scheduled castes is through Special Component Plans (SCP) applied in 20 states and 4 union territories where there is a relatively large scheduled castes population. Such plans are implemented by the state governments with overall financial supports of the Central Government. These component plans serves as transformation pot for "generation uplift" among the scheduled castes. The Seventh Plan (1985-90) intends to continue the thrust towards the socio-economic development of the scheduled castes and to provide them with greater occupational mobility and economic strength. Emphasis on beneficiary oriented programmes and schemes for their better socio-economic living and uplift in the existing generation is objectified to continue through the plan. the Scheduled Caste Development Corporations (SCDC) which constitute one of the instruments of economic development of the scheduled caste families (younger generations) have been given special emphasis to act as catalysts, promoters and guarantors in respect of beneficiary oriented programmes.

Here again, modern education has proved a positive force. Some noteworthy incentives which have led to generational uplift have been the increase in the quota of reservation for recruitment of scheduled castes in different government jobs, admission to higher educational centres and representation in political and administrative structure of society.

At the same time, the continued processes of urbanization and industrialization have also provided several psychological, social and economic incentives as well as job opportunities to the already status conscious, educated scheduled castes. As a result they found themselves in a social climate which is highly favourable to them in making upward mobile from generation to generation. In the context of inter-generational mobility the independent effects of urban experience along with the new value orientation, attitude, thoughts and style of life, new ways of thinking, feeling, perceiving and doing have influenced their social living. Also, the exposure to urban living in cities have further motivated them to tread on the tracks of modernity. Therefore, the process of mobility is concomitant with individual modernization among the scheduled castes leading to individual mobility. Here the inherent conception of "lagging emolution" marshals their interests of social mobility at the individual level where the concept of Sanskritization has no appeal or scope in promoting their interest.

Contemporary India very clearly shows a generation gap among scheduled castes. All this is an outcome of the impact of modern education and democratic privileges which shows an uplift from father to son and to the children. Today's parents hve more prospective expectations about their young children as there is a rapid upgoing trend within their three generations. Thus we can say that given the necessary provisions, the processes of generational mobility will happen with lightening speed out in its vogue, it will revolutionize the society.

After going through the above discussions, we can very well say that Education has played an indespensible role in the mobility of scheduled castes regarding their social position, occupational structure, style of life, modification of caste titles and nomenclature, habits and manners. Modern education has created a generation gap and led to the rapid growth of intergenerational mobility in the social status of the scheduled castes. It has pushed the process of upward mobility at group as well as individual levels. At the individual level the concept of "lagging emulation" under the framework of reference group is perceived where the models of reference are not only the higher caste Hindus but more of the "elite sections" of society.

Education increases potentialities and capacities of adaptability among the scheduled castes thereby, enabling them to compete with the higher castes. Education, special previliges and modern employments lead to inter-generational mobility among them. The main observation can be summed up as follows:

A vast majority of the scheduled castes of all educational, income and rural-urban backgrounds perceive education as the primary factor behind the improvement of their social position. Education has encouraged them to shift from traditional occupations to modern secular jobs.

A large number of them aspire for administrative jobs. The choice for non-salaried profession is very scanty and is generally among those who have technical and professional education. As regards mobility in habits, manners and patterns of behaviour mostly all of them perceive that education helped in the adoption of honourable means of livelihood and the manners and practices of the higher castes. In order to get rid of the age old shackles of casteism, a majority of the scheduled caste functionaries have modified and changed their caste names in the direction of the higher caste Hindus or have adopted secular names "Rastrapal", "Bharti", "Shastri", etc. Those who retain their traditional caste names are very few. Most of them evaluate and accept the impact of education in modifying their sentiments, caste names and nomenclature. It has been observed that those who are highly and technically qualified have more keen interest in the modification of names than the less educated ones. Similarly, the rural-urban analysis suggests that the scheduled castes of urban background are more prone to adopt new names and specially of seculiar connotation than those of the rural ones. Those who have higher education and income have developed a revolting tendency to abolish the caste hierarchy for good.

There has been comparatively much more upward inter-generational mobility among the scheduled castes. It is also perceived that those who are highly educated, their fathers' position was also comparatively better than those of the less educated ones.

Hence, there is no doubt in the fact that education has played a pivotal role in the mobilisation process of the Scheduled Castes.

Six

Related Research and Literature

Over the past several hundred years, from time to time there had been government policies and various national level discussions and debates on the schedule caste community. The Scheduled Caste community have always occupied a low status in the society.

Research on education of the scheduled castes children was brought under priority by National Council of Educational Research and Training in 1975 when a number of research problems were suggested to be subjected to investigation. These problems were:

1. Identifying solutions for the educational needs of the children from the poorer sections of the society.
2. Finding out solution to problems existing in the field of education, as a whole.
3. Identification of talent and its development at all levels of education.
4. Research related to the fulfilment of constitutional directive of Articles 45 providing for compulsory and free education for all children up to the age of 14.
5. Non-formal education.
6. Finding solutions to problems arising out of increased population.
7. Studies on education of the scheduled caste and scheduled tribe children.
8. Relevance of education to socio-economic needs of the country.

Research on education of the scheduled caste children has been very meagre in the past. Out of 729 research studies conducted during 1943-73 only one study was on scheduled caste children. Out of 832 researches conducted during 1972-78 and reported in the Second Survey of Research in Education only 33 studies were on scheduled caste children. Also, some general, social and economic problems in the form of disabilities of the scheduled castes have been studied either in sociology or in some Government surveys by the NCERT and the ICSSR, New Delhi. Similarly, only five studies of the total 536 abstracted in the Dissertation Abstracts and completed during 1973-77 related to the problems of the scheduled caste children. After years of research, it was only two years back that the National Council of Educational Research and Training issued a list of 30 specific problems of research and devlopment on the education of the scheduled castes and scheduled tribes.

General Studies

In the early studies the researchers tried to study the attitudes of the non-scheduled caste students towards untouchability or the Scheduled Castes. Jha, Anand, Patwardhan and Sinha and Sinha all have shown that higher caste students have favourable attitudes towards Harijan students. Anand had found significant differences between Brahamins and Sudras on attitudes of various kinds. The studies conducted by Jha revealed that higher the level of education, the more favourable is the attitude of people towards abolition of untouchability. An important study conducted at B.H.U. (Sociology Department) in 1974-75 concluded that "while there has been an encouraging rise in the number of Scheduled Caste students at the undergraduate level, the rise in their number in the institutions of higher learning lags behind." It was further found that the Scheduled Caste students are highly upward-social-mobility oriented, their aspirations for entering the professions are limited and more often they settle down to school teaching and clerical services mainly on reserved quota. It was also found that the occupational aspirations of the Scheduled Caste students are lower as compared to those of the non-Scheduled Caste students, especially in case of low class families. It was just the opposite of this in case of middle and higher class families. Chitnis and Premi hold that instead of providing equal opportunity to all, the present system of education is creating new inequalities. Only a small proportion of scheduled castes students have been able to reap the major benefits of higher education and modern occupations. The studies also reveal that the incidences of stagnation and drop-out is higher among the scheduled castes than among the non-Scheduled Caste students. Goyal has reported the historic development and progress of depressed classes. Goyal has also surveyed the educational facilities available for the under-privileged communities. The studies Chauhan and others revealed how the students from the Scheduled Castes of U.P. look at the welfare measures undertaken by the State, how the students live in the two worlds of the school and the home, and how traces of modernity have begun making some inroads into their culture.

Studies on Characteristics of Scheduled Caste Children

In recent years, various comparative studies on psychological and other characteristics of the scheduled and non-Scheduled Caste students have been made. Chattopadhyay made a study of intelligence of tribal and non-tribal children of Tripura. When Dubey made a comparative study of the Scheduled Castes and Scheduled Tribes students of Assam, it showed that (1) both the groups had high educational and occupational aspirations, (2) both showed interest in extra-curricular activities, (3) Most of them were exposed to mass media. (4) The general intelligence level is low. (5) teachers felt that the facility of reservation for them was justified. The study conducted by Thakral showed significant difference in locus of control, vocational aspirations and general intelligence level between the scheduled and the non-scheduled caste students. The scheduled caste students had, as compared to the non-scheduled caste students, lower level of vocational aspirations, and general intelligence. Tribal students were found to be less neurotic than the non-tribal students in a study made by Seth and Srivastava. A study conducted by Vageswari in Tamil Nadu revealed that (1) the literary level of Harijan (S.C.) students was lower than that of the non-Harijans, (2) the parents of most of the Scheduled Castes students were illiterate and that they were ignorant of what the government was doing for promoting the education of the scheduled caste people, (3) only 17 per cent of Scheduled Caste people were fully employed as against 50 per cent of the non-scheduled caste people.

On the whole, it was found that most of the Harijans had no agricultural land and that they were living in the very poor conditions. A study conducted by Shah and Thaker in Gujarat on the first generation scheduled caste learner reveal that (1) as the Scheduled Caste and Scheduled Tribe students were, largely, motivated not by self or their family but by the Governmental encouragement, they were likely to lack strong motivation, ability, good study habits, good performance, etc., required for study, (2) the scheduled caste students showed ambivalent attitudes in several areas, (3) they sought shelter in their traditional group ties by sharing rooms with member of their own caste, tribe or groups, (4) they participated less in the politicization process and felt shy of exposing themselves to mass media, and they also felt shy of modernising their attitudes and behaviours. In a study of scheduled caste and scheduled tribe students of colleges in East U.P., Goyal found that the socio-economic background of scheduled caste and scheduled tribe students was very poor. It was also found that the scheduled caste people living in the villages were not, at all, familiar with the educational facilities that the Government was providing to the students of these castes. Further, studies of Singh and Dubey show that (1) the literacy of the parents of the scheduled caste students was poor, (2) sixty-eight per cent of the scheduled caste students were in economically difficult conditions, (3) only nine per cent of the students were receiving scholarships, (4) Most of the scheduled caste students were devoid of congenial home atmosphere for proper study, (5) most of these students were found to be doing well in the schools in spite of adverse socio-economic conditions, (6) a majority of these students did not express difficulty in comprehending the lessons in the class-room, (7) social distance was not found to be a barrier in teacher-taught relations, (8) a few students (only 15 out of 240) expressed that special programmes for them were damaging their self respect, (9) about 63 per cent of the teachers felt that the scheduled caste students have lesser intelligence than other students. Another study conducted by George in Kerala revealed that (1) the reservation on the community basis needed to be changed to consideration like economic backwardness, (2) the amount of scholarship was inadequate, (3) the system of distribution of stipends was complicated, (4) education of parents on the Governmental programmes need to be emphasized in order to ensure proper utilization of recources, (5) the students needed to be educated about the facilities existing and their purpose, (6) separate hostels for scheduled caste students should not be promoted as it would be socially unhealthy, (7) a considerable number of scheduled caste students suffered from inferiority feeling and they needed to be protected through proper guidance, (8) vocational training for these students should be emphasized in order to make them self independent, (9) they did not show high aspiration for technical and professional jobs. A comprehensive study of the status of the scheduled caste students was made by Desai and Pandor, were it was found that (1) the economic status of the majority of the scheduled caste students was not up to the mark, (2) in a large number of cases the scheduled caste students were first generation learners, (3) adult education seemed to have little impact on spread of literacy, (4) they not only feel that they are discriminated from non-scheduled caste students but rather they feel that they are at an advantage because of govt. policies, (5) they cherished the values and norms of their non-scheduled caste counterparts, (6) generally, they believed that their condition had improved, but their status was still lower to that of their friends from non-scheduled castes, (7) They felt that as a result of governmental policies their lifestyle has improved and that the same should be continued, (8) the teachers of these students were of the opinion that the scheduled caste students were comparatively low in academic calibre and performance. In an independent study by Desai it was found that (1) the literacy among the scheduled tribes rose from 11.69 in 1961 to 14.12 per cent in 1971, (2) the enrolment in primary schools increased from 2,02,458 in 1961 to 3,50,000 in 1971 with a rise of 73 per cent in nine years, (3) only six per cent of the students in primary schools went to the secondary schools and only 11.8 per cent of the secondary education population went to the higher education. Another study of Ruth and Misra concluded that a large percentage of scheduled caste students came from rural areas with poor conditions and felt that they were neglected by some teachers.

Problems of the Scheduled Caste Students

Some researchers have concentrated their studies on identifying the problems faced by the scheduled castes students. Adiseshia and Ramanathan conducted a study in Tamil Nadu and found that (1) the wastage in education at primary level in case of the scheduled castes was very high, (2) majority of scheduled caste students came from illiterate homes (67.22 per cent) and lived in difficult financial conditions, (3) the scheduled caste students found it difficult to follow the curriculum, (4) the scheduled caste students formed 7.2 per cent of the total university population, (5) Nearby 78.5 per cent of the scheduled caste population claimed that their status has not improved. Another study conducted by Lal on the progress and problems of the Scheduled Caste and Scheduled Tribes students in Rajasthan revealed that (1) the population of the scheduled caste people according to the census of 1971 was 15.87 per cent of the total population of Rajasthan, (2) There were greater number of the Scheduled Caste and Scheduled Tribes students Arts stream than in Science, (3) economic status and participation in extra-curricular activities did not affect significantly the study habits of the scheduled caste students, (4) encouragement from home and father's education had no significant influence on occupational aspirations of the scheduled caste students, (5) majority of the scheduled caste students lived in villages. A similar study was conducted by Gangrade in Haryana. He found that (1) the parents of the scheduled castes students were mostly illiterate, (2) their social life seemed to be at a transitional stage with little exposure to mass media, (3) the scheduled castes students were found to have lesser mental abilities as compared to non-Scheduled Caste students. The study conducted by Singh in Rajasthan revealed that (1) the number of scheduled caste girls who came for education was lesser than the boys, (2) the Scheduled Caste students were comparatively of higher age, (3) the Scheduled Caste students had poor awareness of scholarships, etc., (4) Majority of scheduled caste students opted for Arts, (5) they felt that there was the need for extra-coaching for them, (6) they had low level of aspiration for technical and professional jobs, (7) generally, there was a lack of enthusiasm for co-curricular activities, (8) Their exposure to mass media communication was minimal, (9) Inspite of having positive attitude towards governmental programmes they expressed dissatisfaction with regard to implementation of these programmes, (10) teachers found them low in calibre and performance as compared to non-scheduled caste students. The problem of the drop-outs of the scheduled tribe students was intensively studied by Vyas and Chaudhary. The study revealed that (1) in class I, the percentage of drop-outs and stagnation among the scheduled tribes students in Kota Panchayat Samiti was very high compared to Jhadol Panchayat Samiti, (2) the diminution of the students in class II onward was very pronounced in both the areas, (3) the distance between the number of boys and girls in each group widened in higher class, (4) there was no evidence to show the incidence of drop-outs and stagnation occurred more among a particular group of boys and girls, In a study conducted by Singh, Pandey, Dubey and Yadav in UP it was found that (1) in the rural areas untouchability still had a strong hold, (2) a majority of scheduled caste students did not have congenial atmosphere for proper study, (3) participation in extra curricular activities was very low Sachchidananda, in Bihar, found that (1) in the absence of facilities for studying science, majority of the scheduled caste students had to offer arts subjects, (2) the Scheduled Caste students did not take much part in co-curricular activities, (3) the level of educational aspiration of scheduled caste students was lower than that of the scheduled tribe students, (4) occupational aspiration, however, was found to be higher, (5) Among the scheduled caste students the scholarship scheme of the government was not working satisfactorily. Their performance due to the lack of proper educational atmosphere at home suffered a lot in school. The same study was repeated on college students of Bihar by the same author, Sachchidananda in which it was found that (1) 0.4 per cent of the scheduled caste girls went to college, (2) nearly 30 per cent of the scheduled caste students were married, (3) three-fourth of them were in arts courses. Science claimed only 17 per cent, (4) they be friended with students from their own castes, (5) due to the absence of conducive atmosphere at home they had lesser mental abilities Rajagopalam conducted a study on the Scheduled Caste high school students of Karnataka and found (1) only 30 per cent of them live in hostels while their parents lived in villages, (2) economically the students were not in good condition, (3) They also take care of domestic work, (4) They feel the need for tuition, (5) have very little influence of mass media, (6) generally, feel that their status continues to be inferior. Pimpley conducted two studies in Punjab, one on school students and another on college student of scheduled castes. He concluded about the high school students that (1) the parents of these students were largely illiterate and their occupation was mainly farming also they are not economically well off, (2) their drop-out rate was very high, (3) they were inferior in their academic calibre, (4) their participation in extra-curricular activities was low, (5) finally, their condition had improved but they still feel that they have inferior status as compared the non-Scheduled Castes section of the population. About the college students of Scheduled Castes he concluded that (1) they were mostly over-aged, (2) in most cases their parents were illiterate and had meagre financial resources, (3) most of them felt that the governmental programme of providing facilities to them was not administered satisfactorily, (4) on the whole, they felt that their status had improved but was still inferior. Scheduled caste high school students of Kerala state were studied by Nayar and it was found that (1) mostly the parents of these students lived in villages, (2) the number of failures increased with the higher classes, (3) about three-fourth of the scheduled caste students found difficulty in following their teachers in the class in a few subjects, (4) nearly 80.65 per cent of the scheduled caste students considered the scholarship as inadequate, (5) fifty per cent of the teachers felt scheduled caste students have lesser mental abilities. Chitnis conducted studies among the scheduled caste students of Bombay. It was found that (1) the scheduled caste people lagged behind the total population in literary, (2) this disparity was more marked in the urban areas and with respect to males than females, (3) Most of them came from disadvantaged homes, having illiterate fathers in rural occupation, (4) Generally they opt for arts stream, (5) most of them were first generation learners, and hardly have any awareness of the educational facilities provided to them, (6) also the facilities provided by the government were not considered by most of them adequate to their needs. In still another study, (7) the failure rate among the Scheduled Caste students was very high. Problems of quite different nature were found by Bindu in a study conducted on the education of the scheduled castes in Uttar Pradesh study showed that (1) literacy among the scheduled caste females was very low specially in rural areas, (2) the per capita expenditure on welfare of the scheduled castes in U.P. was lower in comparison to that in other state, (3) hardly any importance was given to preprimary education (4) girls formed only a fifth of the enrolment of the boys at primary stage in school.

The perceding pages revealed various kinds of problems pertaining to the education of the scheduled caste students in India. Mostly, problems were of socio-economic nature. A few of these relate to their enrolment and academic performance. Nearly all the studies conclude that the scheduled caste students are inferior to other caste students in their calibre and performance. Finally, the scheduled caste students, largely feel that the facilities provided by the governments to them are needed and satisfactory also, but they are not administered properly.

Psychological Studies

There are very few studies in which psychological characteristics of the scheduled caste students have been measured and compared. One of these few studies was conducted by Aggarwal between the scheduled and non-scheduled caste high school students of Thanesar (Haryana). A significant difference was found on locus of control and intelligence. The scheduled caste students were found to be more external (believing in systems, luck and chance for their accomplishment) than the non-scheduled caste students. Also, it was found that the non-scheduled caste students were significantly more intelligent than the scheduled caste students. A study of the personal characteristics and academic achievement of another study conducted on the Scheduled Caste students of Meerut University by Gupta revealed that (1) the scheduled caste graduate students are more affiliative, more in need of feeling inferior, more nuturant and more enduring as compared to the non-scheduled caste students, (2) they are less aggressive less dominant and less succourant as compared to the non-Scheduled Caste students, (3) Generally, the Scheduled Caste graduate students feel comparatively more inadequate and inferior and suffer more from feelings of emotional instability, (4) Intellectually, the Scheduled Caste graduate and post-graduate students both are found to be inferior to non-Scheduled Castes students of the same classes, (5) the graduate and post-graduate students of Scheduled Castes are poor achievers as compared to their non-Scheduled Caste counterparts.

For the first time, Sinha and Sinha studied how non-scheduled caste students perceive the scheduled caste students. They found that the non-scheduled caste students showed favourable attitudes towards the Harijans, the male students being more liberal than the female ones. In a study made by Sharma, it was concluded that significant differences do exist between the scheduled and non-scheduled caste students-teachers on fourteen variables of behavioural dimensions. They were found to be of relatively lower scholastic mental capacity than their counterparts of higher castes. They have a lower capacity to learn. This fact, it was stated by Sharma, resulted into lower level of academic achievement of the Scheduled Caste student teachers as compared to that of the higher caste student teachers. Besides, it was found that the scheduled caste students were less creative, more easy-going, more expressive emotionally, less confident, more prone to adopt withdrawing behaviour and having higher degree of emotional instability. In Rajasthan, Rao also conducted a study of Harijans and concluded that students from Harijans, Muslims, Hindus and Tribals perceived one another negatively. Ethnocentrism was found to be decreasing with lower caste children.

In another study, Bose found that the morale of these children was low; they were educationally backward, had religious-communal feelings, flexible in the aspects of emotion and temperament.

Chattopadhyaya, in his study of the intelligence of tribal and non-tribal children of Tripura was found that the (1) tribal boys did not compare favourably as a group with the non-tribal boys, (2) the higher score by the tribal boys only on Alaxander's Passing Test showed that the problem-solving situation posed by this test might be more akin to the real life-environment of the tribal boys than that of the non-tribal boys. Kundu studied the personality traits of juvenile offenders of scheduled tribes and other communities. He found that instability at home poor parent child relationship, parental objection to the kind of companions they had, feeling of resentment, high level of anxiety, depressive trends lesser degree of satisfaction with self, poor health condition and poor power of observation were, perhaps, the cause of the delinquency of tribal children, (3) low intelligence was also, perhaps, linked with their delinquency.

Similar studies have been conducted in America and Canada on the Negros and other majority groups of society. The personality needs, interests and other psychological dispositions of the Black Americans and other groups have drawn the attention of the researchers. Significant differences on personality traits exists between the Blacks and the Whites was proved by Epstein, Minigione, Kinnick, Grossack, etc.

Conclusions

In the field of education, sociology, psychology, the weaker sections of the society, the scheduled castes in India and the Negros in the West have constituted an important area of research. Since the 1970s when the Government of India policies stressed the need for integrating the weaker sections of the society into the mainstream and emphasized equalization of opportunity for all the scheduled caste have evoked special interest among the researchers. Almost all the studies except two or three reviewed were completed during the period 1974-1978. About 45 studies have been conducted during this period in the field of education, psychology, sociology and economics. Although, the scheduled castes have been a focus of intensive research enquiry among the sociologists, anthropologists, and political scientists, yet the research workers in the field of education and psychology have not paid sufficient attention.

On the whole, we can say that fifty per cent of the studies have concentrated on the study and identification of the problems of the scheduled castes students at various levels of education. A few of them dealt with the study of the attitudes of the non-scheduled caste students towards the scheduled caste ones. Still a few others have studied the attitudes of the scheduled caste students towards teaching facilities provided by the Government in their own states, etc. There are very few studies on psychological characteristics of the scheduled caste students.

Psychological studies which have attempted to study the characteristics of the scheduled caste students on weaker section students in India and in the countries of the West have mainly, focused on personality needs, motivation, belongingness, anxiety, neuroticism,. attitudes, self-esteem, self-concept, intelligence, academic achievement, academic motivation, etc.

Surprisingly, hardly and study have been conducted in India or abroad on the first generation learners of the scheduled castes.

Though here and there researchers did used the word 'first generation learners' but till today this special group of the first generation learners of the scheduled castes have never been studied. Hence, even the term "first generation learners of scheduled caste" is not found being used in literature. It occurred recently in one of the Government of India document where it was stated that, "It seems essential to juxtapose the scenerio of the education system against the internal dynamics of a society in which 64 per cent of the population is illiterate and large percentage of students are first generation learners". This, however, is about the first generation learners of the general population. The first generation learners of the scheduled caste have not received the attention even here. In the National Policy on Education, 1986 the equalization of the scheduled castes with the non-scheduled caste population has been again emphasized. It says, "The central focus in the scheduled castes' educational development is their equalization with the non-scheduled caste population at all stages and levels of education, in all areas and in all the four dimensions—rural, male, rural female, urban male and urban female". The 'first generation learners group' of the scheduled caste population is found missing in this perspective also.

Since this group of the first generation learners of the scheduled caste has failed to receive the attention of the researchers till today as is found from the review presented here and since the group is considered important by this researcher and also by the authors of the Challenge of Education as pointed out earlier, it was decided to make a study of this group. Again, since psychological studies of the scheduled castes were found to be very few it was also decided to make a psycho-educational study of this group. The following chapter presents the design of the study and its details. Hence, this researcher, emphatically would like to say that there is still great need of research on the scheduled caste students. Only more and more studies in this direction will yield stable conclusions about the scheduled caste students.

Implications of Findings and Suggestions

This chapter describes how the information collected on the Scheduled Caste students can be utilized by concerned people in the field of education. Also, suggestions are given for further research in the area of the education of the Scheduled Caste first generation learners.

Implications of Findings

Finding No. 1

The hypothesis No. 1 was that "there is no difference between the enrolment in class XI of first and subsequent generation learners of the Scheduled Castes population". This hypothesis got rejected at 0.01 level and it was concluded that the enrolment of first generation learners is significantly higher in comparison to the children of subsequent generation learners of the Scheduled Caste community. Thereby, showing that the parents of first generation learners are quite enthusiastic about the education of their children. They perhaps, realize the importance of education and seem to be well-motivated to encourage their children to go to schools and study.

The above finding indicates that the Government's policy of helping and encouraging weaker sections of the society, particularly the scheduled castes has been successful to a large extent. The information can be utilized as a feedback for the educational planners and the managers at the level of the region as well as the State of U.P. Also, the information may form a part of the data-bank of the enrolment of students for future reference. The finding has far-reaching implications from the point of view of planning and administration. It suggests that more facilities have to be provided keeping the first generation learners in mind.

Finding No. 2

The testing of hypothesis-5 which stated that "there is no significant difference between problems pertaining to 'finance, living conditions and employment (FLE)' of first and subsequent generation learners". This was not accepted as the difference was found to be significant. It seems the first generation learners have significantly more problems pertaining to finance, living conditions and employment. They have poor living standards and are in need of immediate employment for reasons of being poor.

This information is important from the point of view of planning for the education of the first generation learners for future. Perhaps, specific recommendations for more facilities, financial, and residential have to be made for the first generation learners in future, in order to bring these children at par with the children of other castes. Equalization of opportunity of all people in India has been emphasized in the National Policy on Education, 1986.*

To ensure progress of education of the scheduled caste children especially the first generation learners, scholarships and free hostel accommodation should be provided to them. On the whole, more facilities are to be given or more attention is to be paid or priority is to be given to the first generation learners of the scheduled castes.

Finding No. 3

The hypothesis No. 5.4 which stated that "there is no significant difference between problems related to 'social-psychological relations (SPR)' of first and subsequent generation learners" was tested for significance and it was concluded that the difference, in this regard, between these two groups was significant. It was further concluded that the first generation learners were more worried about social-psychological relations and hence, need some sort of guidance and counselling. This finding would be important to the principals and teachers of these children as this may enable them to understand them better.

---

* *National Policy on Education, 1986*, Ministry of Human Resource Development, Government of India, New Delhi, para 4.1 to 4.13.

Finding No. 4

This finding is a result of the hypothesis that "there is no significant difference between problems related to adjustment to school work (ASW), of first and subsequent genration learners". This hypothesis was rejected because the difference between the groups was found significant on problems related to adjustment to school work. The problem was especially in the first generation learners. This finding is important from the point of view of students' achievement and learning. Poor adjustment may affect their achievement adversely and can demotivate them further. Hence, the teachers, are required to pay special attention to the first generation learners . They should identify the causes of their poor adjustment and, once known should make efforts to eliminate them. The school psychologist or the guidance department of the school as the case may be, should use this information to the advantage of the first generation learners of the scheduled castes.

Finding No. 5

Here, the most acute problems of the first generation learners of the scheduled castes were identified. The most important once are: (i) employment during holidays, (ii) possibility of post-college education, (iii) home being away from the school, (iv) lack of facilities at home, (v) need for borrowing money, (vi) non-availability of time for play, (vii) desire to be popular, (viii) anxieties and worries of varaious kinds, (ix) curiosity about man's post-death phenomenon, (x) no separate room for study at home, (xi) lack of training for any job, (xii) lack of guidance for career after passing their intermediate examination, (xiii) worry about the examination result and division to be obtained.

All these problems seem to be more acute in case of the first generation learners as compared to the subsequent generation learners. Out of these, some problems can be minimized, but cannot be completely eliminated while others can neither be minimized nor can be eliminated. In such cases it is only the guidance and counselling which can be provided. Through counselling the perceptions and the attitudes of the first generation learners of the scheduled castes may be so changed that they do not perceive these problems baffling and difficult. Some sort of motivational counselling that aims at strengthening the ego should be provided to these students of the scheduled castes.

The above findings have serious implications for guidance workers, counsellors and teachers. It would help the administrators such as the principals and the social workers to understand how these first generation learnes of the scheduled castes may be helped.

Findings suggests that special programmes of assistance and guidance should be organized by the Government to help these children of the scheduled castes.

Suggestions for Further Research

The above findings show that there are innumerable problems in the field of educational research. To get results which are more stable and conclusive it is essential to conduct many research studies on a problem. Further, it is also not possible for one research worker to cover all the dimensions of the particular problem. The present problem focussed on "A comparative study of achievement, adjustment, attitudes and problems of first and subsequent generation learners of scheduled castes at higher secondary level". The results of this study cannot be considered conclusive. They need to be substantiated by further research and verification. More conclusive result can be obtained if similar studies are conducted on other similar populations. Besides, there are a few questions that are raised by the present study which need to be answered by further research. These have been discussed in the following sections:

1. Due to the limitations of time, money and energy the present study was confined to the students of scheduled castes community of Meerut region only. Hence, all the conclusions are very much region specific. To make the observations more generic, similar studies need to be conducted on a wider population at state level and national level.
2. The present study was based on the first generation learners of scheduled caste who were males. A similar study need to be conducted on female learners too.
3. In this research, the Mooney Problems Check-List was found to be very relevant for this group of students. But the researcher felt afterwards that the problem check-list

should have consisted of more realistic and genuine problems. For example, instead of courtship, sex and marriage there could be an area of "relationships with class fellows and teachers". This is the area in which the first generation learners of the scheduled castes may be expected to face problems. Hence, a fresh study with a newly constructed problem check-list should be made.

4. The present study restructed itself to the comparison between the first genration and subsequent generation learners of the scheduled castes only. It is suggested that similar studies should be conducted on first and subsequent generation learners of the non-scheduled caste communities also. There is a need to find out whether the problems faced by scheduled caste first generation learners are also being faced by the non-scheduled caste first generation learners.
5. The studies revealed that conducted no significant differences between the first and subsequent generation learners on any dimension of the attitude inventory. But, the researcher still feels that the difference should emerged. Perhaps, the case study method may be more appropriate for this purpose. It is therefore, suggested that a few studies of this kind may be conducted by using in case study method.

Summary and Conclusions

Objectives of the Study

There were five main objectives which encompassed this present study. The objectives have been clearly discussed in the preceding chapter "The Problem and Its Background".

Population

The population constituted of all the scheduled castes learners of XI class of boys intermediate colleges of Meerut region. The study was confined to male learners only.

Sample

The sample consists of 14 per cent (43 colleges) of 595 boys intermediate colleges, randomly selected through systematic sampling method from the consolidated list of schools from the districts of Saharanpur, Muzaffarnagar, Meerut, Ghaziabad and Bulandshahr. The sample table is as follows:

TABLE 6.1
SAMPLE TABLE OF SCHEDULED CASTE LEARNERS

Sl. No.	*Name of district*	*Total no. of intermediate boys colleges*	*Total no. of selected colleges*	*Total no. of learners collected*
1.	Saharanpur	98	8	23
2.	Muzaffarnagar	78	6	26
3.	Meerut	167	12	52
4.	Ghaziabad	94	7	38
5.	Bulandshahr	158	10	27
	Total	595	43	166

The Variables involved in the Study

This study involves following variables:

Dependent Variables — Achievement.
— Adjustment.
— Attitudes.
— Problems.

Independent Variables — First generation learners of SC.
— Subsequent generation learners of SC.

Tools Used

The tools used to measure the problems are Asthana's Adjustment Inventory, Students' Attitudes Inventory and Mooney Problem Check-List. To obtain score the variables have been defined in this pattern:

1. To measure achievement the divisions (I, II and III) of 1985 passed students in high school exam. have been taken for achievement of the learners.
2. To measure adjustment "Asthana's Adjustment Inventory" has been used.
3. To measure attitudes of learners "Students' Attitude Inventory" has been used which was prepared by the researcher.

4. To measure the problems of the students' "Mooney Problem Check-List" has been used.

Summary of Findings

To sum up, the following results were obtained:

1. Enrolment in class XI was found higher in case of the first generation learners as compared to that of the subsequent generation learners of the scheduled castes.
2. In terms of the academic achievement no significant difference was found between the first and the subsequent generation learners of the scheduled castes. Academic achievement was measured in terms of divisions (I, II, III and fail) obtained after class X.
3. There was hardly any difference on personality adjustment between the two sections of learner as defined by Asthana's Personality Adjustment Inventory.
4. The first and subsequent generation learners of the scheduled castes were compared on four dimensions of attitudes—attitudes towards college, teachers, education and society—No significant difference was found between them on any of these dimensions.
5. Problems of these two groups of learners of the scheduled castes were studied under 11 subheads (1) health and physical development, (2) finance, living conditions and employment, (3) social and recreational activities, (4) social psychological relations, (5) personal psychological relations, (6) courtship, sex and marriage, (7) home and faculty, (8) morals and religion, (9) adjustment to school work, (10) The future: vocational and educational (11) curriculum and teaching procedure. Out of these eleven problem areas only on three of them significant differences were found between the first and subsequent generation learners of the scheduled castes. The first generation learners as compared to the subsequent generation learners were found to be worried more about finance, living conditions and employment. The other two problems were in the area of social psychological relations and their adjustment to school work.

6. Most acute problems of the first generation learners of the scheduled castes were also identified. They were found to be (1) employment during holidays, (2) possibility of post-college education, (3) home being away from school, (4) lack of facilities at home, (5) need for borrowing money, (6) non-availability of time for play, (7) desire to be popular, (8) anxieties and worries of various kinds, (9) curiosity about man's post-death phenomenon, (10) no separate room for study at home, (11) lack of training for any job, (12) lack of guidance for career after passing intermediate class, (13) to be self-dependent, and (14) worry about the examination result and division to be obtained.

Seven

Educational Wastage

It has been proved beyond question, that in the development of child's personality, education plays a vital role. But ina caste ridden and hierarchical society like India's, it was only the priviledged classes who had access to educational opportunities, during preindependence days and the lower castes, especially Scheduled Castes were denied the educational facilities. However, after independence, special measures were proposed in our constitution for the education of the scheduled castes and liberal plan allocations were made under different five year plans to improve the lot of Scheduled Castes. Inspite of these efforts, there exists a wide disparity in the educational level of scheduled castes and non-scheduled castes. Various committees have been set up and research studies have been conducted to investigate the reasons behind the wide disparity. Most of these studies have concluded that wastage is the main reasons for hindrance in the way of progress of the scheduled castes.

Different studies, define the term 'wastage' in different ways, UNESCO (1968) defines that educational wastage includes two main components (1) grade repetition, which refers to pupils who are held back in the same grade and do the same work as in the previous year, and (2) drop-out or withdrawal from a school cycle before its completion. However, generally, the term 'wastage' implies premature withdrawal of a child from school cycle before completing the last grade of the stage of education in which he is studying. As research studies show that wastage acts as a road block in the path of progress of education of scheduled castes. One needs to know the causes so as to finally remove it from the system. In the present chapter about fifty studies dealing with drop-outs among scheduled castes have been reviewed.

Research shows that the incidence of drop-outs or the rate of wastage is more in scheduled castes than in non-scheduled castes. One of the main reasons mentioned is the stigma of untouchability (Sharma and Sapra, 1969; Naik, 1971; Pimpley, 1974; Singh, 1974; Nayer, 1975; Chitnis, 1976; Dantawala, 1976; Mehta, 1976; Chitnism, 1977 and Yadav, 1984).

The incidences of wastage is reported at various school stages. Chandrasekhraiah (1969) found that largest drop-out is in the classes I and II, while Adiseshiah (1974), Kariekar (1975) and Mishra (1978) reported that the percentage of detention was highest at the primary stage (I-V classes). But some studies have concluded that wastage exist at the middle stage or after 8th class (Chauhan, 1375; Maurya, 1976).

Another category of studies points out the difference in wastage of education in relation to demographic variables of age and sex. Pimpley (1975) and Shah (1976) found that the largest number of drop-out was of male than female students while Singh (1969) and Gore (1974) found that wastage of education is not less than 80 per cent in lower age groups particularly school-age children (6-14 years).

Further, there are studies which refer to wastage of education in relation to place of living. Chaudhary (1970), Gore (1974) and Mehta (1976) found that the children belonging to rural areas have higher rate of drop-out than the children belonging to urban areas while Pimpley (1978) reported that the urban children had a higher rate of drop-out than rural children. Some studies on.wastage of education refer to income bracket of the parents belonging to scheduled castes. The studies of Kariekar, 1975; Rastogi, 1976 and Yadav 1984 concluded that the parents whose income is less than Rupees 1500 per annum have more drop-out children in the family as compared to the parents having more income.

The above discussion shows that there are a number of social, educational, occupational and economic factors which affect the wastage of education among scheduled castes, and hence study can be broadly classified under these four categories.

Economic

In most of the studies poverty and economic backwardness of the family has been cited as the most important cause contributing to wastage in education. Lack of good clothing, shelter, medical facilities, stationery and cost of education are broadly the reasons which compelled them to give up their studies (Chandrasekharaiah, 1969; Singh, 1969; Naik, 1971; Shah, 1972; Dubey, 1974; Lakshmanna, 1974; Singh, 1974; Nayer, 1975; Chatterjee, 1975; Mehta, 1976; Santhakumari, 1976; Maurya, 1976; Rastogi, 1976; Chitnis, 1977 and Ramanamma, 1978.

Again due to economic backwardness, children are compelled to take up domestic responsibilities. Their help is required in house-hold work such as keeping watch over the house in the absence of adult members of the family and the compulsion to earn or to take a major share in domestic work in order to release the adults for gainful work and the consequent attention to school work (Shah, 1972; Chatterjee, 1975; and Santhakumari, 1976).

Also, studies reveals that employment is a reasons for the wastage of education. Due to poverty; children get employment as unskilled labourers in factories or other organisation. Some children drop-out due to seasonal employment. At the time of harvesting the crops, children being landless labourers, are engaged to cultivate the crops with the whole family (Soni, 1975; Chitnis, 1977 and Kirpal, 1978).

Occupational

Various research studies have concluded that occupation of the parents also lead to wastage in education. As mostly, Scheduled Castes are the artisan, they have their own parental occupations. They generally withdraw their children from school at early stage and engage the children in their own occupations (Shah, 1973; Singh, 1974).

Social

There are instances which show that caste leads to wastage in education. In India, rural communities have still not lost their cultural sterotypes, thus there are villages which are conspicuous by their caste or occupational character. It is not uncommon to hear in this country— This is a Brahmin 'village', This is an Ahir 'village'. This social disease compels children to drop-out from the schools (Sharma and Sapra, 1969).

In case of girls, early marriage or betrothal significantly operates as a cause of wastage. It is more pronounced at the primary and middle stage of education. It is found that children are withdrawn from school after betrothal or marriage particularly in the case of girls in the rural areas (Sapra 1967, Chauhan 1976). Besides, studies refer to the discriminating behaviour as a cause of wastage. The children of scheduled castes faced the difficulty of ill-treatment in school particularly in urban areas. (Singh, 1974). It was also found that mal-treatment and impolite attitude of teachers towards these children and their discrimination by teachers, general indifference and hostility towards them, force them to leave their education, leading to wastage in education (Lakshmanna, 1974; Chatterjee, 1975; Maurya, 1976 and Yadav 1984).

Social and family customs are also responsible for many cases of drop-outs. Because of these, they believe in supersitions (Singh, 1974; Ramaswamy, 1974; Maurya, 1976). Chatterjee (1975) found that many of the parents regret the adverse affects that one drop-out child from the family or neighbourhood have upon the others. Also, as most of the students are the first in their families to attend the school and as such parental help and encouragement are generally lcking for them in their effort to continue their education (Bose, 1969).

We also cannot deny the fact there is lack of condusive environment for the study. The facilities available to them for study are not sufficient. This leads to wastage in education (Singh, 1974; Lakshmanna, 1974; Mehta, 1976).

Educational

Stagnation is a major factor which contributes to wastage. The longer a child remains in one class, the more he is discouraged and probably neglected while his continued presence at school not only confess no benefit on him but also affects adversely the education of other pupils. Stagnation is due to a variety of factors, the main among which are the poor performance in studies, failures, poor quality of teachers, indifferent teaching, defective system of examination, load of syllabus and textbooks, lack of co-curricular activities and non-availability of textbooks, etc. (Chandrasekaraiah, 1969; Chaudhary 1970; Lakshmanna, 1974; Nayer, 1975; Soni, 1975; Maurya, 1976; Santhakumari, 1976; Chitnis 1977).

There are some defects in the system of admission also which affects the education of the Scheduled Castes. Basically, there is no systematic procedure for the admission of these children. In some schools, admission in grade I is kept open throughout the year where as in some schools the admissions are open only in the beginning of the session. As a result thereof those children who join the school towards the fag end of the academic session are treated as stagnation cases because they study only for few months and not for the whole years. Some schools have provision of entrance tests while others have not.

Some studies have revealed that the presence of illiterate parents and larger number of illiterate members in the family, also effects the phenomenon of wastage (Ramaswamy, 1974; Maurya, 1976; Shanthakumari, 1976 and Yadav, 1984).

Being first generation learners the attitude of their parents is also not that inspiring. Parents attitude is not very encouraging motivating, and supportive towards education. They have low aspiration level. (Singh, 1969; Shah, 1972; Naik, 1971; Debey, 1974; Singh 1974; Lakshmanna, 1974; Maurya, 1976; Misra, 1978; Ramanamma, 1978; Pimpley, 1978). Added to this, the inadequate facilities provided at home and school, indifference shown by teachers etc., make children to drop-out. Non-availability of educational aids like mid-day meals, books, slates, uniforms, etc., affect the education of Scheduled Caste children and lead to poor retention in schools (Chitnis, 1972; Dubey, 1974; Lakshmanna, 1974; Maurya, 1976; Yadav, 1979 and Yadav, 1983).

Though the provision of scholarships is provided to simplify their educational endeavour, some studies have revealed that delayed payment of scholarship is the main reason for the discontinuation of studies. Most of the times scholarships are distributed to the students at the end of the session and even after the session (Soni, 1975; Yadav, 1979 and Yadav, 1981).

Premi (1974) found that although there has been expension of elementary education and abolition of fees, yet the facilities are availed of more by "haves" than by deprived sections of society whose children drop-out at various stages.

Besides, these social, economic, educational and occupational factors which lead to wastage in education, there are also certain other reasons which are responsible for discontinuation of education among scheduled castes. For instance, continuous illness of the pupils adversely affects their academic achievement and health which ultimately lead to wastage in education (Sapra, 1967; Mehta, 1976). Collection of money in the form of donation and irregular attendance have also been found to be the most important contributory factors responsible for the phenomenon of wastage in education (Lakshmanna, 1974). Distance between educational institution and home is sometime very long. During rainy seasons, it really acts as an obstacle for the students.

Now, that we are more or less aware of the reasons behind the wastage in education, we need to look at some ways and means to solve this complex problem of wastage in education.

Some researchers feel that as income level of the parents and family is the dominant factor in influencing the extent of retention in schools, one needs to first tackle this fundamental problems. They feel that the parents should do extra work for increasing the income level of the family. (Shah, 1972; Nayer, 1975; Chatterjee, 1975).

Another set of studies suggested that special academic programmes and coaching classes shold be organised for scheduled caste students for recovering their deficiencies in their subjects and in improving their academic performances. This will help in reducing the problem of wastage in education (Rastogi, 1976; Chitnis, 1977; and Yadav, 1984). Santhakumari (1976) found that size of class and teacher-pupil relations also effect this problem. In primary and upper primary.If size of group or class is small, the teacher can adopt a standard of teaching in accordance with their abilities which is suitable to them. This can be helpful in reducing the complex problem of wastage in education.

The studies of Pimply (1978) reveal that the awareness of reservation does have any positive relationship with attendance. Those who are not aware are generally not attenders. He feels that the place of residence, the distance from school however, does not seem to make any significant effect on school attendance. According to him, it is the lack of awareness of reservation of seats in educational institution which should tackled first (Yadav, 1984) also feels the same. For tackling this problem, there should be provisions of free supply of mid-day meals, biscuits uniforms and other materials for the scheduled castes, so that they can be attracted and motivated towards the schools and remain in the schools (Yadav 1981). For the drop-out students, programmes like non-formal education, partial education and adult education can be made, so that they can join schools, again after getting feedback from these agencies (Yadav, 1979).

Eight

Awareness About Educational Schemes

Awareness of scheduled castes about educational schemes is very crucial for their educational progress. This chapter discusses the effect of demographic variables like age, sex, location and other variables like education, occupation and economic status of the scheduled castes on their awareness level about educational schemes for their progress.

The studies in the area of awareness have covered a wide variety of variables pertaining to scheduled caste students and parents. Firstly, awareness has been studied in relation to students, parents and awareness within scheduled castes. Pimpley (1974), Singhi (1975), Dubey (1974), Nayer (1975), Valunjkar (1975), Gangrade (1974), Sachchidananda (1974), Chitnis (1974), George (1975), Shah (1974) and Yadav (1983) in their studies found that most of the students were aware of the scholarship facilities, reservations in educational institutions and also aware of the Constitutional provisions regarding the welfare of scheduled castes, whereas, Soni (1975), Rath (1974) and Rajagopalan (1974), Chauhan (1974) and Sachchidananda (1974) found that some of the school and college students are still not aware of the special reservation in educational institutions, scholarship schemes and Constitutional provisions for the welfare of scheduled castes.

Also, there is a difference in the awareness of parents belonging to scheduled castes about educational schemes. Punalekar (1975), Santhakumari (1975) and Premi (1974) found that the parents were aware of the educational concessions, financial concession, scholarships, stipends, freeships, reservation of seats for admission to educational institutions, coaching facilities provided and administered by Government/Harijan Welfare

Department. However, Naik (1971), Vagiswari (1973), Maurya (1976), Yadav (1979), Nautiyal (1979) and Parvathamma (1973) found that the respondents were still unaware about the various facilities, aids, concessions in admission, special schemes and programmes provided by the government for the welfare of the scheduled castes.

Not only this, there is a differential awareness within scheduled castes as well. Parmar (1978) on Mahayavanshi, a scheduled caste in Surat city found that the development of education in Mahayavanshi caste shows that among these there is an increasing awareness of the need for education which is further reflected in their increasing utilisation of educational facilities such as scholarships, freeships, and examination fees provided by the government. Abbasayulu (1977) and Yadavn (1983) also found that the scheduled caste elite group was more aware about the educational schemes and benefits for their progress than all the scheduled castes taken together.

On the while, the studies reveal that in the area of awareness, there is a whole lot of contridictory finding looking at the area of awareness in relation to demographic variables of age and sex, we find that the girl students were aware about the reservation for scheduled castes in government and public undertaking (Lal, 1974). But in contrast to this, Pimpley (1974), Chitnis (1977) and George (1975) found that the awareness about reserved seats in educational institutions and facilities available for the welfare of scheduled caste, was more in boys than in girls.

The findings of Rastogi (1976) shows that the respondents of different age-groups are aware of the different Constitutional provisions for protecting the interests of their communities. He further found that elder respondents are more aware of various legislative measures as compared to the younger members.

Looking at how awareness of facilities and the location of scheduled castes are related, Pimpley (1978) found that both the rural and urban attending children were equally aware and the place of residence does not seem to make any significant difference in their awareness. However, Rastogi (1976) and Yadav (1983) contradices this finding. He reports that all respondents of urban areas are more aware of the Constitutional provision regarding scheduled castes than the rural ones. Mukherjee (1975) corroborates this finding when he states that women belonging to scheduled castes are more aware about educational schemes in urban areas than in rural areas. Chitnis (1977) on comparing the awareness of hostellers and non-hostellers, reveals that hostellers have distinctly higher level of awareness than non-hostellers about schemes.

Another study shows that the awareness of scheduled caste children about educational schemes differ from district to district (Gangrade, 1974; Dubey, 1974). But Rajagopalan (1974), Soni (1975) and Rastogi (1976) found that the awareness of the respondents at the college stage belonging to corporation districts regarding educational schemes and reservation policies are higher as compared to other districts. So, the place of residence effects the awareness and utilisation of Scheduled Caste about educational schemes for their progress.

The awareness of scheduled castes about educational schemes is also studied in relation to other variables like social, educational, economic and occupational status of the scheduled caste respondents. Social restrictions create hinderance in the awareness of scheduled caste progress. The respondents being aware of this feel the need for protective discriminations (Chitnis, 1977). The awareness of educational facilities increase the social status (Shanthakumari, 1976). The welfare workers most must create an awareness about their rights and an atmosphere to assert them by reporting cases of infringement (Dubey, 1972).

Besides the above discussed, education is one of the important factors in increasing the awareness of Scheduled Caste about schemes for their progress. Regular school/college goers are more aware of the schemes. The lack of awareness was most pronounced in the case of non-attenders (Chauhan, 1967). Education in Mahayavanshi caste shows an awareness in the form of utilisation of educational schemes such as scholarships, freeships, and examination fees provided by the government (Parmar, 1978).

According to Malik (1971) and Malik (1979) also, greater percentage of educated respondents are aware of more important facilities, such as educational facilities, provisions of grants and less educated persons are comparatively less aware of these facilities. Rastogi (1976) also found that the respondents doing their law graduation are comparatively more aware of various legislative measures than the respondents pursuing other courses of study. Overall, quite a good number of respondents of all educational levels are aware of the various constitutional provisions.

While studying on impact of welfare measures on the backward classes in Kerala Shanthakumari (1976) found that the awareness transcends both the educational and occupational level of respondents and the awareness of educational facilities is an incentive for their children for jobs, which brings them a better job. This is an incentive for availing of existing educational facilities.

Further, she feels that economic status also increases the awareness of scheduled castes about educational schemes. The respondents in the large income brackets are comparatively more aware of various legislative measures as compared to their counterparts who are placed in lower income brackets (Rastogi, 1976). It can be the other way as well. They might be economically betters because of their higher awareness level.

On the whole, the research studies reviewed in this chapter highlight the extent of awareness and unawareness among scheduled castes about the reservation in educational and technical institutions, scholarships at various stages, educational schemes and programmes for their progress. Antecendent variables of awareness have also been discussed and presented in this research review.

Utilisation of Schemes

The study of educational schemes would be incomplete without discussing the utilization of them by the scheduled castes. The utilisation of educational schemes provided by the government for the welfare of the scheduled castes differs in different context. This tries to present the findings of different studies pertaining to the utilisation of educational schemes in a systematic way.

The studies in the area of utilisation have covered a wide variety of variables pertaining to scheduled caste students and parents. Firstly the utilisation of schemes by the students and parents have been considered. Lal (1974), Adiseshiah (1975), Goyal (1974), Gangrade (1974), Pimpley (1974), Soni (1974), Dubey (1974), George (1975), Shah (1974), Parvathamma (1974), Chauhan (1975),

Chitnis (1977), Desai (1974), Lakshmanna (1974), Sachchidananda (1974), Singh (1974) and Yadav (1983) found that most of the college and school students considered educational facilities, scholarships, stipends, freeships, reservation in admissions to educational institutions and various educational programmes to be useful, effectively utilised, beneficial for their educational progress and advancement. However, Rath (1974) and Chitnis (1974) found that the educational facilities are not adequate for the scheduled castes. The teachers as respondents also support the finding that scholarships and other schemes are very useful and fair in the promotion of education of scheduled castes (Nayer, 1975; Jha, 1973; Lakshmanna, 1974).

Further, the studies reveal that the scheduled castes differ in the use of educational facilities. It prepetuates the inadequacies within these people (Chauhan, 1976 and Yadav, 1983). The government assistance for education creates inequalities of utilisation between different groups within scheduled castes (Shah, 1974). Chitnis (1977) and Premi (1977) feel that there is a distinct caste and class pattern in use of educational facilities at higher stage.

Singh (1971) elaborated the usage of the scholarship money. He found that scholarship holders utilize a part of received amount on such items as buying books and other educational requirements, purchasing of clothes and on transports and the remaining goes for family expenses. Some spent lessthen Rs. 100 on hostel bills and examination fees, some spent more than Rs. 500 on above items. Some use a part of their scholarship for meeting family expenses. Only the amount varies one obvious reason for this wrong utilisation of money was the poverty.

Another study based on the demographic variable of age and sex shows that the male students considered these schemes more useful and satisfactory than the female students (Dubey, 1974 and Yadav, 1983). Chitnis (1977) found that the scheduled caste women don't use these facilities as freely as scheduled caste men. Shah (1976) also found that male and female postmatric scholars indicate substantial difference in this aspect. More male postmatric scholar are coming for higher education that female postmatric scholars.

The use of educational schemes differ as per age groups also. (Rastogi 1976) found that elder respondents are more aware and utilize the various legislative measures as compared to their younger counterparts.

Studies show that utilisation also depends on the place of residence of the scheduled castes. Rastogi (1976) report that respondent coming from rural areas of U.P. show the maximum tendency of utilizing facilities provided by the government. On the other hand, Shah (1976) found that the proportion of the scheduled caste scholars from urban areas is little less than double the proportion of their population residing in rural areas. Dubey (1974) also found that more postmatric scholars were coming from the urban areas than rural aras. According to Ahmed (1973), different utilisation of government assistance is not due to socio-economic reasons, but due to urban residence. Premi (1974) found that better availability of educational facilities offered by big cities and towns, lead to greater awareness whereas others have to content themselves with lower educational attainments.

Further, we find that the utilisation of educational schemes and government assistance differ from district to district. Surat district in Gujarat State was the highest in utilisation of government schemes. Parmar, 1978; Shah and Patel, 1976). A probable reason for this may be due to the increasing involvement of voluntary organisations and due to the impact of Gandhi and his belief in constructive programmes.

The findings of Dubey (1974) show that highest respondents are from sibsagar district in Assam at college level, who think educational facilities are quite satisfactory, useful, and adequate; while Dubey (1974) at the school stage found that the highest number of scheduled caste respondents from Lakhimpur and Dibrugarh feel that these facilities are not at all useful, adequate and satisfactory.

Hostellers were surveyed to evaluate the also affect the utilisation of schemes. Chinist (1977) found that college hostellers were dissatisfied with the facilities, while Trivedi (1977), Dueby (1974) and Valunjkar (1975) found that most hostellers felt that these educational facilities were useful, adequate and satisfactory.

From state to state also, the utilisation of schemes differ a lot.

In every state certain scheduled caste communities within scheduled castes, which are in comparatively more advantageous circumstances to begin with, were able to get more benefits out of the schemes than other (Vyas, 1969; Chitnis, 1977; Parmar, 1978; Ram, 1976; Ramaswamy, 1974; Patwardhan, 1973; Premi, 1974; Shah, 1976; Chauhan, 1976; Das, 1971; and Hussain, 1972).

Most of the respondents considered various educational programmes to be useful, effectively utilised, beneficial for their educational progress and social advancement (Rajagopalan, 1974; Gangrade, 1974; Pimply, 1974; Singhi, 1975; Singh, 1974; Sachchidananda, 1974; some negative views have been given by Shah, 1974 stating that scheduled castes have to face obstacles in the main stream of Indian social life due to these schemes. George (1975) also found that the system of separate hostels for scheduled caste students was considered socially unhealthy as it widened the gaps with higher caste students.

Utilisation of schemes depends to a large extent on the Parental education, as well. Shanthakumari (1976), Rastogi (1976), Dubey, (1974) and Gangrade (1974) found that higher the education of the father, higher the utilisation of schemes by their children. George (1975) found that the parents needed to be educated about the government programme in order to properly utilise the resources.

Rastogi (1976) found that the incidence of utilisation is higher among the respondents, doing their graduation and after that doing their diploma/LLB Courses and least utilization is conspicuous is medical graduations. Malik (1971, 1979 and Yadvav 1983) also found that higher the education of the respondents, the higher percentage of those who avail themselves of the opportunity, while Premi (1974) found that majority of respondents use educational facilities, i.e., financial concessions such as freeships, stipends at high school and scholarship in college.

Level of occupations also decides the utilisation of schemes. Better occupations increase their utilisation of educational schemes. Most of the postmatric scholars were found from the white collar occupations (Shah, 1976).

The differential utilisation of government assistance is due to socio-economic reasons. Pathsudu (1971), Pimpley (1976), Goyal

(1974), Yadav (1980), Premi (1977) and Saxena (1968) found that greater advantages of the programmes are availed by the people from high socio-economic group, advanced sections and privileged families from scheduled castes. The postmatric scholarship, the central piller of all educational facilities at higher stage, tends to favour the 'haves' rather than 'have not's' or depriveds sections. Dogra (1977) found that low socio-economic status of Harijans has resulted in a massive under utilisation of facilities.

Again, Gangrade (1974) found that all the students belonging to the comfortable and average economic position found the educational facilities useful. The students who were of the opinion that facilities are not proving useful had poor economic condition. In contract to this, Lal (1974) found poor economic status students hold the view that educational facilities are quite useful.

Not only this, Rastogi (1976) found that all those who are better aware of Constitutional provisions have better availed of the benefits provided under the act with regard to other legislative measures. Mailik (1971), Malik (1979) found that educated respondents have greater knowledge of the facilities provided and avail these to a greater extent than the less educated persons.

Aggarwal (1976) found that scholarships are considered most useful among the priviledges. This corresponds closely to high level of awareness of privilege among the respondents. Not only did a large number know this but they list it as the first item when asked to identify the various privileges. Parmar (1978) also found that there is an increasing awareness of the need for education in Mahayavanshi caste.

Premi (1974) found that greater awareness of freeships, stipends and scholarships, suggests that these facilities are universally available and widely used. Lesser awareness of other financial facilities suggests that either these particular facilities have not been properly published or they have not been introduced at many places; while Pimpley (1974) found that they are aware of the facilities provided to them, but in general, a large number of educable age group had not availed of these facilities.

According to Misra (1978) the utilisation and non-utilisation depend on several factors such as family background, attitude of the community members, attitude of non-scheduled caste members, teachers role and attitude of the members of the family toward education, social status of family, and lack of conducive environment. Shantakumari (1976) also found that the above mentioned factors affect the utilisation of educational facilities.

Based on the researchers, this chapter highlighted the utilisation of educational benefits/schemes by the scheduled castes. It also reflected the determinants and antecedents of utilisation of educational schemes in terms of social, educational, economic and occupational status alongwith demographic factors.

Constraints on Utilisation

Though numerous facilities and benefits have been provided by the government for improving the educational status of the scheduled castes, yet it is seen that the utilisation is not happening as desired and hence the results are far below the expected level. In this chapter, an attempt has been made to review the research studies which are conducted so far to evaluate the various constraints and difficulties which generally come in their way of availing these facilities.

Proper publicity of the educational schemes creates awareness among the Scheduled Castes. Soni (1975) found that proper communication of government policies in small and rural areas is found somewhat lacking in effectiveness. Nautiyal (1979) and Yadav (1983) also found that there is not enough publicity regarding the exact nature of concessions facilities permissible to Scheduled Castes. In publicising the educational schemes, mass media can play a significant role. In a few research studies it was found that those who are illiterates have less exposure to mass media, particularly the news paper and fail to get benefits from the schemes. Those who are literate and educated have more exposure to mass media and avail of maximum benefits from the schemes (Parvathamma, 1974; Gangrade, 1974; Goyal, 1974; Chitnis, 1977; Pimpley, 1974; Sachchidananda, 1974; Valunjakar 1975 and Yadav, 1983. According to studies, educated biased way of publicity of educational schemes has creased a privileged class among the Scheduled Castes, and usually, the privileged comes from better off families. This, in turn, leads to intra-scheduled castes inequalities (Chitnis, 1975; Khurana 1980; Sharma, 1974). It is seen that the help tends to benefit the 'haves' rather deprived section of the society (Premi, 1977). Several low levels of occupational categories, (i.e., sweepers, vendors, tanners are not represented among the scheduled caste postmatric scholars (Shah, 1976). So due to inadequate publicity of educational schemes a number of needy students fail to avail of such educational opportunities.

Next, obstacle in the way of utilisation of schemes is the procedural difficulty like difficulty in securing forms, comprehending the language of the forms, getting scheduled caste certificate, attestation from M.P./Gazetted Officer, and submitting application forms. (Dubey 1974). Gangrade, (1974) also found, both at school and college stage that the formal procedure to obtain facilities, consumes a lot of their time. According to George (1975) the parents belonging to Scheduled Castes, face difficulty at the time of taking stipend of their children. The parents reported that the system of distribution of stipend is complicated. This cumbersome procedure effects a large population of the scheduled caste and deprive them from the benefits.

To avail the benefits, one need to satisfy some eligibility criteria, which sometimes, comes in the way of education of scheduled castes. Many students reported that failure in the examination was the main reason for the discontinuation of their studies. The failure in the examination means loss of scholarships and stipend. The student fail not because of their indifference but because of cultural deprivation and biased examination. With out these educational benefits the Scheduled Caste students can not afford to complete their studies on their own and they are virtual drop-outs (Chauhan, 1975 and Yadav, 1983).

Shah (1976) also reports, that the eligibility test conducted by the government for the postmatric scholars succeeds more or less in restricting the award of postmatric scholarship to the children of the scheduled caste who are generally employed in low level occupations. Thus, the conditions of eligibility are biased towards the priviledged one in this disadvantaged group, while the deserving are left out.

Further, it is seen that due to these incentives, many of the Scheduled Caste students and parents face discriminatory behaviour, prejudices and biased attitude of those who administer the schemes. Chandersekharaih (1969) found the discriminatory treatment of scheduled caste children in privates schools. Instances of ill-treatment are often reported in hostels for Harijans run by the government or private management (Pankaj, 1977). Six students from Gujarat complained that they were insulted when they went to collect their scholarship as the clerical staff called them the 'Son-in-law' of the government. Four of them informed that the teacher did not hesitate to insult them before others and made it clear that they were considered as 'drag on the community' (Karlekar, 1975).

Due to this discriminatory behaviour some students feel that the schemes for the facilitation of education of the scheduled caste provided by the government damage the self respect of the community. Scheduled Caste people become dependent on the programmes and their initiative is killed, (Singh, 1974; Debey, 1973; Lal, 1974) studies of Ramaswamy (1974) and Chitnis (1974) show that there are some Scheduled Caste who opine that the provision of scholarship, reservation of seats in educational institutions and legislatures and special allocation of funds for the welfare of Scheduled Caste have served to reinforce the separate identity of the castes rather than integrate them with the rest of the society.

Effective administration and implementation of the programmes for the welfare of the Scheduled Caste is likely to lead to the progress of their education thereby leading to their growth. But prevalent chronic delays, currupt practices and mis-appropriation of funds present hurdles of insurmountable magnitude. Most of the scheduled caste students and parents report the prevalence of the delay in the award of scholarship which create lot of inconvenience to these people. Due to lack of funds, sometimes they need to discontinue their study. And in many cases, they get money after they leave the school/college. (Jha, 1973; Parvathamma, 1974; Dubey, 1974), Commissioner of scheduled castes and Tribes (1969-70). Administrative delays cause irregularities in the reimbursement of scholarships. Therefore, sometime scholarships are given in lumpsum which is commonly spent for meeting the other domestic requirements rather than purpose for which it is meant (Patwardhan, 1973), Commissioner of Scheduled Caste and

Scheduled Tribes, (1968-69). Overall, it is felt that the pattern of social welfare administration, present a very discouraging and dismal picture today. The administrative agencies do not have adequate and competent staff. The absence of healthy relationship between Scheduled Caste students and those who administer programmes present barrier to their utilisation (Sharma, 1976; Lal, 1975; Pimpely, 1978; Goyal, 1974; Rajagopalan, 1974; Gangrade, 1974; Singh, 1974; Soni, 1975; George, 1975; Lakshamanna, 1974; Valunjkar, 1975; Chitnis, 1977; Premi, 1979).

Malik (1979) feels that the malutilisation of educational schemes is due to the faulty government working style. He criticised the working of the government machinery as such on the ground that the heads of the departments and leaders are from the non-scheduled castes. Dubey (1973) and Aggarwal (1973) also found that most of the respondents complained that without an influence, or an approach with the administrative officer, it is not possible to get funds approved. The allocation of funds is faulty.

Besides, Aggrawal (1976) and Pankaj (1977) reported that the officials are found engaged in corrupt practices and there is mis-appropriation of funds. For example, government are providing funds for the construction of the hostels, but the funds are mis-appropriated and fictitious figures are fed. When any inspector or high official visits the hostels, Harijans boys are brought from outside for the purpose of showing the numbers, they are given a day's food and lodging with some money and are sent away as soon as the inspectors back is turned. Lakshmánna (1974) found that during 1973-74 bogus hostels had drawn Rs. 5.87 lakhs in one district alone. This was a clear proof of the prevalent corruption and lack of supervision and strong hold by the government authorities. Malik (1979) writes that every thing is done on paper by the government and nothing is practised in reality. Azad (1976), Rajagopalan (1974), Singh (1974) and Desai (1974) found that general economic position of scheduled castes is so poor that inspite of scholarships they are unable to pursue higher education while (Soni, 1975; Chitnis, 1976; Rastogi, 1976 and Parvathamma, 1974) found that except scholarship they have to depend on their parents. Premi (1974) found that at elementary school stage it could be possible to study without financial support but she found it is difficult to continue higher education without financial support. Financial concessions are important motivating forces by the respondents. In the dearth of caste availability of these concessions, their growth is stagnated.

Another obstacle in the utilisation of schemes is the inadequacy of educational facilities. Most of the students and parents belonging to scheduled caste report that the existing amount of schemes and scholarships are grossly inadequate. With this amount of scholarship they find it difficult even to meet the cost of note-books (Goyal, 1974; Rajagopalan, 1974; Sharma, 1976; Gangrade, 1974; Pimpley, 1974; Singh, 1975; Desai, 1975; Parvathamma, 1974; Rath, 1974; Chitnis, 1977; Trivedi, 1977; Singh, 1975).

Most of the students offered Arts subjects due to absence of facilities because science students have to incur more expenditure on laboratory dress and on technical instruments. (Sachchidananda 1974). This finding is supported by the report (1971-72, 72-73) of the Commissioner for scheduled castes and scheduled tribes. In West Bengal it was found the exemption from payment of tuition fees is not granted to all the scheduled caste students, but only to 41 communities. This causes hardships to many deserving students from the remaining castes.

Hostel accommodation adds upto the difficulties of the scheduled caste students. (Lal, 1975; Rajagopalan, 1975; Gangrade, 1975; Soni, 1975; Dubey, 1974; Shah, 1974; Lakshmanna, 1974; Valunjkar, 1975; Vyas, 1969; Trivedi, 1977; Rastogi 1976 and Premi, 1974) found that the existing number of hostels are not sufficient. Hostel accommodation and facilities provided for them are unsatisfactory and inadequate. Vyas (1969) and Rastogi (1976) further said that all the respondents residing in the hostels run by the central and state government are not receiving the facilities of free lodging, medical and recreational facilities. In addition, even the available facilities are not up to the mark. Dubey (1974) also reported the unsatisfactory conditions of these hostels. They are not only badly managed, but even the prescribed accommodation requirements are not met. They were found to be overcrowded, unhygenic, and the food was inadequate both in this quality as well as quantity.

Most of the students face many difficulties in getting admission to various courses against reserved seats, (Gangrade, 1974). Dubey (1974) found that they did not get admission in Assam Medical College, though there were reserved seats. Frequent refusal to admission in private schools for the scheduled caste children was commonly observed (Chandersekaraih, 1969).

The above discussion clearly shows that though the government has launched a number of educational schemes for the preogress of education of the Scheduled Castes, but the implementation of schemes present a number of problem for the beneficiaries. The problem of inadequate publicity, cumbersome administrative procedure, indifferent implementation machinery, corrupt practices, inadequate hostel facilities, difficulties in admission to educational institutions, delay in disbursement of amount are the some of significant ones.

The Facilitators

The government of India has provided several Constitutional measures and safeguards for the scheduled castes. During implementation, number of problem arises. Earlier chapters have usually concentrated on finding out the solutions of these complex problems and difficulties. Here the review of such research studies have been made to highlight the various solutions and answers of the constraints which generally come at the time of transcation of the various schemes.

The first problem posed by the respondents refer to the inadequacy of publicity. Lakshamanna (1975) feels that the social workers should be put into service for publicity, in addition to the printed materials. Special programmes should be launched through mass-media (Rastogi, 1979). Social workers should personally visit the rural areas and urban localities having a large scheduled caste population for assessing their needs for the educational facilities and take immediate steps to provide them the inputs if they are willing to avail in case are not making their use due to poverty.

Next to publicity problem is the cumber some procedure of submitting application for availing the schemes. To make the procedure funtional, several steps need to be followed. The respondents feel that the application forms should be printed in regional languages. There should be easier accessibility to form the respondents feel that the documents should be accepted even afterward, since some-times it is difficult to obtain these particularly, when the date of submission is very close. This will help the Scheduled Caste students to avail the maximum benefits from these schemes (Rastogi, 1976).

Besides, discriminatory behaviours, prejudicial attitude and fear complex among the schedueld castes poses a serious problem in utilising educational schemes. In order to overcome this problem proper guidance is needed to protect the Scheduled Caste students from inferiority complex through counselling. The students needed to be educated about the existing facilities and their purpose (George, 1975). The scholarships awarded to the students should be sent to their parents directly. This will avoid the possible discrimination among the students in the school (Chauhan, 1975). Rastogi upholds that the reservation of seats in educational institutions should be increased. Encouragement of freeintercaste dining, marriage, children education upto 14 years, improvement in the economic status should be emphasised. Also, Children of the economically well off scheduled caste should not be given such facilities. Instead, these facilities should be extended only to those who are really needy (Sharma, 1974). Gupta (1976) also suggested the solution for overcoming this problem. He suggested that the theory of 'Social work practice' should be such that the profession can lean upon it. One has to create an awareness in the minds of the clientale about the problems they face and at the same time, to make the clientale aware of the resources they own both as individual as well as in collectives situations to solves the problem. This will help in reducing the prejudicial attitude of higher castes.

The problem of delay in the scholarships, corrupt practices in the administration, and mis-appropriation of funds are quite common these days. For overcoming these delays Singh, 1974; Jha, 1973; Dubey, 1974; and Commissioner for scheduled caste and Schedueld Tribe (1971-72, 1972-73) suggested the usage of some fixed procedures, like it was said that the scholarships should be awarded within a month of the submission of application.

Further the scholarships should be paid to him before he is required to pay his fees or spend on maintenance and after he has got into debt (Pisharody, 1972). A separate cell may be set up in the Directorate of Public Instruction for the disbursement of scholarships and for maintaining an upto date record (Jha, 1973; Singh, 1974). To avoid the mis-appropriation of the funds, the teachers suggested periodic checking from the records as well as from the students. Some think that the scholarships awarded to the student should be sent to their parents. This will check the misuse of the money by the students (Chauhan, 1975). A review should be made to see that schemes benefit more the backward amongst these communities or not (Khurana, 1981; Yadav, 1979).

Overall, it is felt that the programmes should be revised and properly implemented. The placement of persons for administering these schemes should be either from the scheduled caste themselves or if they are to be from the other communities it may be insured that only those who have sympathetic attitude towards these castes are allocated work in this respect (Dubey, 1974). Unless government brings forward a law which fixes responsibility for administrative lapses and provide for punishment of those officers who fail to implement the constitution safeguards, these safeguards will continue to be floated with inpunity (Ramdhan, 1978). For a better implementation of various schemes it has been suggested that welfare programmes should be conducted and implemented through voluntary organisations particularly because the worker will be from the strata of the society to which the problem and programme pertain (Sahai, 19788).

According to Acharya (1971) the work should be entrusted only to such officers who have been exhibited a real sense of service to the cause of the backward community. Merely mechanical utilisation of funds alloted for the welfare of the scheduled caste will never solve this vast problem. Added to this, is the corrupt practices and mis-appropriation of funds, which is common these days. It should be ensured by all means that the funds alloed are utilised on schemes, drawn up with thought and imagination, so as to achieve the desired effect within the shortest possible time.

Moreover, it is seen that there is lack of coordination amongst the various administrative agencies. For formal action and implementation of programmes, high level coordination committee should be set up at the headquarters and the districts levels. Monitoring arrangements should be made with the coordinating function resting with education department. There has to be constant monitoring for proper utilisation of funds. At the centre also there should be an institution which may be assigned monitoring of the progress of education of these communities by undertaking evaluation studies at the national level (Premi, 1979).

The problem of administration implementation of scheme is followed by the inadequate amount of scholarships. Khurana (1980) and Yadav (1979) suggest that the rate of scholarships and distribution of concessions will have to be revised and the amount of scholarships should be sufficient to meet the cost of their education.

Facility of hostel accommodation is also not well managed and fails to provide benefit to the needy. Several suggestions have been put forth to overcome this problem. (Singh, 1974) and Commissioner for scheduled castes and Scheduled Tribes (1971-72, 1972-73) suggested that hostel facilities for both boys and girls need to be improved particularly for the latter. Dubey (1973) also recommended opening of "Model government hostel", training of the wardens, matrons, taking over the subsidised hostel by the government and auditing of the accounts in order to prevent mis-appropriation of funds. SCERT Tamil Nadu (1974-76) recommended that there is need to improve the percentage of residential scholarships so that they may stay in special hostel with better facilities for study. Pimpley (1975) suggsted that women hostels should be attached with every women's and co-educational college where sufficient seats should be reserved for the scheduled caste students. This will help in tackling the hostel problem of scheduled caste students.

The problem of admission in various educational institutions against reservation seats is still faced by the scheduled castes. In order to overcome this problem, Pimpley (1975) suggest that sufficient seats should be reserved for scheduled caste students in various types of educational institutions, so that they can avail the benefits easily for their educational progress. Rastogi (1976) suggested that the sympathetic attitude towards these people can help in tackling this ticklish problem.

Some remedies have been suggested in this chapter to overcome some problems faced by the Scheduled Caste in the utilisation of educational schemes for their progress.

Motivational Tendencies, Intelligence, Academic Achievement and Adjustment

A baseless fact which is commonly accepted among the people is that Scheduled Castes are inferior in academic achievement, motivational tendencies, intelligence and have adjustment problems as compared to other castes. But this kind of generalised statement can't be made without the availability of large number research studies. No doubt some researchers have been conducted in this area and have shown a mixed findings. An attempt has been made in this chapter to review all the psychological studies on scheduled caste conducted so far in this area and presented them in a systematic order so that some conclusions can be drawn on the basis of the findings of these researches.

1. Motivational Tendencies

Motivational tendencies are the most important for the development of the child's personality. The available studies have been classified under achievement motivation, fear, anxiety, aggression and learning task etc.

Achievement Motivation

When we compare the result of the most of the research studies about the achievement motivation of backward classes particularly of the Negros abroad and Scheduled Castes and Scheduled Tribes in India, we donot find unanimity. In some cases (Bradburn, 1963; Cameron, 1965; Poussaint Alvin, 1968; Himes, 1973; Minigione, 1965 and Mossback, 1969), the coloured population have been found inferior in achievement motivation. But in some other studies no such discrimination was found (Barial, 1966; Hall, 1975; Mehta, 1967; and Minigone, 1968). In few other cross cultural studies of white and coloured, South African Adolescents, only certain minority group who were subjected to discrimination, were found having low achievement motivation (Lazarus Kessel and Botha 1969). In India, surprisingly in some studies socially backward classes have shown higher achievement motivation than socially upper classes (Gokulnathan, 1972). But in this case, the study was on students who migrated from a village to some urban areas and were studying in some urban based schools.

Anxiety

When Julka (1963) and Choksi (1975) compared Bhills and non-Bhills on anxiety and found that two groups did not differ in their anxiety level in any significant level. Study of Amita Chokri also, showed no difference in the anxiety level of persons from different socio-economic background. But, in the studies of Joshi (1980) and Singh (1982), majority of the scheduled caste students suffered from fear complex, anxiety and lack of confidence and they were more worried and had anxiety towards examination and scholarship. They had positive attitude towards schools and mothers but had negative attitude towards society, elite group and the opposite sex. Similarly, Usharri (1978) found that the disadvantaged pupils were less keenly interested in their academic pursuits and had poor personal efficiency in the planning and use of their term due to anxiety and depression. Laxmidevi (1980) reported that the major problems of the Harijan children as perceived by the teachers were inferiority feeling. As regards fear motivation, Kamlesh (1981) reported that the mean scores of the urban non-scheduled caste was above average and it was below in case of scheduled castes.

Aggression

The study of Julka (1963), revealed that non Bhills hvae significantly more themes of aggression than Bhill children. Poussaint Alvin Etal (1968) also found impeded aggression in the Negroes. Modsen (1967) in his study on cooperative and competative motivation found that the middle class boys from urban areas were more cooperative than urban low and rural middle class ones. Besides, Parkash (1981) indicated factors namely assertive and self critical domination attitude, low integeration, negativism and apprehensiveness, preference for one's own decision, obstructiveness and aggressiveness, escapasim attitude and self opinion for the caste Hindu group, for the scheduled caste group the factors were assertion and collective action, practicalness and not free from obstacles, free from inhibition and participation, independent and self confidence attention, getting behaviours and lack of self criticism, demoralised emotion and action, accomplishment and developing collectives.

Academic Motivation

In this area Amita Choksi (1975) conducted a study in five english medium schools of Baroda and could not find any significant differences among students from various socio-economic status. Elearnor R. Hall (1975) also observed that racial differences in academic achievement may not hold true for particular sub-groups. However, Cameron (1965) found middle class students better than working class and Canadian Indians on learning task under non-material rewards. Similarly Mishra (1968) and Chitra (1969) found culture background playing a significant role in the determination of learning. Katz (1967) also found achievement gap existing among white and Negroes students. Further according to Bose (1969) unattracted school environment and school curriculum leads to loss of interests of the child in the school. Inappropriate teachers and faulty supervision were found to be the reasons which did not motivate the students to learn in an effective manner.

Fear Motivation

Though, Julka (1963) in his study on Bhills and non-Bhills did not find significant difference in these two groups in their fear motivation but Singh (1982) found significant difference between scheduled caste and non-Scheduled Caste students in fear motivation.

2. *Intelligence*

Many research studies have been conducted to find the level of intelligence between Scheduled Castes and non-Scheduled Castes. The findings of these studies are not uniform and common. Das, (1969); Singh, (1974); Gangrade, (1974); Karlekar, (1975); Singh (1975) and Nayer (1975) conducted the studies on teachers to investigate the intellectual level between scheduled caste and non-

Scheduled Caste students. Studies showed that Scheduled Caste students were much poorer in calibre and intelligence than the other students belonging to higher castes. The teachers perceived that the Scheduled Caste students had lower level of intellectual capacity than the other castes. When, Aggarwal, (1975); Thakural, (1977); Singh, (1981); Rath, (1979); Parkash; (1981) and Gaur (1987) conducted the studies on the students, they found that between scheduled castes and non-scheduled castes there is a difference in the mean intelligence scores. The non-Scheduled Caste students were found more intelligent on the average than the Scheduled Caste students. It was stated further that the level of intelligence was affected by the places of their livings. The rural non-Scheduled Caste groups showed significantly higher verbal intelligence than Scheduled Caste group. The same significant difference was found on intelligence in urban areas between the two groups (Gaur, 1987). The sex differences were also noticed on the scores of intelligence between the two groups. The male students scored higher on intelligence than female students (Rangari, 1981). According to Parkash (1981) the students belonging to Scheduled Castes whose parents had better houses, better education and are from higher income group scored higher score on intelligence than those scheduled caste parents who belong to lower income group and uneducated families.

Some studies of Barial (1966), Ushasri (1978) and Sutradhar (1982) did not find any significant difference in the intelligence level of the students belonging to different social classes. However, Shanthamani (1970) found that caste has an influence on intelligence of students. Singh (1978) emphasised that due to age old atrocities made on the Scheduled Castes they almost had no opportunities to develop their intellectual capacities and abilities. Besides, our orthodox caste based society has also made the scheduled castes far away from scientific development, industrialization or modernization, thereby helping them in sustaining their orthodoxy and conservative feelings. Their orthodoxy manifests more in the rearing of their children. No doubt orthodox parents find themselves unable to develop their children's knowledge, intellectual level and raise them in a proper way.

3. Academic Achievement

In the studies of academic achievement of Lal (1975), Lakshmanna (1975), Valunjkar (1975) and Nayer (1975) most of teachers reported that Scheduled Caste students were poor in studies in comparison to non-Scheduled Caste students. They also pointed out some reasons like poor in intelligence, poor comprehension, uncongenial home environment and poverty etc., which are responsible for their poor academic achievement. They had suggested that the teachers should pay more attention towards these children and reservation Policy can also be useful for them for their academic achievement.

Studies conducted on the school students are at par with the studies conducted on the teachers studies. Higher caste students achieve significantly higher than the scheduled caste students (Singh, 1975; Sharma, 1975; Kumar and Murlidharan, 1978; Suri, 1979; Ameerjan, 1979; and Aikara, 1980). The other studies like Sharma (1982), Vastisri, (1978); Sutradhar, (1982); Khobragade, (1981) and Laxmidevi (1980) reported that the percentage of retention was highest in class X and the percentage of detention was highest in class I. Dantawala (1976) and Suri (1979) expressed the five main characteristics of educational backwardness. These were (1) poor enrolment in terms of numbers at different stages of the educational system, (2) consistantly poor performance (3) heavy rate of drop-out, (4) clustering in inferior and less prestigious institutions, (5) inability of students from the weaker sections to enter professional and technical courses. Shivashan Kara (1981) reported that the intelligence, personality adjustment and school adjustment variables were responsibles for their poor performances but Nagaraju (1977) in his study found that the average achievement of the scheduled caste students was same as that of the general group.

Another set of studies were cnducted on the college students and revealed the same results. The mean academic achievement index was found higher in non-scheduled caste College students than the scheduled caste students (Gupta, 1979; Bindu, 1974 and Barkar, 1982). The difference between scheduled caste and non-scheduled caste students in academic achievement was also noticed in engineering and professional colleges. It was due to the past academic background (I.I.P., 1982). But Adiseshiah and Ramanathan (1979) reported that the percentage of Scheduled Caste literacy had increased from 14.66 per cent in 1966 to 26.00 per cent in 1971 showing an increase in the annual ratio at 1.26 per cent over 0.8 per cent for non-Scheduled Castes. Chitnis (1975) reported that inferiority of Scheduled Caste students was even more pronounced with respect to performance at college level. The percentage of enrolment in engineering and mmedical college was very much small.

Usually, the Scheduled Caste students opt for arts stream in higher education whereas, the students from other castes generally offered the science subjects (Sachchidananda, 1975 and Adiseshiah 1979). In the study of Rao (1976), overwhelming enrolment of Scheduled Castes students was found in bachelor of arts courses, whereas, the enrolment in bachelor in science courses was from the higher castes. Singh (1982) reported that three commulative report cards of the students over a three years periods indicated an improvement in performance. Sixty four per cent of these students had been in residential school for over three years. The majority of the students had academic problems like poor handwriting, difficulties in english and mathematics subjects; lack of books and food etc. They suffered from uncertainity about future, inferiority and indecision particularly in regards to vocations and higher education. But Nagarajun (1977) reported in his study that the achievement in science and mathematics among Scheduled Castes students staying in hostels was the same as that of the day scholar of the higher caste.

Alongwith these negative figures, we have data which shows that some sub-castes within scheduled castes like Kanwar and Sansi have crossed over the line of achievement of the total population in respect of literacy at primary and junior basis educational level. Singh (1986) also felt that the academic performance within scheduled castes vary a lot. The respondents belonging to four castes Qusadh, Chamar, Dhobi and Passi did better than other Scheduled Castes. Dom and Mehar also leave behind other castes. Here three cluster were formed. Cluster one consisted of Dushad, Chamar, Dhobi and Passi. Cluster two consisted of Dom and Mehar. Cluster three consisted to other castes. The castes in cluster one were different from other castes as far as their desire to achieve more is concerned. These castes respondents seem to be set for achieving higher and higher. This showed better academic culture developed among these castes.

Genderwise also, Academic achievement differed between scheduled castes and non scheduled castes. Sachidananda (1974) and Aggarwal (1982) conducted a study on girls of both the communities and found that Scheduled Caste girls were poor in academic achievement than non-Scheduled Caste girls. Sharma (1975) investigated that both male and female children were found inferior in academic achievement than high caste group. Singh (1969) reported that upper caste people have almost 100 per cent literacy whereas in the Scheduled Castes, 50 per cent males were literate. It was also marked between males and females (Chitnis, 1975) and Scheduled Castes women did better than men (Rangari, 1981). The place of living was also put as a reason behind the academic achievement of the children. Chitnis (1975) conducted an intensive analysis of scheduled castes literacy in Maharashtra and indicated the disparity between the Scheduled Castes and the rest of the population in the district having largest Scheduled Castes population. It was more marked in urban areas than in rural areas.

Economic factor plays a crucial role in the academic achievement. Studies show that lower academic achievement among the Scheduled Caste students who belong to lower economic strata (Sharma 1975 and Singh 1982). In the Bombay study, Chitnis (1975) provided several indicators to prove that the academic performance of Scheduled Caste students does not compare favourably with that of their non-Scheduled Caste students on economic basis. Harijan, poor and rich were found to be backward in word reading and speech. The Brahmin children with comparable economic level did better than Harijan in short term recall. The Harijan students committed a large number of errors in writing auditory material and the Harijans children were found to have less relatively, less facility with cross model coding than with unimodel coding although this they shared with poor Brahmin children.

4. *Adjustment*

In the study of Singh (1982) found that majority of the Scheduled Caste students were well adjusted with the non-Scheduled Caste students. Choksi (1975) also suggested the social background does not create much difference. But Sharma (1979), Rangari (1981), Sharma (1982), and Sen (1982) found significant difference on adjustment between Scheduled Caste and non-Scheduled Castes students. Rangari reported that there was significant difference between scheduled cast and non-Scheduled Caste students on the sub-variables of adjustment also. By and large the non-Scheduled Caste students showed better adjustment in different mean scores than the Scheduled Caste students. Sen (1982) said that negative adjustment was very high in Scheduled Caste students. Ushasri reported that the socially disadvantaged and the socially non-disadvantaged group significantly differed with regard to academic adjustment scores. Sharma found that the adjustment of Scheduled Castes and backward students was very much unsatisfactory as against the condition of general upper class students which was reported as satisfactory.

In some other studies, the adjustability of the students of both the communities have been studied with regard to their place of livings and their sex. Kamlesh (1981) found that the level of adjustment among the urban Scheduled Caste students was lower as compared to rural scheduled caste students whereas the non-Scheduled Caste students both in rural and urban areas did not have adjustment problems. These findings were supported by Sharma (1979) and Rangari (1981).

Studies reveal that the sex had significant impact on adjustment. The females had higher adjustment scores than males and also the females had more psychological problems and complexes than the males (Sharma, 1979). The same findings was found in the study of Rangari (1981). Besides this, Sharma (1979) reported that the adjustment of both the comparable groups in 1977 indicated that the adjustment of the Scheduled Caste and backward class students had considerably improved. The faculty differences did not affect the adjustment scores and the levels of education. The socio-economic status had no effect on adjustment but Kamlesh (1981) felt otherwise and emphasised that the level of adjustment among the Scheduled Caste belonging to lower socio-economic status was below normal.

According to Aggarwal (1970) adjustment problems in home, school and social areas decrease themselves with increase of the age of the children but it increases in case of health and emotional areas. It was also found that teacher perception of pupil adjustment is by and large in agreement with that of the parents. Shivashankara (1981) also conducted that study on factors which influence adjustment of Scheduled Caste students with the higher caste students. He reported that the variables which influence the socially disadvantaged including the Scheduled Caste students were intelligence, personality adjustment and school adjustment.

The preceding discussion has focussed the motivational tendencies, intelligence, academic achievement and adjustment problems of scheduled castes in relation to non-Scheduled Caste including their different dimensions. these psychological factors have made clear that Scheduled Caste people are much behind the people of other caste and great effort and attention is required for improving their status by the government.

Nine

Training Scheduled Castes

The thrust of our study in this chapter has been directed to the marginal farmers. We chose those who were marginal because they eke out a miserable existence, and farmers because they serve a national need. In illustrating how our new approach works with the weaker sections of society we have chosen the Scheduled Castes. We have also chosen two courses which shaped up according to our expectations and one which did not. This we hope, will give, a balanced view of our performance.

The term Scheduled Caste refers to those downtrodden sections of society which have been lowest in the class hierarchy. Our training was given to only one of them called Vankars or weavers. The number of participants in the first course was 29. Though all of them were Vankars, by religion they belonged to two groups, one Christian and the other Hindu. Their village is a fairly large one in the Bhal region in Gujarat. The soil there is very good for agriculture. They rely mainly on rain water for their crops as the sub-soil water is brackish. By the time we held this course we had grasped the importance of agricultural technology and much of the course was devoted to it. The purpose in describing these courses is to give a clearer idea of how one course differs from another. In all the courses we dialogue with the participants but the subject matter is always different. It is these differences that will be the focus of the following description.

The First Course

Concentration of the first course was on two points : Their exploitation and a desire to achieve unity as the best means to liberate themselves from oppression and also to achieve some economic progress. Another concern voiced was the need to improve their agricultural methods and to reduce their indebtedness.

In response to their concern about exploitation they were asked to identify those who had the resources in their village, i.e., had power, money and prestige. After analysing the social structure of their village, they came up with the opinion that, (1) they had no power; consequently, (2) they were unable to satisfy their legitimate needs; (3) they were often treated unjustly by others; and (4) the only way out of these difficulties was to unite themselves though at this point we wanted to make the group aware of the problem of self-respect, but due to dearth of response from the group, this problem was not pursued.

To accept in principle the need for unity and to achieve unity are totally two different aspects. Our effort as trainers at that moment was to allow differences and divisions to surface and later to help the group resolve them. The main division within this group was along religious lines. Though the Christians in the group were fewer in number, they were better organised and had better leadership. The same feature was brought out in the village as well where there were two religious organisations, one Hindu and the other Christian. Both held meetings but while the latter attended them, the former did not. The Christians were very proud of this fact and the Hindus naturally resented it.

On top of that there was an unresolved conflict. The Vankar community jointly owned a piece of land which was leased to a third party for cultivation in return for half of the produce. The previous year the Christian decided to cultivate the part of the land that proportionately should belong to them. The rest was given for cultivation to the brother-in-law of the main leader of the Vankars. During the harvest time, though the Christians distributed the whole crop among themselves, the farmer who had tilled the land for the Hindus gave half of the crop of bajri to their leader. This leader, refused to distribute the bajri stating that the Christians too should have given half of their share and the total amount distributed among them all. Though we are unaware of this conflict, bμt we did notice that the Hindus were not taking an active part in the sessions. We therefore decided to devide the group along religious lines.

Though, the Hindu group was a little suspicious to meet separately but later, agreed and pointed out that there was a reason for it. They were afraid of the Christians and especially of their leader Shilanand. In the past he had not given food-for-work to their main leader and his followers mainly, they felt, because of what had happened with the bajri. Now, they felt, if they said something which he did not like he might again penalise us.

At this stage, it is better to be aware of the leadership pattern among the Vankar community in the village. The Vankars have six leaders (mahetar), each having authority over about 10 families. Matters of common interest are decided by all the leaders, though one of them is accepted as the main leader. These leaders are all Hindu yet among their followers there are some Christians. The leaders play an important role during marriage, disputes, etc., Therefore not even the Christians can do without them.

Besides, the Christian community has its own leaders, one of them being Shilanand who was attending the course. Only one Hindu leader and the son of the main leader were in the course. Shilanand had considerable power as he was entrusted the task of relief work in the village which was started by the catholic priest of the area. It was to this that the Hindus were referring. One of the six leaders and all his followers had been deprived of food-for-work by Shilanand. This was interpreted as an act of revenge and was the reason why they were afraid to speak in his presence.

Among Christian sub-group, the discussion was on a different note. There was a list of complaints against the leaders but these were variations of a single theme : if we could get rid of these leaders things would improve considerably. Seeing this, the instructors turned a direct question on them. Could they really fight against the leaders? They knew very well that the leaders would then turn to the Rajputs for help and that would be bad for all of them. The instructors also pointed out that there seemed to be a power struggle going on. What was the point of fighting among themselves? Who would profit from it? This question now became the central issue for the rest of the course.

The following day we had a joint meeting of Hindus and Christians. Though the Hindus were much more active that day but it was mainly because they came up with their internal grievances. But soon the whole group started moving in the direction of unity and its requirements. During the day through a number of informal meetings, they were trying to work out a common organisation for economic and social purposes while the two religious associations (Hindu and Christian) would be exclusively for religious purposes. The idea was approved in principle but there was a practical difficulty with the Hindus. While the Christians were very clear as to who should be their leader, there was no one who was acceptable to all the Hindus. Moreover, they could not agree without the approval of all their mahetars (leaders), or else the latter would sabotage the whole scheme.

As we moved to Ahmedabad from the Farm, Shilanand, the Christian leader had to leave us. To our surprise a absence led to power struggle in the group. The first sessions went on smoothly but by afternoon, it became clear that we had lost contact with the group and hence, we went into consultation. Some of our participants were not involved, some had withdrawn psychologically, others give signs of a veiled hostility. Should we change the activity? On reflection we concluded that we need to re-establish contact and the best way is to allow them to talk. This is exactly that we did. Our silence created a double power vacuum and one of the Christians, Natu, took the initiative to assert himself over the group. First he fought with other participants until he had them apologise to him and then he argued with one of the trainers about a point. We refused to be drawn into the power struggle which had taken the shape of a verbal duel. We intervened only to make the group aware of what was happening. So far the group had tried to patch up the differences between Hindus and Christians, but now that the undisputed Christian leader had left, another Christian wanted to establish his position by fighting his fellow participants and challenging the education.

The events of the day had totally gone haywire. The group had moved from disunity to unity and during most of the morning our activities had taken places smoothly. In the afternoon when the trouble started we were in the midst of an activity encounters in a T-group. A sudden yet subtle boycott of on-going activities so late in the programme was rather unusual and frankly irritating.

Our session has changed from a structured into a totally unstructured one. We moved into a sensitivity training group.

It was a good learning situation. But as long as the contenders for power had to face the whole group, they would find it very hard to accept and reflect on their behaviour. Besides, there were many silent spectators. At this point, we divided the group according to age. The younger people welcomed the more as they now had the opportunity to be all by themselves. For some it was the first time they dared to speak. Those not involved in the power struggle found it easier to understand the whole situation but others were very defensive about the incident. Gradually, the whole group became aware of the dangers arising from power struggles. There were still deep divisions within the group and our assessment was that unless the problem of the bajri was solved the struggle would go on. So it was decided to make an attempt to solve the problem by concretising it and discussing the issues as objectively as possible. Written below is what we came up with.

The total number of households belonging to the Vankar community were 76. Of these 14 were Christian who had cultivated their share of land in the jointly-owned plot. Their claim was that the whole produce of the land should belong to them since both the labour and the property was theirs.

On the other hand, the Hindus argued that one could not cultivate the land without permission from the leaders, which had not been granted. Therefore, the Christians should give half of the produce to the leaders and this would be added to the share given by the brother-in-law of the main leader who had cultivated the rest of the land. Till that time, the share of bajri had not been distributed. The total amount of bajri given to the leaders was 520 kgs. the amount to be given by the Christians would be 280 kgs. and the total amount to be distributed would be 800 kgs.

The proposed solution given by the Christians was that neither do we ask for our share nor do we give our share. In this case the Hindus would have lost only about 6 kgs. of bajri per person. The Hindus objected to this primarily because of the fear that others would believe that the Hindu participants in this group had been pressurised by the Christians. On the other hand the Christians now said that their bajri had already been consumed.

In terms of money, if they were to give their share, it would amount to Rs. 30 per person. In other words the Christian families would have to give Rs. 420 to the others.

At this point, we directed their attention on the losses they were incurring because of the fight. Because of a maximum of Rs. 30 per person they were not coming to an agreement over the land which would produce as much as Rs. 76,000 a year. This would mean Rs. 1000 per family. In other words for the sake of Rs. 30, each of them was losing Rs. 1000! Further, as the bajri was not being distributed it was getting spoilt, eaten by rats and even the hay had been stolen. These losses were all due to their lack of unity.

The Hindu participants then said that they were ready to forego their share. But what about those at home? At this point one of the Christian proposed that the Christians pay up Rs. 30 per person provided the others agreed to cultivate the land themselves (i.e., all the Vankars on a co-operative basis). Hearing this, the Hindus replied by saying, "Well, if we tell our people that you are ready to pay they will not ask for the money, they may be satisfied with the gesture."

The end of the meeting was marked by a great sense of euphoria and joy and it definately showed that a new step had been taken towards unity. It was, however, only the first of many more important steps that would have to be taken back home. But this forms part of the follow-up work which is described in Chapter 13.

The Second Course

The course we are going to describe now was a brave attempt on our part to be always with the participants, no matter what their pace was, nor what their choices were. It was a continuous effort to open up the channels of communication. To the extent to which we failed to do this (and we cannot claim to have been successful all the while), our course was a failure.

During this course we had to overcome a number of difficulties. The very first one was that of recruitment. The contact with this village, in a district of the Saurashtra region had been made through a member of a Trust that had been helping these people. This was our first difficulty. As the villagers took the city people as "givers" of help, it was a major obstacle in our course. Hence, recruitment was left to Kantibhai an accepted leader among the poorer people of that village. Kantibhai took it upon himself to recruit more than 20 participants from far and wide, belonging to various castes. These were few in number but enough to inhibit free communication among the rest.

From the very first session, this group showed great interst in receiving material help. They wanted a deep tube-well to provide the village with sweet water. They wanted houses built in their fields, and training in agriculture.

Though it was made very clear to Kantibhai the purpose of our visit, still when the groups expectations rose, he would tell the group : "If you learn what you are taught and pass the examination you will receive whatever you need."

As the course progressed it became clear that they wanted two things : material help and conversion to Christianity. All that we said and did was interpreted accordingly. Thus, for example, during the ring-toss the word spread around that the longer the distance chosen the more the money that would be given. But, as our motive was different and we were pulling them in different directions, there was a breakdown in communications.

Again we made an attempt to make our position clear. "We are educationists", we said, "and all that we can give you is training." While explaining this at length one of us drew circles on the blackboard. The explanation over, we left the meeting place hoping that we had made our point clear. As we walked out one of us was approached by Kantibhai. "I know what those circles on the blackboard mean," he said. There was a slight pause, an anxious look at the instructor and then he continued with a smile : "They mean that we should come into your circle, your religion." Though the remark was amusing but the instructor in question was a Muslim and Kantibhai was referring to Christianity. As we are reflecting with the group on the losses made in a simulation game, and we explained the factors which should be taken into consideration for a good decision, suddenly Kantibhai spoke up, "all these things happen because you are not united and, as a punishment they do not give us help." This clearly showed that we would be able to communicate with the whole group. Accordingly, we decided to form three small groups in this manner: one group would be made up of the most vocal members, the second of the younger participants, and the rest would form the third group.

The vocal group drew up a long list of requests for material help. The younger group had realised the need of training and complained that the 'elders' had come with a fixed idea from which it would be difficult to make them move. The third group was very quiet for a long time. Finally, when the only non-Scheduled Caste left the place they became more vocal mentioned how they were despised by other castes and constantly humiliated. Then they went to say: "The best remedy is to leave Hinduism and become Christians. Whenever they ask us what caste we belong to, we shall be able to say that we are Christians. That is all."

So, gradually we were beginning to communicate, at least with some of the participants . Now, that it was more or less clear to them that this course was not meant either to give them material help or to make them Christians and that the purpose of this course was just to give them training, they became more involved in the course activities. We took advantage of this to play the simulation game in which they had big losses. As we explained things all over again, we tried also to instil confidence in them with a pep talk : "You are now convinced that you cannot do it. But that is not true. You CAN do it. Come on, make up your mind and say, "We can!" and let us see what happens." They agreed and we played the simulation game a second time. They did it differently this time : they got together, helped each other and made a big profit. This experience provided ample matter for reflection and dialogue.

Now, it was time to give them training inagriculture at Xavier Research Farm. During the first day at the Farm the group seemed interested and involved in the explanations given by the agricultural expert. But soon the participants were again divided into three sub-groups, those who wanted conversion, those who wanted material help and finally those who wanted to learn. Again we divided the group accordingly, but this time the elders objected. "This procedure is followed only when someone accused of a crime is taken for cross-examination", they said. "Have you taken our youngmen into custody?"

It was apparent by now that unless Kantibhai changed, very little would be done in the group. Hence, we decided to meet him alone and talk things over. "You are the unquestioned leader in this group," we said. "The others believe what you say. If we work together, something will be achieved. If we work at cross purposes the course will be a failure. To that extent, you have a great responsibility. We have no money to help you. Our duty in this course is to train you and nothing else."

But this time, even he was adamant and even he could not accept that this course was meanta just for training. He used every argument to convince us, from stubborn resistance to fear. At one point he turned to me, the only Christian in the team and, with the smile of a soldier who senses victory, asked defiantly : "Do you mind if I become a Christian? Can you object to that?"

"Not in the least, Kantibhai. But if what you mean to say is that conversion should be part of this course, then my answer is negative. Everything has to be used for its own purpose, food to eat, spades to dig and books to read. If I were to use this course for another purpose I would be wrong and I would be committing a sin in the name of religion—a horrible thing to do."

This reasoning seemed to impress him and he asked what his responsibility was. "Just tell the group that no matter what might have been said before, the aim of this course is to learn and nothing else", he was told.

We let him explain the situation to the group. We rejoined the group when he came back telling us that everything was now all right. But, it was very apparent that Kantibhai had not conveyed the message. We let the group talk things over. In the end the pleas to have training become so loud they could not be ignored. The agricultural expert was recalled and he joined the group rather despondently thinking that these people were not interested in agriculture and that nothing could be done about it. He was in for a pleasant surprise.

Though, the participants who were yearning for material help and conversion had not been convinced, yet they had been silenced by the others. This difference of opinion kept the group divided till the very end. But some learning was taking place. This became evident when we conducted a brain-storming session.

The question that each one of the four sub-groups was supposed to answer was, "How will you achieve development?" The sub-groups managed to generate 112, 85, 82 and 75 ideas respectively. As the sub-groups proceeded to choose the four best ideas from their lists a new list was ready for the whole group. The participants decided that they would vote on each one of them. The results of the voting was interesting :

First preference	:	to keep accounts
Second preference	:	to grow trees
Third preference	:	to bund the fields and make use of manure.
Fourth preference	:	to form a cooperative.

This was a very tough course as we were fighting against odds all the time. Still, it would be useful to recall the difficulties that had to be faced. The first one was that, although the majority of participants were Vankars, there were some who belonged to other castes. This made it difficult for the Vankars to speak about their problems which would have created a common platform and served to unite them. The second difficulty was that these people had already been conditioned by other agencies to receive material help and had been attracted to this course by the hope of receiving more. While we tried to understand their position we told them frankly about our constraints. The frankness and patience we managed to maintain was a sign that we, too, had learned from past experience The sad part about the course was the fact that some participants did not believe what we said. This wall of distrust we had managed to break on other occasions at a relatively early stage. In this course, if it was broken at all, it was only right at the end.

The memories of this course was painful. We were unable to achieve our goal. Deep down in our heart we felt that we had been unfair to the participants. It was only when we conducted the evaluation that this truth dawned on us. But this experience will be analysed in a later chapter.

Ten

Societal Background of an Individual

The subsequent pages discuss the demographic features, family background and economic status of the Scheduled Caste students.

(i) The Demographic Characteristics includes sex, age, religion, caste and marital status.

(ii) Family Background includes place of residence of parents, education of parents, education of siblings and occupation of parents.

(iii) Economic Status of the Students include students' self-image of their own economic status, their employment, economic obligation to the families if the students are employed, sources of financing education, financial obligation of the family and number of scholarship/ freeship holders.

Demographic characteristics are external to an individual, on which he/she has no control. Some determinative social characteristics are sex, age, religion and caste, which are vested in the individual at the time of birth.

On studying, it was found that except three (1.3 per cent) all the Scheduled Castes students are males (98.7 per cent). This reflects the low educational attainment of Scheduled Castes females. The literacy rate in the females of Rajasthan is only 8.5 per cent and it is much less among the Scheduled Castes (1.2 per cent). Hardly, 0.01 per cent of the women of Scheduled Castes has received education up to High School or more.

Age of students ranges from 16 or less years to 22 or more years. There is only one student (0.4 per cent) of 16 or less years while 12.9 per cent of the students are of 22 or more years. Majority of students (25.3 per cent) are of 20 years of age. The average age of Scheduled Castes college students is 19.8 years.

Generally, Scheduled Castes belong only to the Hindu or Sikh religions. The Scheduled Castes of Rajasthan are predominantly Hindus and 1.3 per cent of the Scheduled Castes persons follow Sikh religion. The same is reflected among the college students where 96.1 per cent are Hindus and only one student (0.4 per cent) is Sikh. Some students (2.2 per cent), however, have reported that they follow Neo-Buddhism. One (0.4%) is a Christian. One student (0.4 per cent) has said that he belongs to no religion and the remaining one (0.4 per cent) has not mentioned his religion.

The largest single group (43.4 per cent) of the entire Scheduled Castes population of the State belong to the group of Chamars. Balai constitute 9.1 per cent of the total Scheduled Castes population of the state. Bairwa forms only 0.3 per cent of the state Scheduled Castes population and Meghwal constitute 9.4 per cent of Scheduled Castes population, Khatik constitutes 3.1 per cent of the Scheduled castes population. All these castes are traditionally associated with leather work. Kolis form 4.4 per cent of Rajasthan Scheduled Castes and Gawarias form only 0.15 per cent of Scheduled Castes population. These castes are traditionally associated with crafts. Rest 6.4 per cent of the students belong to Daroga, Harijans, Kalal and Laskar castes. According to Census of 1961, the castes traditionally associated with leather work constitute 65.88 per cent of all the Scheduled Castes and they are people who also return the largest number of Scheduled Castes college students (79.1 per cent). The castes traditionally associated with crafts form 6.6 per cent of total Scheduled Castes population of Rajasthan and they send 10.3 per cent of college students. The remaining Castes (27.6 per cent) are traditionally associated with scavanging/music/entertainment/criminal activities or those which belong to miscellaneous/unidentified categories.

More than half the population consist of married students 39.9 per cent are married and gauna has also taken place while a little more than one-tenth (12.4 per cent) are also married but in their case gauna has not taken place. three percent of students are engaged and 1.3 per cent are widowed. Only 43.4 per cent of the students are unmarried.

Family background plays an imporatant role in the life of an individual. Discussed below are some selected aspects that have been chosen for investigation.

Parents' Place of Residence

It was applicable only to the students who live either in the hostel or in the rented room, or in families other than those of parents. Of 233 Scheduled Castes students the question is applicable only to 72.1 per cent.

The parents of a large number of students (56.2 per cent) live in villages whereas 12.0 per cent of students' parents belong to towns and parents of only 3.9 per cent of students reside in the cities. Hence, it is very clear most of the students' parents come from rural background.

Parent's Educational Level

Fathers of a sizable proportion of students (47.2 per cent) are unlettered. Fathers' of 40.3 per cent are who can only read and write upto primary level. Father's of only 6.9 per cent of students have passed middle school examination. There are only 3.0 per cent of students whose fathers have attained the educational level of high school.

Further, Students whose fathers have been educated upto intermediate level are 1.3 per cent. Fathers of two students (0.9 per cent) are graduates. One student (0.4 per cent) has not mentioned anything about the education of his father.

As far the educataion of mothers was studied, it was quite low. Mothers of a huge majority of the students (91.0 per cent are unlettered and mothers of only 8.6 per cent of students have received education upto primary level or below. Mother of one of the students (0.4 per cent) has passed middle school examination.

Brothers' Educational Level

It was found that 81.5 per cent students of this study are the most highly educated persons in their families. Only 9.9 per cent are those who have reported that there are others who are more educated than them. A very small percentage of the students (2.6 per cent) has mentioned that their other brothers are as much educated as the respondents. The question is not applicable to six percent of students since they have no brother. On the whole, the study shows that these students form the first generation of college students.

Sisters' Educational Level

It was found that for 87.5 per cent they are also most highly educated compared to their sisters. Sisters of only two students (0.9 per cent) have received education more than they have while sister of one of the students (0.4 per cent) has read equal to that of her brother. Two students (0.9 per cent) have not responded. The question is not applicable to 10.3 per cent of students as they do not have any sister. The above statistics shows that female education has not been given importance. But at the same time the fact that 13.8 per cent of students of Scheduled Castes have siblings who had also been to college, suggests the chances of their upward mobility.

Fathers of more than a half of all the students (52.4 per cent) work in the villages, in conventional rural occupations. Fathers of only 23.2 per cent are in service. A negligible proportion of students' fathers is found in business and agriculture. Fathers of 3.0 per cent of students are in no particular occupation. Fathers of 6.0 per cent of students are old and retired and 7.7 per cent of students either do not know the occupation of their fathers or their fathers have died.

Mothers of a vast majority of students (92.7 per cent) are not in any occupation. The mothers of 1.3 per cent of students are housewives. Mothers of 4.3 per cent of students do agricultural work in their own farm and 0.9 per cent of students' mothers are either land labourer or do other manual work. Mother of one of the students (0.4 per cent) is a peon and of one (0.4 per cent) is engaged in other work.

Occupational pattern clearly shows that like parents' poor educational background the Scheduled Castes students come from families with low occupational background.

Though, Education and occupation provide an objective measure of economic status of a person or a community, to know the subjective views of the respondents about their economic status. They were asked to designate their own economic status. Three categories of the economic status have been worked out which are as follows:

(a) *Comfortable:* The students who feel that they are economically well-to-do,

(b) *So-So:* The students who find themselves in between well-to-do and bad economic condition,

(c) *Difficult:* The students who consider their financial position to be precarious.

1.3 per cent have refused to classify themselves under these categories. A majority of the students (47.2 per cent) consider their economic status to be difficult while 45.5 per cent of students think their economic status to be so-so. A very small proportion of students (6.0 per cent) has exhibited signs of comfortable economic status.

It is found that in spite of the fact that a majority considers that their financial position is stringent yet a proportionate number of students do not seem to go for employment during their college life. A large majority of the students are unemployed (89.7 per cent) while only 6.9 per cent of students are employed full time and 1.3 per cent are part-time employed.

Only 2.1 per cent of all the students get into employment only occasionally. Therefore, there are only 10.3 per cent of students who study while they work which is a characteristic feature of 'Self help' students.

Only 5.1 per cent of full time employees work in government offices and a very small proportion of the students are working in the private firm (0.9 per cent) and the remaining 0.9 per cent are self employed. The question is not applicable to 93.1 per cent of students.

Most of the students (4.7 per cent) who earn and are in full time employment give money to the parents regularly and 0.9 per cent of students only occasionally. Two students (0.9 per cent) give money seldom and one of the students (0.4 per cent) has not mentioned anything about contributing his share. The question does not apply on 93.1 per cent of students.

As it is clear from the preceding pages that the financial standing of these students is not good, it is necessary to enquire into the sources through which their eduation is financed.Studies reveal there are five sources of financing their education .

1. Part of the expenditure is covered by scholarship/freeship, the rest of it they get from parents/relatives.
2. Parents/relatives finance education,
3. Part of the expenditure is covered by the scholarship/freeship and the rest from students' own earnings,
4. Through scholarship/freeship, and

5. Through the students' own earnings

For 74.7 per cent of the students, part of their expenditure is covered by scholarship/freeship, the rest of it they get from their parents/relatives. Parents/relatives exclusively finance education of 8.6 per cent of students. In case of 8.2 per cent of students, part of their expenditure is covered by their scholarship/freeship and the rest from their own earnings. Six per cent students depend exclusively on scholarship/freeship and only 2.1 per cent bank exclusively on their own earnings.

Overall, the study shows that even though government provides assistance for the education of children of Scheduled Castes, the students are not in a position to pursue their college studies without the assistance of family or of any other source.

To summarize, the college students of Scheduled Castes receiving education in Rajasthan are predominantly males, having an average age is 19.8 years. Except a few, they follow Hindu religion. Scheduled Castes students are generally married. The students whose parents are largely the village dwellers live in hostels. The rate of illiteracy among the mothers of the students is much-much higher as compared to their fathers. The students are also the most highly educated persons in their family as compared to the education attained by their siblings. While fathers of the students are generally engaged in economic activities and most of them work in the villages for their livelihood, mothers generally seem to be housewives. As the economic condition of these students is not well off some of them go to work to supplement the family income, alongwith financing their education.

Scholarship is also a source of financing education. Almost nine out of every ten students get scholarship and most of them get freeship.

Lastly, we can say that whatever may be their economic status, family background and demographic state, they are trying their level best to enhance their status in society, slowly and gradually.

Multifarious Aspects of their Academic Life

This chapter deals with some aspects of their academic life, the courses they have offered, the colleges they have chosen for their study, the reasons for such choices. Where do the students live in, hostel or elsewhere?, How much time do they devote towards study?, their participation in extra-curricular activities, Educational and occupational aspirations, and finally contribution of the home-environment.

For undergraduate studies, three year degree course is prevalent in the state of Rajasthan. The distribution of these students according to class shows that a little less than a half of them (48.1 per cent) are the students of first year degree course. In second and third year they are 30.9 per cent and 20.6 per cent respectively.

About seven-tenths of Scheduled Castes students (69.5 per cent) have sought admission in Arts and a little less than one-fifth of the students (18.0 per cent) has offered Science. In Commerce the percentage is still lower (12.4 per cent). The higher percentage in Arts is due to its being less expensive, less time consuming and easily accessible.

The study reveals that the educational background of father acts as a selective factor in deciding the course of study by the students. About three fourths of the students (74.5 per cent) whose fathers are unlettered have offered Arts courses whereas about two-thirds of the students (66.4 per cent) whose fathers have received education upto middle level and below have offered Arts courses. With the increase in the level of education of fathers there is a decrease in the percentage of those students who have offered Arts courses and increase in the percentage of those who have offered Science. Statistics shows that economic status do not act as a deciding factor for the stream of course opted by the students.

The students with so-so economic status (70.8 per cent) are highest in opting for Arts stream, very closely followed by students with difficult economic status (69.1 per cent) and then the students of comfortable economic status with 57.1 per cent. Though compared to Arts, the percentage of students in Commerce and Science is much smaller, still a trend seems to emerge that with an increase in the economic status, there is decline in the percentage of those who have offered Commerce and an increase among those who have offered Science. Chi square test shows that economic status does not significantly influence the choice of the students in offering the course. When asked: "Why did you choose the particular course that you are doing?" Nearly 50.6 per cent answered that they opted for it as it is relatively easy.

Seventeen students out of every twenty (85.4 per cent) maintain that they have offered the course because it consists of their favourite subjects. More than seven-tenths of students (72.5 per cent) have said that they have offered the course because it is the best and it will be of help in getting a job. Finally, only 12.0 per cent of students have offered the course because they were not able to get admission in the subject of their liking.

While enquiring at the reasons for the choice of a particular college, they were given a questionnaire. The students were desired to say 'yes' or 'no' on each one of the six items indicating the reasons. The items are given below:

" I came to this College Because

(a) It is the only college in this place,
(b) It is the best of the colleges in this area,
(c) I could not get admission elsewhere,
(d) It offers special facilities for Scheduled Castes students,
(e) My parents/relatives advised me, and
(f) It is nearer my home."

There was no single factor determinative factor in the choice of the college. It was a combination of several factors. There has practically been no choice in the case of 55.8 per cent of students because of the non-availability of any other college in their locality and 52.8% of the students have joined because of nearness to their homes. According to 54.5 per cent of the students it is the best college in the area. In the opinion of 37.3 per cent of the students, the college offers special facilities to Scheduled Caste students. A small proportion of students (10.7 per cent) has joined the college on being refused admission elsewhere. Inspite of the above reasons as many as 62.6 per cent of the students have mentioned that the advice of their parents/relatives have acted as a deciding factor.

The academic life of the students is also influenced by the place of residence, i.e., whether a student is a hosteler or a non-hosteler. In the case of non-hoteler is essential that he should be able to have there an adequate place, sufficient time and environment for study. Hence, a study into the pattern of their life and study habit is necessary.

More than two-fifths of the Schedued Castes students (42.1 per cent) reside in hostels while even less than three-tenths of the students (27.9 per cent) live with their parents and a very small proportion of students (3.8 per cent) lives with their relatives. A little more than one-fifth of the students (22.7 per cent) lives in rented rooms. Five students (2.1 per cent) live with their own famileis. Two students (0.9 per cent) stay with their friends and the remaining one (0.4 per cent) as paying guest.

While looking at the study hours, we found that 36.5 per cent spent more than four hours on their study closely followed by 36.1 per cent of those who spend four hours. Three hours on study have been given by 17.2 per cent of students and 7.3 per cent of the students have spent two hours. Some students (2.1 per cent) have mentioned that they devote only one hour daily on their study. One student (0.4 per cent) was not certain about the time that he devoted towards his study.

The no. of study hours devoted by a student is also affected by variables like father's education, economic status, employment of respondents, course of study and student's extra-curricular activities.

It was found that largest is the percentage of those whose fathers are unlettered (76.8 per cent) followed by those whose fathers have read upto middle school or less (70.9 per cent). Relatively lower percentage is of those whose fathers have read upto high school or more (58.3 per cent). The study shows that with the increase in the level of education of father, the percentage of students who spend more hours declines and increase of those who spend less time on study. Further, Chi square tests brings out that economic status does not significantly influence the study hours of the students.

Employment of the students seems to have a direct bearing on the time the students spend on study. 76.8 per cent of the unemployed students spend more time on the study.

Further, the kind of course opted by the students also determines the time which the student will spend on his studies. Data shows that the students offering Commerce courses are spending more time on studies than those of Arts and Science students. Also as compared to Arts students (69.7 per cent), a larger proportion of science students (73.8 per cent) devote more time on study.

Statistic reveals that a higher percentage of the students who have registered average participation in extra-curricular activities (84.8 per cent) devoted more time on study than those who have shown higher participation (74.1 per cent) or low participation (65.8 per cent). Hence, we can say that educational background of fathers, economic status of students and courses offered do not significantly affect study hours, but students employment and the level of participation in extra-curricular activities significantly influence their study hours.

Another aspect related to study time is associated to those students who stay with their parents. Their study is likely to get affected as they get time for study after performing domestic duties. On an average, 3.5 hours are spent on domestic work by these students.

As a result 62.3 per cent of the students are of the opinion that they should spend more time as against 30.0 per cent of those who feel that there is no need to spend time more than what they spend at present. Some students (7.3 per cent) appear to be uncertain and one student (0.4 per cent) has not replied. It is also to be seen that more Scheduled Castes school students of Rajasthan (73.0 per cent) want to devote more time for study than college students.

When enquired about the factors responsible for their not being able to devote more time for study, the reasons varied to a large extent. A great deal of work at home / hostel prevents 37.8 per cent of the students from devoting still more time to study and 9.4 per cent of the students do not get time to study as they are employed on some job. A new students (4.7 per cent) feel that either they have no interest in studies or they find the subjects difficult. There are others (3.0 per cent) who do not have adequate facilities such as room, electricity and peaceful atmosphere. Family problems do not allow 1.3 per cent of students to devote more time for study. Sickness is another cause in the case of one student (0.4 per cent). The reasons for not spending more time to study are not known to 5.6 per cent of students. The question is not applicable on 37.8 per cent of the students. Lastly, whether there is a place or not to study at home, those who stay with their parents, do study at home.

The Career of the Students

Now, that we have studied about the courses, the colleges they opt for, their study habits etc., its time to look into their performance of these students. Are they able to pass examinations uninterruptedly?, Are they able to follow lectures of their teachers?, Do they go to the teachers for help and guidance?, Do the students feel that they need coaching in order to make them well versed with the subjects they study and facilities for coaching, etc., are available to them?

To guage the performance of the students, they were asked to mention (a) the number of years they spent in each class from class VI. (b) whether they have to discontinue their studies at any level after primary school and (c) reasons for discontinuity.

As an answer to the first question, it was found that a vast majority of the students right from class VI to XI spent only one year in their respective classes. A decline in their proportion is observed after class XI.

Regarding the second question as well as the third, according to 97.9 per cent of the students there was no discontinuity in their study after primary school and before joining middle school. Only 1.3 per cent of the students had to discontinue for one year and one student (0.4 per cent) for two years. One student (0.4 per cent) did not give any response. They had to discontinue mainly because of economic reasons.

After passing middle school also, discontinuity has not been reported by 98.7 per cent of the students. Only one student (0.4 per cent) had to discontinue after passing middle school and before joining high school. Two students (0.9 per cent) did not give answer. The student had to discontinue the study because there was no college in nearby place. Financial difficulty was stated to be the second reason for discontinuity.

Further, the data showed that nearly 87.6 per cent of the students joined the college immediately after passing the qualifying examination, except 3.9 per cent of the students who joined after a year, 3.0% of the students joined after two years, and 5.1 per cent of the students joined after three years of more. One student (0.4 per cent) didn't give any response. Primarily economic factor was cited as the cause.

Let's now move on to access the comprehension level of the students. Whether the students understand the lectures or not and if there is any difficulty, what exactly was the nature of the difficulty?

Nearly, 76.4 per cent have no difficulty in understanding the lectures in the class as against a negligible percentage of those students (2.1 per cent) who feel difficulty in following the classes while 20.6 per cent of the students had felt difficulty ina few subjects only. One student (0.4 per cent) said that generally he felt no difficulty but at the times the lecture could not be comprehended by him and the remaining one student (0.4 per cent) did not respond.

Besides, comprehension may depend on the time students spend on study and also possibly on the exposure to mass media of communication.

It was found that 77.5 per cent of the students who spend more time on study do not feel any difficulty in the comprehension. At the same time 74.6 per cent of those who spend less time also do not feel any difficulty in the comprehension. Thus, it shows that comprehension is independent of time which students spend on study. Chi square test also indicates the same.

Alongwith this it is found that more than three-fourths of the students (77.5 per cent) having low exposure to mass media and 75.8 per cent of highly exposed students do not feel any difficulty in comprehension. Chi square test illustrates that comprehension of the students is indepenent of the exposure to mass media.

Hence, again it is obvious that neither study hours nor exposure to mass media plays a significant role in comprehension.

Those students who were not able to follow class lectures were also asked to give the reasons. According to 14.2 per cent of the students the teachers did not explain well while the subject was very hard according to 3.0 per cent of students. In the opinion of 2.5 per cent of students the teacher used difficult language and 1.6 per cent of them attributed it to a lot of disturbance in the class room. One of the students (0.4 per cent) said that since he was not regular it was difficult to follow the lectures and the two of the students (0.9 per cent) could not specify a particular reason and remaining two students (0.9 per cent) did not respond. The question was not applicable on 76.4 per cent of the students.

Special efforts like guidance and counselling are required to improve the educational standard. For want of these facilities, the Scheduled Castes students are generally in a disadvantageous position specially at the level of higher education. It is, therefore, essential to make for these facilities, otherwise they are likely to remain handicapped.

A cordial relation between students and teachers is very essential to provide a healthy environment for study. In an hesitation free environment students may seek guidance and advice from the teachers. This depends on the teachers' willingness to be available to help the students and the desire on the part of the students to seek help and guidance from the teachers. Only 25.3 per cent of students went quite often to teachers for seeking guidance and advice while 46.3 per cent went only some times. There were 26.2 per cent of the students who never went to teachers and one student (0.4 per cent) said that he went only rarely. Four students (1.7 per cent) did not respond.

Generally, students feel that the teachers are very helpful and sympathetic towards the Scheduled Caste students. 57.9 per cent of the students upheld this view, while 36.5 per cent of the students said that teachers did not pay extra attention towards them. Only 3.9 per cent of the students reported that the teachers were not at all helpful. Four students (1.6 per cent) said that except a few, in general teachers were helpful.

On being asked whether they need extra coaching to facilitate them to remove their deficiencies was found that a little over three-fourths of the students (76.0 per cent) do not need coaching while more than one-fifth of the students (22.7 per cent) need but they do not go to the coaching classes. Two students (0.9 per cent) were already getting coaching and the remaining one (0.4 per cent) was uncertain of this need.

Students' Participation in Extra-Curricular Activities

Sports/NCC/Students' Union, debates, literary and cultural activities such as drama, dance, painting, music, etc. all come under the bracket of extra curricular activities. It provide an opportunity for the students to come closer to one other in college irrespective of their social background. This study reveals that

Scheduled Castes students participate mostly in sports/NCC, nearly 73.5 per cent. Only 38.2 per cent of the students have evinced participation in the activities of Students' Union (Table 39). In debates and other literary activities 37.3 per cent of students have registered their participation.

The participation in extra-curricular activities may depend on several things, e.g., district in which the college is located, fatahers' education, economic status and level of politicisation. The influence of each one of these is examined here.

The districtwise participation in extra-curricular activities clearly shows that except Kota students (34.9 per cent), 50 per cent or more students of each district under study have shown low participation in extra-curricular activities. The percentage is the highest of the students of Jodhpur in this regard (71.4 per cent).

Further, Chi square test shows that fathers' education does not significantly affect students participation in extra-curricular activities.

Similarly, Economic status also does not significantly affect students' participation in extra-curricular activities.

Research reveals that with the increase in the level of politicisation, there is a decrease in the percentage of the students who have shown low participation in extra-curricular activities and an increase has been found among those who have registered high participation. Chi square test shows that level of politicisation does significantly affect the level of participation in extra-curricular activities.

Thus, the above discussion shows that while the level of politicisation significantly affects the participation in extra-curricular activities, fathers' education and economic status do not play significant role.

The Educational and Occupational Aspirations

The study of the level of aspirations of the college students of Scheduled castes reveals that a majority of college students has the desire to get post-graduate degree. When asked, "Upto what level would you like to study?" About 59.2 per cent have shown their inclination to study upto post-graduate level as against 16.3 per cent of the students who want to study only upto graduate level. 9.9 per cent want to get Ph.D. A small percentage of the students is inclined towards professional education like M.B.B.S. (9.4 per cent) and Bachelor of Engineering (0.4 per cent). Some of the students (4.3 per cent) have shown a desire for law, diploma in engineering, graduate and post-graduate degree in education. Only one student (0.4 per cent) has not indicated educational aspiration. Overall, the data show that Scheduled Castes students are more inclined towards liberal education than towards the professional. When asked from the school students it showed that they 24.2 per cent aspire for graduate degree, closely followed by those (23.7 per cent) who want to study upto high school level only. 10.4 per cent want to study upto intermediate level. The analysis thus reveals that the college students have comparatively higher educational aspirations than that of school students.

Further analysis showed that of the students who spend more hours on study, 60.3 per cent are those who aspire for post-graduate degree. Not only this, irrespective of the educational level of the fathers, a majority of the students aspires for post-graduate degree, highest being the percentage of students whose fathers are unlettered (66.4 per cent).

Even the study revealed that not a single student with comfortable economic status aspires for graduation only. With the increase in the economic status there is an increase in the percentage of those who aspire for Ph.D.

Irrespective of the level of politicisation 55.0 per cent of the students aspire for Post-graduate degree, highest being the percentage of those whose level of politicisation is average and lowest is the percentage of highly politicised students.

It seems, therefore, that the educational aspirations of the Scheduled Castes college students vary in terms of districts and economic status but study ours, fathers' education and level of politicisation do not significantly affect the educational aspirations.

Occupational Aspirations

Since time immerorial, occupation in traditional societies is generally hereditary. Each caste in the system has more or less a fixed occupation to depend on for livelihood. There is actually no choice for one to select an occupation according to ones' own aptitude and interest.

But, with the spread of education and modernization, are gradually changing. Now-a-days, one finds some freedom in the choice of occupation according to one's education and training. The Scheduled Castes students are also not untouched by these changes. It is surmised that the new changes would lead them to look forward for better occupational opportunities. It is high time to investigate into occupational aspirations of the college students of Scheduled Castes. At the outset an attempt is made to know whether the students will like to follow the occupation of their fathers. When asked the question "Would you like to enter into the same occupation as your father?" 96.6 per cent answered negatively. There are at least 3.4 per cent of such students who wish to fall in line with their fathers' occupation.

A natural corollary of this is to ask the Scheduled Castes students, as to what they would like to be. 9.0 per cent seem to be indefinite in regard to their choice. Others were able to indicate the broad main categories of occupation they intended to do like 41.2 per cent want to be government officers and 35.2 per cent will like to do high level professional work, 12.4 per cent like to be teacher, gram-sewak, clerk, typist etc. Only 1.7 per cent of the students like to be social or political workers. One student wants to join any other occupation (0.4 per cent). When a similar survey was conducted on the Scheduled Castes school students, it also showed that a large number of students (62.4 per cent) aspire for the post of government officers while only 8.7 per cent out for high profession. Teachers and gram-sewaks draw only 5.2 per cent of students. Only a few students want to be police officer (1.7 per cent) busienss man (1.7 per cent) social or political worker (1.1 per cent) clerk and typist (1.1 per cent). Only one student (0.4 per cent) wants to be a farmer. It may be seen that 15.0 per cent of school students want to follow the occupation of their fathers.

There were varied differences found when districtwise occupational aspirations were studied. Major cause of difference are the districts in which the colleges are located. Clearly one-half of the students of Jaipur and of Jhunjhunu district want to be government officers and the remaining students' choices are divided into different occupational categories. Two-fifths of Ajmer students (40.0 per cent) intend to be government officers and another two-fifths (40.0 per cent) wish to join some high level professions. A majority of the students of Jodhpur and Kota districts also aspires for high professions.

An interesting fact to notice is that with the increase in the level of education of the father there is decline in the percentage of students aspiring for becoming soldier/police/government officer and a reverse trend is seen among those aspiring to become teacher/gram sewak/nurse/clerk/typist.

Economic Status and Occupational Aspirations seems to have a co-relation. Nearly 42.9% of the students who perceive their economic status as comfortable choose high profession for their future career and 35.7% of them want to be government officers. On the other hand those who think that their economic status is just so-so or difficult, they set low goals for themselves.

Extra-curricular activities seems to have no effect on deciding the occupational goals. Inspite of active participation in college activities, most of the students are inclined to be government officers. Mass media also reaffirms the same occupational aspirations.

Further, we find that most of the students whose level of politicisation is low or average in the College have aspired for posts of government officers whereas most of the highly politicised students want to go for some high profession.

While evaluating the motivators behind the occupational aspirations of these students it was found that the students who have decided about the occupation on the suggestion of fathers, 38.2 per cent of them have opted fot profession and another 38.2 per cent for the post of government officers. Whenever the students have decided on suggestion of teachers, 41.7 per cent of them have opted for profession. Of the students who alone decide for themselves, 43.8 per cent want to be government officers and 34.4 per cent opt for profession.

After knowing the kinds of occupation they would like to pursue in future they were further asked, "Given the choice, would you prefer government service or would you prefer some other employment?" They were desired to specify the order of preference from among the alternative provided: (a) government service, (b) semi-government service, (c) private service, and (d) self-employment.

Around 91.4 per cent has given first preference to government service probably because, it is easier for them to get employment in government sector due to reservation of seats. There was no one who preferred semi government sector as first preference. Service in private sector has been given first preference by only 3.0 per cent of the students while self-employment has been accorded first preference by 6.0 per cent of students. Thus, we find that terms of occupational aspirations, government service holds the imagination of the students.

Encouragement and Discouragement from Home

Parents' attitudes to education in general, and to that of their children in particular, are usually seen to be manifest in an important factor behind the child's success in the educational field is the degree to encouragement given to him by his parents. A positive association between attitudes of parents and attitudes and actions of children as regards higher education seems to help children in the building of their career.

Shows that parents of more than a half of students (51.1 per cent) have encouraged them for higher education. Brothers and sisters have encouraged 28.8 per cent of students while 11.6 per cent of students have been encouraged by their uncle. Only one student (0.4 per cent) has received encouragement from grand parents and one (0.4 per cent) from father-in-law. Only 2.1 per cent has named some other persons as the source of encouragement and 4.7 per cent have said that they had no one to encourage them. Two of the students (0.9 per cent) have not given any response.

A majority of those students who were encouraged by parents (58.0 per cent), siblings (65.7 per cent) and uncle (55.6 per cent) aspire for post-graduate degree. At the same time as many as 63.6 per cent of students who are not encouraged by any one also go for post-graduate degree. Hence, we find that there is no co-relation to the encouragement from home and educational aspirations.

Similarly, data shows that of the students getting encouragement for the study from their parents, 37.8 per cent aspire for the post of government offiers followed by 35.3 per cent of students who opt for high profession. When it was enquired, whether along with motivatoes there anyone who discouraged them for higher studies, 93.1 per cent of the students have said that they have not been discouraged by any one but 6.9 per cent of the students mentioned about varied relatives who discouraged them in the pursuit of higher education. The relations mentioned by students were uncle (2.5 per cent), brother and sister (1.3 per cent) parents (0.9 per cent), grand-parents (0.9 per cent) and spouse (0.4 per cent). No response was given by two students (0.9 per cent).

To summarise, the academic life of the students, we can say that Arts courses are more popular with them than Science and Commerce. Though there is a significant relationship between fathers' education and courses offered by the students, there is no significant relationship between perceived economic status and courses offered.

The students mostly offered the courses of their choice and the reason behind joining a particular college has largely been the advice of parents/relatives. Most of the Scheduled Castes college students do not reside in hostels and they spend on an average 3.6 hours on their study. Educational background of father, economic status and courses offered do not significantly affect study hours but employment and level of participation in extra-curricular activities significantly influence their study hours. As the students devote time on domestic work also they felt that they should spend still more time on study than what they are spending now. It was found that from class VI to XI, a vast majority of the students spent only one year in their respective classes but there was decline in percentage after class XI. There did not take place any remarkable discontinuity in their study. Generally the students are able to understand the class lectures. It has been found that neither study hour nor exposure to mass media has significant influence in comprehension. A majority of the students feel that the teachers are very helpful. Participation in extra-curricular activities by these students is restricted to sports/NCC. Activities of Students' Union, debates and other literary activities is not that much. Inter-district variation is found in participation in extra-curricular activities. While level of politicisation significantly affects the level of participation in extra-curricular activities, fathers' education and economic status do not play any significant role.

On research it was found that the educational aspirations of a majority of the students seem to be high and they want post-graduate degree. Through, the educational aspirations vary according to the district and economic status but fathers' education, study hours and level of politicisation do not seem to affect the level of educational aspirations.

It is interesting to note that only a microscopic minority wants to enter the occupation of the father and a vast section of students want to go for government services, followed by high professions. Overall it was found that more than a half of the students have got encouragement from their parents for both educational as well as occupational aspirations and only a very small percentage of students has been discouraged in their pursuit of higher studies, and profession.

Eleven

Training for Development

The foregoing pages discusses two aspects — first, reasons which led to the evolution of our distinctive training approach. second, aims and objectives of the courses and the methodology we have adoopted or developed to achieve them.

To begin with, any kind of developmental work, be it buildings, machine, technology or even the state should be man-centred. Man has to be at the centre of development not only because he must be its chief beneficiary, but also beacuse development essentially means man's development. Human development takes place when there is personal growth. Actually to us development and personal growth mean the same thing.

Personal growth means awareness: self-awareness, awareness of what is going on within us and awareness of world around us; awareness of our own feelings and needs; awareness of the impact that the world around has on us and the impact that we have or could have on the world; and in this interaction of the world and the self, awareness of our own experiences of growth as those blocking growth. The whole gamut of awareness runs from body awareness to the highest type of spiritual awareness. Nothing is excluded.

Personal growth also means differentiation. In medical parlance, differentiation means the process of development in which a part of the organism is modified into a special form or for a special function. Since the moment of conception till full physiological maturity this process goes on. In the foetus the organism goes on differentiating until various parts develop into specialised organs which are able to perform specific functions. So the organism develops eyes to see, ears to hear etc. In simple words, differentiation, means development from one to the many, the simple to the complex. It is the evolution of a being towards a more complex or specialised form. The result of this evolution is the ability to perform tasks which the organism had been unable to do before. Differentiation in personal growth also means development from the simple to the complex. It implies the development of different capacities which enable us to perform higher tasks and to cope with situations which we had not been able to face before.

The process of differentiation is unending and goes on uninterruptedly unless the individual or society blocks it. Unfortunately, this growth is very often blocked by either societal or natural factors and often cause personal problems. For example, lack of money is an economic obstacle. But it may lead to an inferiority complex or a fatalistic attitude to life or cyncism. This is how an economic difficulty results in a psychological block to personal growth, which further, retrads the progress of society.

Keeping this in mind, when we speak of progress in the context of rural India, we pay more attention to human aspects than to its material implications. In the prsent scenario, due to economic progress people can do something now which they could not do before ; it is the fact that an inner energy has now been released and development can take place in a better way.

But we should not forget that development should be measured in terms of the whole person, and personai growth should be the aim of all development. The craze for economic development, when an increase in GNP became an end in itself, with little attention given to its disastrous consenquences in cultural, ecological and even psychological terms should serve as a warning. Again, the reasons why so many good schemes eventually fail should be sought in the fact that they have not paid enough attention to the personal growth of its recipients. For example, our lack of faith in the people we help might destroy their faith in themselves. This would mean doing more harm than good.

Conversely, any development work will be good if it helps the personal growth of the recipients, if, that is, (1) the recipients have become increasingly aware of themselves and the world they live in, especially of their capacity to transform it; and (2) the recipients are helped to remove the obstacles to personal growth. By obstacles are meant especially all those external conditions which bring abaout in man loss of self-respect, lack of self-confidence, all those conditions which make man lose faith in himself and in others.

Generally, our development approach is conditioned by our professional limitation as educators, meaning thereby, that our developmental efforts our backed with the skills of our profession, leaving other forms of development work to the professionals in other areas. It is within this limited area that we backed help our trainees to live and work more effectively by enabling them to face and overcome the obstacles created by the economic, social or political difficulties existing in society.

In practise, it has two implications. First, it means that we as educators do not show to our trainees the groowth path. That is left to them. Second, this attitude presupposes an important belief which is the foundation of our educational philosophy that every individual has in himself the power to reach full maturity when the obstacles to growth are removed. This faith is the most important element in our educational programme.

It is a proven fact that when you make a group of persons aware of their needs and of the fact that they can do something about them, you open the gates of an inner reservoir of eneregies. They then want to do something and, in planning and executing it, experience a new joy. Faith is then the most important element in our educational programme. This calls for further elucidation.

During the research activities, we realised that diffidence was fairly widespread and that it was a great obstacle to personal growth. And of the many ways to restore self-confidence we found the transactional analysis method very useful. We saw people transforming, developing self-confidence and also how this effected important changes in their lives. We saw shy persons turned into popular class leaders, under-achieving students doing well in the examinations and, more important, we saw that these people became eager to look for opportunities, more creative and joyful.

Self confidence is but an aspect of faith—faith in oneself. To instil confidence in a person means to give him faith. And, conversely, the greatest handicap is lack of faith.

When self-confidence is seen as an aspect of faith it ceases to be a facile, everything-is-all-right attitude. Faith does not ignore the past; but it gives more importance to the present and keeps on looking to the future.

Without faith in God there is no religion; without faith in the students there is no education; and without faith in oneself there is no future but only a repetition of the past. Fortunately we have faith to a greater or lesser extent. But faith is susceptible of growth and the more encompassing the faith the greater becomes the range of man's activity. There are no limits to this, as the great spiritual leaders have taught us. And the wonderful thing is that a man with faith can communicate it to others.

De Charms (1968) has brought out the importance of "personal causation", "the personal knowledge of being an agent of change in the environment". Therefore, to feel like an 'origin' leads to "a strong feeling of personal causation" while to feel like a 'pawn' "constitutes a strong feeling of powerlessness or ineffectiveness."

Our attitude towards rural development changed along with our changing attitude towards development itself. It became more person-oriented. In defining our attitude towards our participants we learned much from NTL trainers. But there was also another influence which helped us very much to define ourselves vis-a-vis our participants—Paulo Freire. He altered us to the dangers and evils of a cultural invasion, (Freire, 1972) and taught us to respect our participants "cultural universe".

Dialogue which takes a central place in Freire's pedagogy is based on love, humility, faith and hope and leads to critical reflection. Very helpful also is the analysis he makes of the relation of oppression to submersion (Freire, 1972 : 27).

> "One of the gravest obstacles to the achievement of liberation is that oppressive reality absorbs those within it and thereby acts to submerge men's consciousness. Functionally, oppression is domesticating. To no longer be prey to its force, one must emerge from it and turn upon it. This can be done only by means of the praxis : reflection and action upon the world in order to transform it."

Freire speaks of making "oppression more oppressive still by adding to it the realisation of oppression." Paradoxically, we found that this realisation had a liberating effect on the minds of low caste people who after the course saw reality not as a consequence of their sins but as a result of well-known sociological forces set in motion to defend the privileges of those in power. Freire's analysis has enabled us to work with the weakest sections of society in a truly effective manner.

Discussing his adult literacy programme, Freire (1973 : 43) says that it should be a programme which itself would be "an act of creation, capable of releasing other creative acts, one in which students would develop the impatience and vivacity which characteristics search and invention." One can lead to creativity by teaching the ABC as Freire does; but one can also teach creativity by asking the group to resolve a conflict which has been plaguing them for a long time, for example, by asking the group to devise a method which will enable them to utilise cattle urine for the enrichment of the land without 'losing face' in their society.

This brings us to the ways in which Freire's theories have been adapted to the requirements of our programme. One of the topics of our dialogue with the participants is their feelings and ours. In the T-group tradition we believe that "sharing feelings with each other is more importance than sharing ideas, opinions or beliefs about each other." The language of feelings is much more effective in reaching the person. Feelings not only take us very quickly to the real needs of those with whom we interact and enable us to perceive the underlying causes of their needs, but feelings unite us as well. This unity further builds the relationship of trust between us. Besides feelings, motives also form an important topic of conversation. This enables us to know one another better and open the door to a true personal communication. When this personal encounter takes place we are in a position to speak to them about the world around them and their work. Much time is devoted to this. It provides a common platform where we all can speak and understand other.

In our programme we have not felt the need to politicise our participants. We want to remain educators believing that our task is to train citizens who are fully aware of their civil and political rights, one of which is to choose their own political creed and their own mode of political action.

Now that we have discussed the various influences which helped the evolution of our distinctive training approach, it is time to explain the aims and objects of the courses and the methodology we have developed to achieve them.

The objective and means of our rural development programme could be stated in schematic form as follows:

1. To organise special courses for the leading members of a homogeneous group, preferably from a backward community of a village. As explained in Chapter 2, the reason for taking people from one village only is that the support of a group is necessary to effect changes in rural India. We also insist on having a homogeneous group. Which means that all should belong to the same caste or to those castes which consider themselves equal. It is very hard to train groups which are very heterogeneous.

We prefer for backward communities because otherwise, our courses would be bringing benefits to those who can best take care of themselves, thereby increasing the gap between the rich and the poor.

2. To increase the self-confidence of the participants, in other words, to effect a behavioural change from a state of diffidence (we cannot!) into a state of confidence (we can!).

3. As behavioural change bring about creativity, we conduct exercises to help the participants to look more creatively at themselves (improved personal behaviour), at others (improved interpersonal relationships), and at their world (more imaginative creative ways of working).

4. At the social level the aim is to resolve the polarity of inferiority and superiority. Oppression of society had adverse psychological reactions on the people. Our courses attempt to restore our participants' sense of self-respect so that they may overcome their feeling of inferiority before the upper castes.

5. The realisation of the feeling of self-respect leads to co-operation. Co-operative effort is the only way by which the poor can make economic progress.

6. These aims are sought to be fulfilled in the process of achieving the objective of improving their agricultural methods. Since the majority of the participants are farmers it is very necessary that we help them to improve agriculture by using HYV seeds, fertilizers, pesticides and larning basic farm management practices.

AIMS AND METHOD OF TRAINING

Initial State	*Transformation Process*	*Goal*
Diffidence	Reasuring questions	Defreeze
	Interesting activities	Confident behaviour with trainers
	Non-verbal warmth Sharing personal information, acceptance, concern, respect	Warm inter-personal support
	Trainer's attitudes of acceptance, concern, respect	'I'm worthy of respect': self-respect
	Positive feedback	Self-confidence
	Helping them to succeed	
Personal blocks	Reflection on activities: how did I act? Why?	Self-awareness Improved behaviour
	Feedback by trainers	
	Reflection on social structures	Social awareness
Factional fights Lack of unity	Meaning of co-operation	
	Reflection on social structures	
	Exercises testing their co-operative spirit	co-operation
	Reflection on their performance: role of feelings, reason	
	Analysis of existing conflicts: analysis of facts: role of feelings	Co-operation: conflict resolution here in the group
	Options open to them; possible solutions	
Low agricultural technology	Scientific knowledge about agriculture Reflection on it and its application back home	Realisation of the possibility and ways to improve their fields
Low agricultural productivity	Knowledge of helps available in Govt., other agencies	
	Experiential knowledge about decision-making:	Final choice
	How many options open?	(a) Individual's
	Difficulties, possible helps, advantages...	(b) Group's
	Calculated risk, concrete	

In order to achieve these aims this is the procedure we follow:

1. *Defreezing*: The initial stages are marked by embarrassment, shyness and even suspicion on the part of the participants. Hence, to break the ice we engage them in external, absorbing activities

and asking them simple questions which allow them to make themselves known and establish rapport with the trainers.

2. *Warm interpersonal support*: Graudally, relationship of trust relationship develops between trainers and participants and among the participants themselves so that all the members of the group can come closer without being afraid to appear as they are. In this climate of trust it is easier for the participants to give up the defensive attitudes which stand in the way of effective learning. To achieve this, the trainers adopt a uncritical attitude of acceptance and respect towards the participants.

3. *Faith*: The major thrust of course is to communicate faith to our participants, the latter can achieve the rest themselves. The effort is to make them aware of their own latent powers and thereby increase their self-confidence. Thus we make them realsie their ability to learn new things by making them repeat what they have been taught in agriculture, by making them succeed in exercises they were unable to do before. But the most effective thing is the educators' faith in them !

4. *Cooperation*: To develop the cooperative spirit in them they are engaged in activities where their cooperative spirit will show. A very effective method of doing this is to help the group to resolve existing conflicts.

5. *Decision-making*: Besides, our main motive is to ensure that before the course ends, they should learn how to make decisions, and see to it that they make some for themselves individually and for the village as a whole. This implies (a) giving them information mostly about agriculture. This is primarily done at the Research Farm at Mogar where they learn modern methods of agriculture (improved seeds, fertilizers, pesticides, and farm management, (b) Along with agricultural methods, they are also given information about banking, government schemes and agro-industries and (c) practical informaion about decision-making with suitable exercises to put it into practice. All this enables them to prepare themselves for the "final choice".

6. *Final choice*: At this stage, the partaicipants are made to set concrete individiual and groups goals, which have an element of calculated risk in them. Their decision is backed by consideration on various options open to them and other factors such as, likely

sources of help, and the advantages and the disadvantages of any particular courses of action.

7. *Follow-up*: To ensure lasting success emphasis is laid on the need of group support. In order to keep up the spirit of the group the trainers are required to visit the village and offer their services to solve any difficulties which may arise while carrying out their plans. Whenever necessary refresher courses are organised.

It will be appropriate here to explain the teaching methods that have been found more effective for the training programme.

The training is primarily based on the laboratory method. The term laboratory should not be confused with that of a scientist's laboratory. Rather, it is an agricultural land where one can experiment newer techniques. In short, it is an artaificial environment. Being artificial it has certain advantages. One can be more free to try new behaviours without fear of graver consequences. It is also away from home and therefore the participants are not subjected to the pressure of what often is an alienating culture or, atleast, of those elements in that culture which are alienating. Further, brings the participants together since they now are in an enemy territory, in unfamiliar surroundings. This togetherness is also a powerful means of creating a climate of trust without which no creativity can be fostered.

In a laboratory situation the participants can undergo an experience and then they and the trainers talk about it. In this method, the partaicipants themselves and on their actions so that they could learn something about themselves and the way they behave. It is clear that this type of education does not presuppose literacy. It does not aim to give much information but to help the participants gain insights which may enable them to function more effectively.

Alongwith this self realisation, some information must be given to them. This is done when the participants are exposed to a more advanced agricultural technology and then their experience is talked about. What happened when the expert spoke to them about agriculture? Did they learn something new? If they did, we make them reflect on the fact that they can learn. If they reject the new knowledge as 'impractical' or as not applicable to their fields, then this defence mechanism becomes the topic of our dialogue.

When the participants manage to overcome their defence reactions they reach a point of reflection on their work. At this stage it is the educators' duty to be there with them, in there moment of innovational creativity. This is the point when the participants to figure out how what they have heard from the expert can be implemented in their own fields. This stage is important because it marks the beginning of change in their agricultural methods and the beginning of a great transformation in their attitude. It revolution sizes their way of looking at the world and at oneself. Unless there is this change of attitude creativity is impossible and, without innovational creativity, agricultural technology cannot take roots.

As mentioned earlier, one of the subjects of dialogue is the participants' feelings and our educator's. The feelings are very important in this type of training to bridge the gap between their value and his. The moment we feel angry or frustrated at their behaviour, it is time to introspect and look for their cause : what did we want to achieve and why ? Who has to make the final choice? We or they? It is this introspection, which helps us to come closer to our participants. Actions and words prompted by unexamined emotions tend to generate negative feelings towards our participants which further alienate them from us. The result may very well be either a vicious circle or lack of authenticity on their part, together with an unhealthy desire to please us.

In rural development team work is very essential. We have striven hard to work as a team. We have spent well over 250 hours during these last years in T-groups ourselves only, trying to resolve our inter-personal difficulties, work out our personal problems and find out the role which each one of us should play in the team. We have spent hours listening to the recordings of our training sessions to criticise ourselves and develop better ways of handling a situation. The greatest difficulty one encounters is that of understanding the people, their feelings, their needs, even what they are actually telling the group. It is imperative on our part to know the impact of our words and actions on them. All this requires keen observation. While one of us intervenes, the others watch the reactions of the group. Each one of us keeps on checking his perceptions with the others' two. It is a known fact that team work gives mutual support and encouragement, the pooling of ideas, resources and creativity. We offer a model to our participants of how to work together. This model is all the more telling in India in as much as three of us belong to different communities and religions and have been brought together only by our profession as educators. There is no point in telling your participants that they should co-operate if you yourself are unable to do so. In making the effort to co-operate with others one learns the difficulties of cooperation and the means of solving these difficulties, and enjoys the experience of working together.

Twelve

Aspects of Social Life

With change in time, the identity of every individual changes. It is the task of the Social Scientists to look into the problem of identity and change. It is felt that the college students of Scheduled Castes who come from unprivileged sections of the Indian society, and have been kept almost isolated from the main currents of cultural life might have social life quite different from that of the other sections. The exposure to mass media and their participation in political oriented activities are likely to break their isolation and in the process, they are likely to look for some one who may provide the frame of reference for their behaviour. Therefore, these aspects should become part of a study which is related with the exploration of the various aspects of Scheduled Castes students. The study of changes in parental authority is another aspect which needs probing. Further, the social circles in which a student belonging to a scheduled caste participates helps to indicate his identification, adaptation or isolation from others. In the process of interacation with friends, one is likely to experience differential treatment. All these are important aspects which one needs. Therefore, this chapter deals with the following aspects :

1. Exposure to mass media, to study to to get a wholesome picture of the behaviour of the Scheduled Caste,
2. Politicisation,
3. The ideal and the people the students admire,
4. Outlook on marriage, and the authority of parents,
5. Friendship-integration and isolation, and
6. Experience of discrimination.

Exposure to Mass Media

In today's world, various communication medias have revolutionized the society. It has changed the man's perspective of his world. While written words provided facilities for the accumulation of culture within the national boundaries, the new electronic media have internationalised it resulting in the abolition of space and time. These mass medias are introducing a wide audience to urban, Westernised values and the style of life and have immediate and direct effect on the society. The modern techniques of communication, in India, are mostly available to urban centres, though gradually they have been reaching in rural areas also. This section, attempts to study the extent to the use of these media by the college students of Scheduled Castes of Rajasthan. The focus would be to examine the utilisation of the mass media by these students, in terms of their going to cinema, listening to radio and newspaper reading.

Cinema

It is being recognised now that cinema functions both as a means of recreation and education. While the commercial films act as recreational media, it is the documentaries and arts films which impart education also.

To study the cinema going habit of Scheduled Castes students may be of interest as it requies money to see a film and most of the students come from unpriviledged homes.

Of 233 Scheduled Castes college students, two (0.9 per cent) have given no reply and 11.1 per cent of the students do not see films at all. A considerably higher percentage of Scheduled Castes school students of Rajasthan (46.0 per cent) does not go to see a film. On the basis of the frequency of visit to cinema by the college students to see films. Scheduled Castes students may be classified into following categories:

1. *Occasional cinema goers* : The students who go to cinema once in two or more months,
2. *Habitual cinema goers* : Those who go to cinema once a month, and,
3. *Cinema addicts* : Those who go to cinema once a fortnight or more,
4. *Non-cinema goers* : The students who do not see the films at all.

An analysis of the frequency of visiting cinema with a purpose to see a film in terms of these categories reveals that the habitual cinema goers constitute three-tenths of the students (30.9 per cent) and a little less than this (29.6 per cent) are cinema addicts. Somewhat less than this is the proportion of those (27.5 per cent) who are classified as occasional cinema goers. Some students (11.9 per cent) have not gone to see any film and they are non-cinema goers. Two students (0.9 per cent) have not given any response.

Radio

Radio is another popular media of mass communication. It not only restricts itself to the broadcasts of national, international and state news but also broadcasts educational and youth programmes separately. Useful and popular lectures also form part of the radio programmes. It imparts knowledge and increases the awareness of the students. Except 8.1 per cent of the Scheduled Castes students all others (91.9 per cent) listen to the radio. The percentage of students who listen to radio regularly is pretty small (16.3 per cent). A large percentage of students (61.4 per cent) however, listens to radio only occasionally and 14.2 per cent of the students listens to radio rarely.

Newspaper Reading

Newspaper is a very strong media of communication. Exposure to newspaper tends to effect the outlook of the readers on public affairs at the international, national, state and also at the local level. They get to know the latest happenings around them.

It is heartening to find that out of 233 students of Scheduled Castes, only one student (0.4 per cent) does not read any newspaper and all the remaining 232 students read newspaper. A majority of the students (59.2 per cent) are daily readers while 32.6 per cent read newspapers occasionally. There is a considerable difference between the Rajasthan school (39.0 per cent) and college students (59.2 per cent) who read newspapers, daily. A small proportion of the college students of Scheduled Castes in Rajasthan (7.7 per cent) reads newspaper very rarely. It is possible therefore to say that Scheduled Caste students are mostly exposed to printed media.

As to the number of newspapers they read, it is found that 48.1 per cent of the students read three newspapers. One student (0.4 per cent) reads five newspapers and another one (0.4 per cent) reads even six or more newspapers. Only one newspaper is read by 22.3 per cent of students. On an average Scheduled Castes students read 2.06 newspapers. College students are mostly interested in advertisements pertaining to employment.

Hindi being the predominant language of the state approximately four out of every five students of Scheduled Castes (79.4 per cent) read Hindi newspapers. Only 17.6 per cent students read regional language newspaper. 1.7 per cent of all students read English newspapers. There are two students (0.9 per cent) who read newspapers other than regional but not Hindi/English. The question is not applicable on one student (0.4 per cent) as he does not read newspaper.

Overall Level of Exposure to Mass Media

To have a better understanding of the responses pertaining to the exposure of the students to different mass media, namely cinema, radio and newspapers, we need to colate the data.

The composite scale of exposure shows that 65.7 per cent of the students are fully exposed whereas only 34.3 per cent of the students have low exposure to mass media.

In districtwise categorisation Jhunjhunu (75.0 per cent) was found to be most exposed and Ajmer (60.0 per cent) was lowest exposed. The chi square test shows that there is no significant inter-district difference in the level of exposures to mass media.

Further, Irrespective of the parental education more than three-fifths of the students are highly ejxposed to mass media. The chi square test shows that exposure to mass media is not significantly related with fathers' education.

Besides, the study reveals that with the increase in economic status, there is an increase in the percentage of students who have shown high exposure to mass media and there has been corresponding decline in the percentage of students who are less exposed to mass media. However, the chi square test does not indicate a significant relationship between economic status and exposure to mass media.

Politicisation

Centres of education do not exist in social or political vacuum. They are perhaps more responsive to politics in a large society. Politicisation refers to role-enactments oriented to power acts and participation in community decision-making. It is expected that education tends to increase people's acceptance of those values which sustain democratic processes and institutions. In developing societies, the students are participating in larger number in the political life of the country and India is not different. The students consider colleges as a place for anticipatory socialisation for adult political life. Therefore, a study of students' participation in political activities is of immense use. The current study tries to explore the relative state of politicisation among college students of Scheduled Castes in terms of their participation in political parties. The Scheduled Castes students are likely to participate in the political activities to raise their own status and that of the caste people by accumulating pressures on decision-making. The investigation in this sphere begins with asking a question from Scheduled Castes students, "Have you ever participated in the meetings, processions or rallies organised by any political leader or party?"

The answer showed, approximately two-fifths of the students (39.9%) have participated in the meetings organised by political leaders or parties as against three-fifths of those (59.7 per cent) who have not participated. One student (0.4 per cent) has not given any response to this question.

Like meetings, in processions also, 38.6 per cent of the students have participated as against 59.2 per cent of those who have not participated. Some students (2.2 per cent) have not given any response to this question.

On asking as to the type of work they had done for the political parties, more than a half of the students (52.8 per cent) had not done any work for any political party. Slips and pamphlets had been distributed by 24.5 per cent of the students. Canvassing for candidates had been done by 13.3 per cent of the students. The remaining students had participated in processions (3.0 per cent), had shouted slogans (2.6 per cent) and 2.1 per cent had done other work. Four students (1.7 per cent) did not respond. These responses were given by the students when asked to indicate first party work. They were also asked to indicate second party work if they had done it at all. A large percentage of students (55.4 per cent) had not done any second party work. Canvassing was done by 14.2 per cent of students, 9.0 per cent students had shouted slogans,

8.6 per cent had participated in processions and 6.9 per cent had distributed slips and pamphlets. Only 2.6 per cent of the students had done other work and 3.3 per cent had not responded. No third or fourth party work had been indicated by any one of the students.

The above survey, showed that the participation in these activities may even be casual and momentary. But to enquire whether a student is an active worker of a party, two additional questions were put to the respondents : One question sought to know the student's own position in the party and another question sought to know the position of family members in relation to political party. As an answer to the first question "Are you an active worker, supporter or sympathiser of any political party, it was found that a sizable proportion of the students (34.3 per cent) has no association with any political party. Only (65.2 per cent) are either active workers or supporters/sympathisers. About three-fifths of the students (52.8 per cent) are members of the Indian National Congress (R). A much lower percentage of the all India college students (24.0 per cent) than that of the Rajasthan Scheduled Castes college students (52.8 per cent) belongs to this category. The differences is considerable. Republican party draws 3.4 per cent of students, 3.0 per cent of the students are members of the Congress (O). The remaining students are associated with other political parties such as Socialist party (2.6 per cent), Communist (1.7 per cent), Swatantra party (1.3 per cent) and Jan Sangh (0.4 per cent). One student (04 per cent) did not reply. In all, total strength of students having some affinity with opposition is of 12.4 per cent only as against those who hold middle of the road ideology represented by the ruling Congress party.

As an answer to the other question "Is or was any member of your family an active worker, supporter or sympathiser of a political party?", a little less than half of the students (48.9 per cent) replied negataively. Of all the students, 46.4 per cent said that their family members were with Indian National Congress(R). Their proportion is considerably higher than all India College students (19.0 per cent) and also than Rajasthan school students (22.0 per cent). Republican and Congress (O) had drawn 1.3 per cent each. There were only two students (0.9 per cent) whose family members belonged to Swatantra party. One each belonged to Communist, Socialist and Jan Sangh parties.

The sympathies of students and also their family members indicated that they were largely oriented to the ruling party and opposition parties had not been able to draw them in any substantial proportion in their fold.

After going through the above discussion an overall picture of politicisation of the students can be built.

It is clear that most of the Scheduled Castes students (45.1 per cent) have low level of politicisation, 17.6 per cent have reached the medium level and 37.3 per cent of students attained high level of politicisation.

As is evident, Jhunjhunu and Kota are the only districts where the Scheduled Castes students are, highly politicised, their percentage being 68.2 per cent and 55.8 per cent respectively. Jaipur, the capital district of Rajasthan have low level of politicisation. The chi square test reveals a significant inter-district variation in the level of politicisation of the students and the difference is significant at 0.01 level.

Irrespective of the level of education of the father of the students, most of the students have low level of politicisation. Chi square test does not show a significant relationship between fathers' education and politicisation.

There seems to be a direct relationship between economic status and politicisation. With the increase in economic status there is a decrease in the proportion of highly politicised students and there is corresponding increase in the proportion of low politicised students. The chi square test does not show any significant relationship between economic status and politicisation.

Further, shows that the level of politicisation is low of a higher proportion of those students whose exposure to mass media is either low or high. The chi square test also shows that exposure to mass media is not significantly related with politicisation.

The Ideal and the People the Student Admire

The importance of the family as an agent of socialisation can not be minimised but with the increasing differentiation in the society, family is gradually losing its predominance. Earlier, the elder members of the family used to be the 'role models' for the young generation. But, in todays' society family no more plays as role model. People look for other sources. Under such circumstances Scheduled Castes students were asked a question, "Each of us has before our mind some person(s) to whom we consider as our ideal and wish to be like him. Name three persons whom you consider your ideal?" The students were desired to give name out of the following categories:

1. Historical figures,
2. National leaders,
3. Scientists or men of literature,
4. Local leaders,
5. Scheduled Castes leaders,
6. Family and caste members,
7. Religious leaders,
8. Government servants,
9. Anmy other and
10. No one.

The students were to give three names at the first instance, whom they considered to be their ideals.

A small proportion of the students (4.3 per cent) does not consider any one as their ideal but a large majority of them (95.7 per cent) does have one or the other person as ideal. The students seem to have been oriented towards national leaders (59.2 per cent). Only one student (0.4 per cent) has local leaders as his ideal. Those leaders who have immensely worked to uplift these unprivileged people received admiration. Students generally mentioned the names of Gandhiji, Pt. Nehru, Shri Lal Bahadur Shastri, Shri Patel, etc. among the national leaders.

Schedule Castes' leaders like Dr. Ambedkar, are ideals for 15.0 per cent of the students. An equal proportion of the students have mentioned historical figures (3.4 per cent) like Vir Durga Dass, Rana Pratap and Shivaji and scientists (3.4 per cent) as their ideals. Government servants are ideals for only 3.0 of students. Only 1.3 per cent of students have regarded religious leaders as their ideal. When asked to give second name of ideal pesons, 6.9 per cent of the students have not given any name. 61.8 per cent gave the name of national leaders. There is slight increase in the proportion of the students naming historical figures as ideal (5.2 per cent). No change has taken place in case of scientists. Only 4.7 per cent of the students give the name of Scheduled Castes leaders. A decrease in proportion is found also among those who recalled family and caste members (3.9 per cent). The proportion of those naming religious leader is doubled (2.6 per cent) and also there is some increase in the proportion of students who mention Government servants (4.3 per cent) but the increase in both cases is negligible.

When the students were asked for the third name of the ideal person 14.6 per cent did not give any name. 15.6 per cent mentioned the name of national leaders. This time the proportion of students mentioning Scheduled Castes leaders, family and caste members and religious leaders have further declined. Thus, it shows that Scheduled Castes students are largely oriented towards national leaders.

Authority of Parents: Outlook on Marriage

Over the years, there have been many chanages on various aspects of the Indian society including the position of parents in family power-structure. Does this change characterise the Scheduled Castes families also? To understand this phenomenon, an attempt is made to study the extent to which the students have been able to assert themselves in the area of family decision-making. Only two areas of decision-making have been considered here (1) the decision about future career, and (2) decision about marriage.

Decision about the Future Career of the Students

It was found that students have started asserting their right to decide about themselves. About seven students out of every ten decided about their future caraeer by themselves. There is a cognizable difference on this point between Rajasthan college students (68.7 per cent) and those of all India college students (57.0 per cent). Similar is the result with respect to school students (42.0 per cent).

Only in the case of 14.6 per cent of students, fathers have decided about their future career. Only 6.0 per cent of students have mentioned relatives. A very small proportion of students (5.2 per cent) has acted according to the decision of their teachers in deciding about their future career. Friends are very rarely influencial in deciding the career. They are instrumental for a lone student (0.4 per cent). One student (0.4 per cent) has not responded and another 3.9 per cent of students are undecided about their future career. In the case of two students (0.9 per cent), persons other than those mentioned here have decided. The responses as indicated above are the first response given by the students.

An attempt is made here to see as to what factors are kept in view while deciding about the marriage and whose voice will ultimately prevail in the decision about marriage. The respondents were asked: "When deciding about your marriage what importance will you give to the following?"

1. The economic status of the other party,
2. The social status of the other party,
3. Caste,
4. Education of the girl/boy,
5. Boy's/girl's look.
6. Girl's ability at house keeping (for boy)/The quality of job the boy holds (for girls) and
7. Girl's ability to get alongwith boy's parents (for boy)/The income that the boy earns (for girls).

This question was not applicable to 56.7 per cent of students of Scheduled Castes because they are married.

21.9 per cent consider economic status to be very important. But 15.0 per cent of the students take it to be unimportant.

The proportion of students who regard social status to be very important is 16.3 per cent and 23.2 per cent think that it is important. In the opinion of 3.9 per cent of the students, it is not an important consideration.

According to 17.6 per cent of students caste is a very important consideration in selecting marriage partner and 15.0 per cent of students consider it important while a small proportion of students (10.7 per cent) consider it to be unimportant.

Education seems to be a very important consideration according to 11.2 per cent of the students and it is important according to 28.8% of them while it is considered unimportant by 2.6 per cent of the students. Two students (0.9 per cent) have not given any response.

Fifteen per cent of students consider the physical look of the partner to be very important and 24.9 per cent consider it important.

Only 2.6 per cent of students do not consider it important. No response was given by two students (0.9 per cent).

Girl's house keeping ability or the quality of job held by the boy was considered very important in the opinion of 30.5 per cent of students and 11.2 per cent of the students consider it important. Only two students (0.9 per cent) consider it unimportant and other two students (0.9 per cent) have not given any response.

Girl's ability to get alongwith boy's parents or the income of the boy was considered by 32.2 per cent of the students to be very important criteria and 9.9 per cent hold it to be important. Three students (1.3 per cent) did not respond.

From the above, we can infer that the income of the boy and the job he holds are very important considerations for selecting husbands for girls and the girl's ability to adjust with parents and her ability at house keeping are considered very important as far as boys are concerned. It is striking to see that economic status finds the lowest favour.

Marriage and Final Decision Makers

As mentioned earlier, the young men and women now feel that they should have their say in decision about marriage. Further, when the Scheduled Castes students were a question, "Do you think that you will ever marry a girl/boy whom your parents do not approve of?" 23.6 per cent answered that they will not go against the wishes of their parents. While 8.6 per cent of Scheduled Castes college students of Rajasthan are willing to go against the wishes of the parents if in their opinion, the partner is found to be very good, some students (11.1 per cent) are undecided. The question is not applicable on 56.7 per cent of students.

On the whole, the students, will follow their parents in regard to their marriage and would exert themselves as far as their career is concerned.

Friendship — Integration and Isolation

When the Scheduled Caste students join college they are likely to have friendship with persons of their own caste or even with those who are not of the same caste. The more the Scheduled Castes students get the opportunity to mix freely with those who are not of their caste, their integration in wider society will be facilitated. In this study relationship between caste Hindus and the Scheduled Castes students is given focus. Students of Scheduled Castes were asked, "Do you think that the fact that you belong to the Scheduled Castes affects the behaviour of classfellows towards you?"

As a response, 13.7 per cent claimed that the behaviour of the classfellows is affected to a large extent and according to 44.3 per cent of the students it is affected at least to some extent. However, 42.0 per cent of students think that the behaviour of the classfellows is not affected at all. Looking at the statistics, we find that the weight of opinion is heavier towards behaviour being discriminated.

As more than 40% of the students were of the view that the behaviour of caste Hindus is not affected, it was natural to ask whether the classfellows know or do not know the fact that the respondents are of Scheduled Castes. 68.2 per cent maintains that most of the classfellows know about their belonging to Scheduled Castes and another 25.3 per cent have said that at least some of the students know about it. Doubt about the knowledge of their being Scheduled Castes has been expressed by 1.7 per cent and 4.3 per cent of the students do not seem to be certain about it and one student (0.4 per cent) has not responded.

After analysing the behavioural aspect of the classfellow, they were asked to name their three best friends in or outside college indicating their castes.

While naming their first friend, it was found that 43.8 per cent has friends of the same Scheduled Castes only 14.2 per cent has friends of the other Scheduled Castes. Around 41.2 per cent has friendship with non-Scheduled Castes persons and two students (0.9 per cent) have not given any response.

Reporting about the second friend a majority of the Scheduled Castes students (49.2 per cent) has friendship with own caste persons and 17.6 per cent have friendship with other Scheduled Castes persons while 38.2 per cent of the students have friends among non-Scheduled Castes also. No response was given by 1.3 per cent of the students.

Finally, speaking about the third friend, it was clear that 40.3 per cent have friends in the same caste and 17.6 per cent have friends in other Scheduled Castes. About 40.3 per cent have friends among non-Scheduled Castes also and 1.7 per cent of the students have not responded.

Similarly, 14.6% of the Scheduled Caste students have reported that all their friends belong to non-Scheduled Castes while 26.2 per cent of the students have two non-Scheduled and one Scheduled Caste friend. Twenty one per cent of students have one friend of non-Scheduled and two Scheduled Caste friends. Six per cent of the students have one friend of their own Scheduled Castes and two of other Scheduled Castes. Another 6.0 per cent of students report that two of their friends are of their own Scheduled Caste and one of other Scheduled Castes, while 19.7 per cent of the students have all their friends from their own Scheduled Castes.

Thus, it is very apparent that a majority of the Scheduled Castes students have friends among the Scheduled Castes and that most of them have friends in their own castes. But, at the same time it also shows that Scheduled Castes students like to have friends not only in their own castes but also in non-Scheduled Castes and secondarily in the other Scheduled Castes.

Experience of Discrimination

Inspite of modernization instances are not lacking where persons belonging to Scheduled Castes meet severe ill-treatment from the persons of caste Hindus. To deal with this aspect, a question was asked: "Have you or any member of your family ever experienced ill-treatment from any one because you belong to Scheduled Castes ?" A majority of the students (65.2 per cent) does not recall any such experience but 32.6 per cent of students do recall. Similarly 81.5 per cent of school students of Scheduled Castes, have not reported any ill-treatment except, 18.5 per cent who felt such ill-treatment.

Districtwise, we find that around 55.8 per cent of Kota students had experienced discrimination themselves or by family members.

As stated earlier, the level of education of their fathers, more than three-fifths of the students have no experience of discrimination. Few of the harassments or ill-treatment are of kind—

1. Refused to serve them with tea in restaurant.
2. If tea served in restaurant, they were forced to wash the cup and plate.
3. Not permitted to stay in Dharmashalla.
4. Not allowed entry into the temple.
5. When went into a temple, they were harrassed.
6. Practice of untouchability continued. As a result harrassment and assault frequently occur.
7. Not allowed to use the public well.

After going through the various aspects of social life of the Scheduled Caste, we can conclude that firstly, students of Scheduled Castes are largely exposed to mass-media of communication. Interdistrict variation is not found in the exposure to mass media. Fathers' education and economic status also have not played significant role in determining the level of exposure to mass media.

Secondly, a majority of the students have low level of politicisation. They do not attend meetings and procession organised by political partaies in large numbers. Most of them do not work for any political party. Fathers' education, economic status, exposure to mass media, have no significant relationship with the level of politicisation.

Thirdly, it was found that through the students would like to decide themselves about their future career but they generally would not like to go against the wishes of the parents as far as decision about marriage is concerned, until a very special situation arises. It was also apparent that the students of Scheduled Castes are most likely to have friendship in their own castes and would like to increase the area of friendship with non-Scheduled Castes persons. Lastly, it was analysed that discrimination has not been experienced by a majority of the students, ever.

Thirteen

Students' Outlook

Since Independence, government of India has been trying to uplift the condition of Scheduled Castes people by launching various programmes for their welfare. Different programmes were formulated and attempts were made to implement them to help these people to raise their living conditions. Through these schemes the government intends to bring about a radical transformation in their outlook and status the scheduled caste people and to make them feel independent, self-confident and able to stand on their own legs. It is time to analyse as to what extent the policies and programmes have been able to achieve the objectives. College students of Scheduled Castes, being the beneficiaries of the schemes, were desired to express their opinion on the following aspects:

1. Students' impression regarding the status of the Scheduled Castes,
2. Students' outlook on educational facilities,
3. Students' awareness of reservation of jobs,
4. Students' outlook on the policy of reservation,
5. Students' views on the programmes viewed as a whole, and
6. The difficulties that the students have personally encountered with reference to the programme.

Students' Impression Regarding the Status of the Scheduled Castes

To ameliorate the lot of scheduled castes the Government of India and the State Governments have enunciated certain policies and initiated certain programmes. To what extent the measures have been a success can be ascertained by those who are being affected the most. The college students of Scheduled Castes are supposed to have better knowledge about this because as an educated section, they are expected to know the policies and programmes and as they come from the unprivileged section for which the schemes are meant, they are appropriate persons to give a sound appraised of the situation. With this in mind, their opinion was solicited. They were given three statements to comment on—

"1. The status of the Scheduled Castes has improved as of before but it continues to be inferior to that of non-Scheduled Castes Hindus.

2. The status of the Scheduled Castes is equal to that of non-Scheduled Castes Hindus in the country, and

3. The status of the Scheduled Castes has not improved. It continues to be backward."

The responses show that only a small percentage of students (23.6 per cent) feels that there has been improvement in the status of the Scheduled Castes as of before but it still continues to be inferior to that of non-Scheduled Castes Hindus. As against this, 68.2 per cent of the students consider that there has been no improvement in the status, rather backwardness still continues. At the same time, it is imperative to mention here that 52 per cent of all India college students think that there has been improvement in the status and 37.0 per cent feel that status has not been improved. It shows considerable difference between all India and Rajasthan college students. Only a small minority of Scheduled Castes college students of Rajasthan (3.9 per cent) maintains that the status of the Scheduled Castes has improved to such an extent that it has now come upto the level of non-Scheduled Castes Hindus in the country. The general inference shows that only 27.5 per cent thinks that government measures have helped to improve the status while the majority (68.2 per cent) think otherwise. It may further be said that according to 91.8 per cent of the students, the status of Scheduled Castes is still inferior compared to that of non-Scheduled Castes Hindus. Three students (1.3 per cent) seem to be uncertain about the status and seven students (3.0 per cent) have not given any answer. Another aspect to be considered here its the possibility that the students while speaking of improvement in status might be referring to the status pertaining to the areas of education, occupation, economic political and while saying that status has not improved they might be having in view their social status vis-a-vis that of the caste Hindus.

Irrespective of the districts, a majority of the students feel that the status of the Scheduled Castes has not improved and that it continues to be backward. The response is highest in Jhunjhunu (97.7 per cent) and the lowest in Kota (51.2 per cent). The percentage of Kota students speaking of improvement is the highest (44.2 per cent) compared to that of other districts. No student of Jhunjhunu has agreed with response. Twelve per cent of students of Ajmer are of the opinion that the status of Scheduled Castes has become equal to that of Caste Hindus. This is the highest percentage in comparison to that of all other districts, lowest being the proportion of Jhunjhunu students (2.3 per cent) as is evident.

Again, Fifty per cent or more of students, irrespective of the educational level of fathers, hold the view that the status of the Scheduled Castes people has not improved and it continues to be backward. But with the increase in the level of education of the father of the students this opinion declined but reverse is the case of those who feel that the students of the Scheduled Casts are equal to that of non-Scheduled Castes Hindus in the country. Chi square test does not show a significant relationship between the level of education of fathers and students' impression regarding the status.

Students' Outlook on the Admission Scheme

As per the central and state government policies, various provisions have been made for the admission of Scheduled Castes students in the various colleges. Special reservation in terms of seats and also some concession in the qualifying marks for admission are given to avoid any difficulty in their admission. Let's review the usefulness of these schemes.

Around 66.1 per cent of students consider the schemes to be very useful and 29.2 per cent consider it fairly useful. The scheme has not been useful according to 2.6 per cent of the students and 2.1 per cent of students are not able to say about the usefulness of the scheme.

With the increase in population, the number of students seeking admission at various levels of education is also increasing. So, the number of seats reserved for admission a decade back may not hold true in the present scenario. Hence, the need for more seats as otherwise they may not be able to compete with the general students. This difficulty may be more perceptible in Science classes where an increase in seats is not easily possible because of laboratory requirements. It is in this context, that they were asked, "Would you say that the reservations provided are adequate in terms of the number of Scheduled Castes students seeking admission ?"

The reservation of seats for admission has been considered as adequate only by a small proportion of students (14.1 per cent) while most of them (74.7 per cent) maintain that it is not adequate. Some of the students (10.3 per cent) do not know whether it was adequate or not and two students (0.9 per cent) did not reply.

Students' Outlook on Hostels

While education is an instrument of progress for Scheduled Castes students, hosels help them to develop corporate feelings. They learn to live independently in the company of others. With the increase in the number of students, the rush for admission in the hostels also increase. The existing hostels may fall short of the requirements. Though the Scheduled Castes students have reserved quota for seats in the hostels of the colleges as well, but owing to heavy rush, they might find the number of seats are inadequate. Hence, they were asked to give their assessment of the situation. The question asked was "What is your opinion regarding hostel facilities for the Scheduled Castes?, Is the number of hostels provided adequate?"

Only a small proportion of the students (12.9 per cent) thinks that number of hostels provided is adequate whereas 58.8 per cent of students do not consider it adequate. A relatively lower percentage of school students (47 per cent) considers the existing number of hostels to be inadequate. It may be noted that a sizable proportion of Rajasthan Scheduled Castes college students (26.2 per cent) has made no comment or they do not know about it and five students (2.1 per cent) have not given any response.

The students' opinion was sought on. Further, as an answer to the question "Are the facilities provided in the hostels satisfactory?", only (2.1 per cent) is of opinion that the facilities provided in the hostels are fully satisfactory and to 25.7 per cent the facilities are quite satisfactory. As many as 30.5 per cent of students maintain that the facilities provided are unsatisfactory. Only 12 per cent of school students considered the facilities unsatisfactory. It is to be noted that 40.8 per cent of Rajasthan Scheduled Castes college students reserved their comments. Two students (0.9 per cent) did not reply.

Students' Outlook on the Scholarship Scheme

To promote education among the scheduled castes, government has provided many incentives in the form of scholarships to them such as Pre-Matric scholarship, Post-Matric scholarship, Merit-cum-Need scholarship, Special scholarship and Scholarship to facilitate study of employed persons.

The Scheduled Castes students are expected to utilise the opportunities so that they may be able to stand on their own legs. Depending upon the extent to which these facilities are utilised and put to proper use, the scheme may be considered as useful.

Hence, to know about the usefulness of the scholarship schemes, the students were asked: "Do you think that the scholarship scheme is useful?" A vast majority of the students (72.1 per cent) thinks that the scholarship scheme is very useful and another 2.45 per cent of students consider it to be fairly useful. Only a negligible proportion of students (1.3 per cent) is of the opinion that it is not useful. Some of the students (2.1 per cent) do not know about it.

Moreover, the purpose of the award of scholarship will be fulfilled only when the amount of scholarship awarded to the student is adequate. Study showed that only 12.9 per cent considered the amount of scholarship awarded to Scheduled Castes students to be adequate as against 85.8 per cent who found it as inadequate. Surprisingly, thirty two percent of school students of Rajasthan feel that the amount of scholarship is adequate. Two Scheduled Castes college students of Rajasthan (0.9 per cent) could not say anything about the adequacy of the amount of scholarship and one student (0.4 per cent) has not given any response. Probably, those who are economically better off feel that the amount of scholarship is adequate, whereas it is inadequate in the eyes of those who are not well off.

On the whole, except seven students (3.0 per cent) all others find the educational facilities provided by the Government to the students of Scheduled Castes to be useful. A majority of the students (66.1 per cent) considers it quite useful while 30.9 per cent think that it is very useful.

Most of the students of each and every irrespective of the district majority of them are of the opinion that educational facilities provided by the government to the Scheduled Castes students are quite useful, the highest percentage being that of Jaipur (74.1 per cent) and the lowest being that of Jhunjhunu (52.3 per cent).

Again, irrespective of the fathers' education, more than a half of the students maintain that facilities are quite useful. Data also show that with the increase in the level of education of father, the percentage of those considering the facilities very useful has declined and on the other hand percentage of those considering these facilities not useful is increasing.

An interesting feature which becomes apparent from the study is that students with difficult economic status feel the advantage of the scheme in comparison to those who are somewhat better off.

Also, as many 48.3 per cent of highly politicised students have rated the educational facilities to be very useful whereas only 19.5 per cent of the average politicised and 20.0 per cent of the low politicised students have considered it very useful. So, we can say that whatsoever may be the level of politicisation, more than a half of the students consider the educational facilities available to them to be quite useful. Chi square test indicates that level of politicisation and opinion about educational facilities are not independent of each other.

Students' Awareness of the Reservation of Jobs

The Central and the State Government have reserved certain seats for them in public appointments. The purpose of this is to bring them at par with the non-Scheduled Castes people by increasing their representation in public appointments progressively. These provisions are beneficial to the Scheduled Castes students. Therefore, in order to analyse, whether the students are aware of such provisions or not, the students were asked: "Are you aware of the fact that certain posts in the Government and in public sector enterprises are reserved for the Scheduled Castes?"

All the Scheduled Castes college students except one are aware of the fact that certain posts in the Government and in public sector enterprises are reserved for the Scheduled Castes. As far as Scheduled Castes school students are concerned, 89.0 per cent of them are aware of this. From the responses of the Scheduled Castes college students, it is also understood that close relatives as well as distant relatives of 40.3 per cent of the students hold one or the other of these reserved posts. Some of the close relatives of 30.9 per cent of students hold these posts and some of the distant relatives of 15.5 per cent of students have got employment on such posts. According to 12.4 per cent of the students, some of their friends are also in such jobs. One student (0.4 per cent) has not replied this question and the question does not apply to one student (0.4 per cent).

Generally, it is seen that government service is the most prefered sector for job. Nine out of every ten students have given first preference to government service and the proportion of students giving first preference to other services is very negligible. Further, irrespective of the districts, fathers' education and economic status the students' prefer to go for government service.

Students' Views on Extending the Policy of Reservations to the Private Sector

Though, a high proportion of the scheduled castes prefer government service compared to that of semi-government or private service, yet when they were asked to give their opinion on the question of extension of the policy of reservation to private sector, atleast seven out of every ten students (70.4 per cent) want unequivocally the extension of the reservation policy to private sector also and they consider that it will be useful and 14.2 per cent of students accept this view grudgingly. They say that reservation in private sector may be introduced but that will not be of much use. Only a small proportion of the students (8.6 per cent) is not in favour of introducing reservation in private sector. A few of the students (6.9 per cent) are quite uncertain about their assessment.

The fact that Scheduled Castes students want the introduction of reservation in private sector is indicative of their desire to get a larger area of opporunity for employment.

It is observed that with the increase in the level of politicisation of the Scheduled Caste students the proportion of the students who want the extension of reservation policy to the private sector and consider it useful increases. Chi square test shows that there is no significant relationship between the level of politicisation and the students' views on introducing reservation in private sector.

Students' Outlook on the Policy of Reservation

The policy of reservation of seats for public appointment of the person of Scheduled Castes is very well written in the Article 335 of the Constitution of India. Accordingly, various State Governments including the government of Rajasthan have also made provisions for reservation for these people. According to the records of the State Government of Rajasthan, there has been substantial progress in the scheme and that Scheduled Castes people have been benefitted by the policy of reservation. But, it is the reaction of the Scheduled Castes people themselves, about these policies, the satisfaction they derive and the benefit they have been getting from the policies of the government that will show the exact picture when the Students were asked: "Do you think that the policy of reservation has enabled Scheduled Castes persons to obtain jobs?"

About three-tenths of college students (29.3 per cent) answered in affirmative. Almost one-fifth of the students (19.3 per cent) are of the opinion that it has not helped much to obtain jobs. However, 41.2 per cent of students have said that the policy of reservation has only enabled them to secure government jobs. It has not enabled them to obtain private jobs. Some students (10.2 per cent) did not know whether it helped or it did not. A thoroguh analysis of the responses of the students indicate that the policy of reservation has served the interest of the Scheduled Castes people but not to the extent they wanted and also that at least some of them wish that there should be opportunity for them to be employed in private sector also. The responses of school students indicate that as many as 63.0 per cent of students are of the opinion that reservation policy has helped to get employment to a large extent and 16.2 per cent said that it helped in securing only government jobs. Only 12.1 per cent are of the opinion that it has not helped them much in getting employment. Some school students (8.7 per cent) have not been able to assess the situation.

Further, they were also asked, has the policy fulfilled a useful purpose on the whole or not?

As an answer, we find that 11.6 per cent felt that the policy of reservation has fulfilled a useful purpose to a large extent while as many as 69.1 per cent have said that it fulfilled the purpose to some extent as against 9.0 per cent of those who maintain that it has served no purpose. As far as all India college students are concerned, 29 per cent of them are of the opinion that reservation policy has fulfilled its purpose to a large extent and 53 per cent of the students maintain that it has fulfilled its purpose to some extent.

That it has served the purpose to some extent only is also held by only 44 per cent of school students of Rajasthan and in this respect there is considerable difference between Rajasthan college and school students also. Some students (10.3 per cent) do not seem to know whether it fulfilled a useful purpose or not. Though there is difference of opinion about the extent and degree, but by and large, the scheme has fulfilled a useful purpose.

Considering that enough of reservations have been given to the Scheduled Castes persons, is it plausible to think that now they can go ahead without protecion being given and more? An answer to this can be had from those who are directly concerned with this. Therefore, the opinion of Scheduled Castes students was solicited on the question, "Would you agree with the statement that the Scheduled Castes have advanced so much that they can stand on their own in open competition with others and do not need reservations any more?"

Approximately seven out of every ten students (69.5 per cent) do not agree with the statement mentioned above while almost one-fifth of the students (19.3 per cent) agree to some extent. Only 6.0 per cent of the students agree with this statement to a large extent. Some of the students (5.2 per cent) do not know. These numbers indicate that it is not possible for the Scheduled Castes people to be independent of the government protection and that they have not been able to develop in them a sense of confidence to stand on their own legs.

To assess their over all views about these programmes taken as a whole. The question raised was : "On the whole, would you consider the programme that the Government has launched for Scheduled Castes beneficial ?"

88.8 per cent considers the programmes to be beneficial and only a tiny minority (4.3 per cent) does not consider them beneficial. A further breakup of the data reveals that 40.3 per cent of the students consider them very beneficial and 48.5 per cent consider them fairly beneficial. Some students (6.9 per cent) were not sure whether the programmes were beneficial or not. Besides, the students' outlook on the policy of reservation on the whole, indicates that a majority of the students (55.8 per cent) considers it fairly useful and 9.4 per cent consider it very useful. As many as 34.8 per cent do not consider it useful.

Except in Ajmer, more than fifty per cent of the students of other districts are of the opinion that the reservation policy has been fairly useful. Chi square test shows that there is significant interdistrict variation among students as far as their outlook on the policy of reservation is concerned.

Also, irrespective of the education of the fathers, a majority of the students holds the view that reservation policy is fairly useful. With the increase in the level of education of fathers the percentage has slightly declined.

In contrast to this, with the increase in the economic status, the percentage of the students who maintain that the reservation policy has not been useful to the Scheduled Castes increases. Chi quare test, however, indicates no significant relationship between economic status and the students' outlook on the policy of reservation.

It is accepted the success or failure of the programme depends on its proper administration. A very good scheme may appear useless if its implementation is faulty. Also, the programme would not be able to deliver the needful if it is not implemented propertly. The same holds true for all the government sponsered initiatives. The Government have, no doubt, launched several programmes for the benefit the Scheduled Castes people but it is the administration or implementation, which decisdes results. Therefore, the students opinion was sought on the question of administration also. A question was asked: "Do you think that the Government programmes for the welfare of the Scheduled Castes are satisfactorily administered?"

At least 47.6 per cent of the Scheduled Castes students answered negataively. The same opinion is held by 36 per cent of all India college students and 10 per cent of Rajasthan School students. A relatively small proportion of them (41.2 per cent) feels that the administration of programme is satisfactory. A further break indicates that only 6.9 per cent of the students maintain that the administration of programme is fully satisfactory and 34.3 per cent are of the opinion that their administration is fairly satisfactory. One-tenth of the students (10.7 per cent) have said that they wer not able to say anything and one of the students (0.4 per cent) has not responded.

Students' Opinion on the Programmes Viewed as a Whole

Now that we have separately analysed the major schemes for the uplift of the Scheduled Castes, such as reservation of admission in colleges and hostels, scholarship and job launched by the Government. It is time to assess as to how these beneficiaries. view the impact of various programmes in totality. An appraisal of this would help the policy makers and social workers to decide their future course of action in this regard. And hence, the students were asked: "On the whole, would you consider the programmes the government has launched for Scheduled Castes beneficial ?" As stated earlier, 88.8 per cent of students consider the programmes beneficial as against 4.3 per cent who do not think so. Though the percentage of those who have answered negatively is very small, still it is very essential to know as to why they have this feeling inspite of the government endeavour to provide necessary assistance. Some of the possible arguments given are that they think that the programmes damage self-respect of the Scheduled Castes people or the programmes make them completely dependent and they can not help themselves, or the schemes destroy the initiative which should come from them if they want to lead a self-respecting life. Let's analyse the responses of these arguments separately.

When this question was asked to ten students (4.3 per cent) who have said earlier that the programmes are not beneficial, we find that they are equally divided among those who agree fully (3) partly (3) or do not agree (3) with the statement that the programmes damage the self-respect of the Scheduled Castes people. One student has not given any answer.

The same categorisation happened when they were asked to assess whether programmes make people dependent — those who agree fully (3), or partly (3) or do not agree (3) and one student could not say anything.

Finally, when asked whether programmes destroy the initiative of the communities, eight of the students fully agreed with the statement. One student agreed only partly and one student does not agree with this view.

Though these responses indicate that the ten students who are of the view that the government schemes are not beneficial to Scheduled Castes people, have some reason to feel so, but the reasons are not strong enough for any further discussions.

The Difficulties that the Students have Personally Encountered with Reference to the Programme

As our study has revealed that there are some of the students who feel that the various government policies meant for the uplift of Scheduled Castes people have not been administered satisfactorily, we need to know what type of difficulties these students themselves have come across. They were asked to enumerate these difficulties, so that the policy makers and those responsible for carrying them out may be able to plug the holes. The specific question raised was : "Have you yourself ever encountered any difficulty with reference to any of the programmes? If you have, please specify the nature of the difficulties, you have faced."

More than one half of the students (56.6 per cent) have themselves encountered difficulties and 42.9 per cent have not faced any. One student (0.4 per cent) has not given any response.

Generally, they mentioned economic difficulties, like scholarship given very late, the students are not in a position to purchase books and they feel that officials who distribute funds do not behave well. The students have also given some suggestions to make improvement in the situation, like enhancement in the amount of scholarship, free books, provision of houses on nominal rent, more reservations, and lastly, part-time services to those who do not get scholarship.

To summarise, the overall picture that emerges from the responses of the students is that only a minority thinks that there has been improvement in the status of the Scheduled Castes. The number of seats reserved for admission and the number of existing hostels are not considered adequate. Also, the facilities provided in the hostel are not considered up to the mark. The usefulness of scholarship is not doubted but it is considered to be inadequate. On the whole, the educational facilities provided to the students by the governments have been viewed useful. Except one, all students are aware of the constitutional provision about reservation of jobs.

As far as the reservation policy in job is concerned, students feel that it has been effective and largely, it has served its purpose. The students want the continuance of the reservation policy still and feel that the administration of the programmes need to be improved. The students want the extension of reservation of jobs in private sector also. If various programmes of welfare are seen in totality, overwhelming majority of the students views them favourably. Exceptions are found everywhere, and here also the same applies. A few students do not think good about these programmes and feel that the programmes damage the self-respect of the community. They feel that Scheduled Castes people become dependent on the programmes and their initiative is killed. Excluding this negative trend shown by a small minority, the general feel is that the reservation policy in education, job, the scholarships and the various welfare programs have been really beneficial to them. Only the administration of these programmes need to be monitored.

Hostelers Vs. Day Scholars

A good hostel can act as a stepping stone in an individuals life. It can change the overall personality of an individual — internally as well externally. Besides educational facilities, the hostel emphasizes character building. It may function as an agency of social integration and broadens one's outlook of the society. It may inculcate a sense of independence as student come to stay here leavaing their parental homes and also imbibe the responsibility of a democratic living. It also creates initiataive and leadership qualities among students.

The hostel facilities were not available upto higher secondary school level in Rajasthan. As the educational institutions were located far away from the villages, students had to go to long distances. Lack of transportation facilities and distance used to take enough time and effort and acted as a barrier to education. Though the students coming from better-off-sections of the society could afford to live in rented houses near the centre of education even if hostels were not available but it was not possible for weaker sections to do so. Therefore, governments made arrangements for these people. Even students receiving higher education were allowed to say in those hostels. But later the college/university students were required to stay in the general hostels and seats were reserved for them.

This chapter tries to focus on the difference between hostel students and non-hostel students, with a view to bring out the influence of the hostel on the life of students.

The survey showed that 57.9 per cent of the Scheduled Castes college students of this study do not reside in hostels and the remaining 42.1 per cent live in hostel.

There are two main sources of maintaining hostels. (a) Hostels that are run by college/university, and (b) hostels that are run by private agencies. As many as 35.2 per cent of students live in hostels run by colleges/university forming 83.7 per cent of all the Scheduled Castes college students living in the hostels and 6.9 per cent of the students live in hostels which are run by private organisations. They accommodate 16.3 per cent of hostelers.

Mostly students share a room as single-bedrooms are not available in large number in the hostels. 81.6 per cent of hostelers share room with others whereas only 18.4 per cent of the hostlers have a single-bed room. when the students were asked to indicate with whom they shared room, it is found that 51.2 per cent of the hostelers live in the hostel alongwith the students of their own castes whereas 20.0 per cent of the hostelers live with students who are not of their own Scheduled Castes but of other Scheduled Castes and 3.7 per cent of the hostelers reside with Scheduled Tribes. Only 6.2 per cent of hostelers share room with non-Scheduled Castes/Scheduled Tribes students. With this numerical data in hand we start our analysis of comparison of hostel students and day-scholars. The comparison commences with analysing data about their social background.

Social Background of Hostel Students and Day-Scholars

Let's have a brief discussion on the demographic characteristics.

Sex

In the sample taken for our study there are only three female Scheduled Castes college students and they do not live in hostels. All the hostelers and except three, all the non-hostelers are males.

The age of hostelers ranges from 16 or less years to 22 or more years but the age of non-hostelers ranges from 17 to 22 or more years. In both the groups, students' concentration is found in 20 years. The average age of both hostelers and non-hostelers is 19.3 years.

Religion

More non-hostelers (97.8 per cent) than hostelers (93.8 per cent) are Hindus. But the difference is negligible.

Caste

The hostelers and non-hostelers differ in terms of caste distribution. Though Chamars are the largest groups both among hostelers and non-hostelers, their percentage is higher among hostelers (44.9 per cent) than the non-hostgelers (34.1 per cent). Next to them is the group of Balais who form one-fourth of the hostelers. Their proportion among non-hostelers (3.7 per cent) compared to the hostelers (25.5 per cent) is very small. It is also to be noted that while there is one Koli (1.0 per cent) who resides in the hostel, 11.1 per cent of the non-hostelers are Kolis.

Marital Status

There is hardly any difference in the marital status of hostelers and non-hostelers. It may, however, be noted that the proportion of non-hostelers (43 per cent) is a little higher than that of the hostelers (35.7 per cent) who are married and whose gauna has also been performed.

Family Background

Parents' Place of Residence

The parents of three-fourths of teh hostelers (7.5 per cent) live in villages. On the other hand parents of only 42.2 per cent of the day scholars live in villages. Further, parents of about one-fifth of hostelers (19.4 per cent) live in towns whereas only 6.7 per cent of the non-hostelers parents live in towns. Parents of 5.1 per cent of the hostelers live in cities whereas parents of only 3.0 per cent of non-hostelers are city residents. The question is not applicable to 48.1 per cent of the non-hostelers.

Fathers' Education

More than a half of the hostelers (53.1 per cent) are those whose fathers are unlettered whereas the fathers of less than a half of the non-hostellers (43.0 per cent) are unlettered. The proportion of hostelers (40.8 per cent) and non-hostelers (40.0 per cent) whose fathers have read upto primary level is almost equal. The number of non-hostelers (8.9 per cent) whose fathers have ready upto middle school is twice the number of hostelers (4.1 per cent). There is not a single hosteler whose father might have read upto intermediate or graduate level.

Mothers' Education

Compared to non-hostelers (86.7 per cent) mothers of a higher percentage of hostelers (96.9 per cent) are unlettered. While the non-hostelers whose mothers have received education even less than primary level is 12.6 per cent the percentage of such hostelers is only 3.1 per cent. One of the non-hostelers' mother (0.7 per cent) is educated upto middle school.

Brothers' Education

As compared to other siblings of their family a majority of both hostelers and non-hostelers are most educated for the hostelers the percentage is 91.8 per cent which is considerably higher than that of non-hostelers (74.1 per cent). A reverse situation is found in the case of those whose brothers are more or equally educated.

Sisters' Education

Similar to the brothers, a vast majority of both hostelers and non-hostelers are more educated than their sisters but the percentage of hostelers is higher (92.9 per cent) than those of non-hostelers (83.7 per cent). There is not a single hosteler whose sister is more or equally educated.

Fathers' Occupation

Fathers of more than three-fifths of hostelers (62.2 per cent) work in village for their livelihood, whereas fathers of only 45.2 per cent of the non-hostelers work in villages, Fathers of more non-hostelers (31.1 per cent) than hostelers (12.2 per cent) are in service.

Mothers' Occupation

There is hardly any difference in the occupations of mothers of hostelers and non-hostelers. More than 90 per cent of them are housewives.

The Economic Status

The percentage of hostelers with so-so economic status is higher 48 per cent than non-hostelers (43.7 per cent) whereas there is no difference in the economic status of hostelers (46.9 per cent) and non-hostelers (47.4 per cent) who report difficult economic status. The percentage of hostelers with comfortable economic status is lower (4.1 per cent) than that of non-hostelers (7.4 per cent). One hosteler (1.0 per cent) and two non-hostelers (1.5 per cent) refused to classify themselves. Chi square test reveals that there does not exist a significant difference in the economic status of hostelers and non-hostelers.

Employment

96.9 per cent of hostelers are 84.4 per cent of day-scholars are unemployed. None of the hostelers is employed full or part time, whereas 11.9 per cent of the non-hostelers are employed full time and 2.2 per cent part time. Three hostelers (3.1 per cent) and two non-hostelers (1.5 per cent) are occasional earnes.

Sources of Financing Education

Scholarships, freeships and own earnings are primary source of financing education. Almost an equal proportion of hostelers (6.1 per cent) and non-hostelers (5.9 per cent) depend exclusively on scholarship/freeship for their study. Respondents' own earning as exclusive source of financing education has been reported by three times more non-hostelers compared to the hostelers. Similarly parents/relatives as exclusive source has been mentioned by fourteen times more non-hostelers in comparison to that of hostelers..

Other Financial Obligations of the Family

According to 67.3 per cent of hostelers and 63.0 per cent of non-hostelers, their parents have to spend on the education of other member in their families.

Scholarship/Freeship Holders

The percentage of scholarship holders among hostelers is higher (95.9 per cent) than those of non-hostelers (85.2 per cent). More non-hostelers (67.4 per cent) than the hostelers (48.0 per cent) are freeship holders.

Hostel as a Factor in the Life of the Students, Students as Scholars

Distribution of Courses

Class

In the first year of three year degree course, the percentage of non-hostelers is higher (54.1 per cent) than that of hostelers (39.8 per cent). Similarly, in the second year also, as compared to hostelers (28.6 per cent), a higher proportion study non-hostelers (32.6 per cent) study. But in the final year the proportion of hostelers (31.6 per cent) is consideraboy higher than that of the non-hostelers (12.6 per cent). It may be that in final year the students prefer to stay in the hostel to enable them to devote more time towards study and therefore, their number in hostel is higher in a financial year.

Course of Study

A majority of both hostelers (63.2 per cent) and non-hostelers (74.1 per cent) opt for Arts courses but the percentage of non-hostelers is higher. For the science stream, non hostelers (20.0 per cent) are higher than that of the hostelers (15.3 per cent). Considerably more hostelers (21.4 per cent) than non-hostelers (5.9 per cent) have offered Commerce. Chi square test reveals a significant differnce in offering the course by hostel students and day-scholars.

Reasons for the Choice of a Particular Course

For both the hostelers and non-hostelers their personal liking towards the course have been the primary reason for the choice. The percentage of hostelers is some what higher (87.7 per cent) than that of non-hostelers (83.7 per cent). But, both of them feel that the course they have offered will help them in getting a job. About three-fourths of the hostelers (74.5 per cent) and 71.1 per cent of the non-hostelers have chosen the course because of this. In the opinion of 47.9 per cent of the hostelers and 52.6 per cent of the non-hostelers, the course is easy and therefore they decided to offer it. It seems, therefore, that for both hostelers and non-hostelers, decision to join a particular course is the same.

Reasons for the Choice of a Particular College

More than a half of the hostelers (54.1 per cent) and non-hostelers (57.0 per cent) selected the college because it was the only college in the area. It is interesting to note that whereas only 45.9 per cent of hostelers have considered their institutions as the best of the place, a considerably large proportion of non-hostelers (60.7 per cent) held the same view. In the case of 4.1 per cent of hostelers and 15.6 per cent of non-hostelers the reason of selection was the fact that they could not get admission else-where and hence there was no choice open to them. About one-third of the hostelers (32.6 per cent) joined the college because of the availability of special facilities of Scheduled Castes. This was also the reason for 40.7 per cent of non-hostelers. A higher proportion of hostelers (55.1 per cent) than non-hostelers (51.1 per cent) chose the institutions because they were located near their homes. It appears, however, that the advice of parents/relatives was important in selecting college for as many as 71.4 per cent of the hostelers and 56.3 per cent of the non-hostelers have mentioned this reason.

The Pattern of Hostelers'/Non-Hostelers' Life and their Study Habits

Study Habits, Hours or Work

Generally, the hostelers devote more time to study than non-hostelers. 57.1 per cent of the hostelers devote more than four hours on study as against 21.5 per cent of non-hostelers. While a small proportion of hostelers (11.2 per cent) spend three or less hours on study, a higher proportion of the non-hostelers (38.5 per cent) spend three or even less than three hours on their study. On an average, hostelers spend 4.14 hours on study whereas non-hostelers 3.38 hours.

Need to Study More

Survey reveals that non-hostelers (74.8 per cent) feel to study more than hostelers (44.9 per cent). Chi square test reveals a significant difference in responses of hostelers and non-hostelers.

Reasons for not Devoting More Time on Study

The question related to reasons for not devoting more time was applicable only to 44.9 per cent of hostelers and 74.8 per cent of non-hostelers. Research shows that the main reasons for not devoting more time on study was a great deal of work at home/hostel. As many as 46.7 per cent of the non-hostelers and 25.56 per cent of the hostelers gave this answer. Also as 14.8 per cent of the non-hostelers and 2.0 per cent of the hostelers do jobs, they devote less time on their studies.

The Career of the Students

Performance

Number of Years Spent in Each Class

For both hostelers and non-hostelers it has been a smooth sailing from class VI to XI. and a vast majority of them had to spend only one year in their respective classes but a sharp decline takes place after class XI and decline in percentage is more among non-hostelers than the hostelers.

Discontinuity

Data shows that neither hostelers nor non-hostelers discontinued the study in large number. After completing primary school education and before joining middle school only two hostelers and one non-hosteler had to discontinue study for one year and there was only one non-hostelers who discontinued study for two years. The only reason mentioned by them was economic. Only one hosteler had to discontinue the study after middle school and that too was due to economic reason. A vast majority of hostelers (93.9 per cent) and non-hostelers (83.0 per cent) joined the college immediately after passing higher secondary/high school examination. The main reason for discontinuance as mentioned by the students was again economic.

Comprehension

Though there was no major understanding issue for both hostelers and non-hostelers, the proportion of hostelers is higher (80.6 per cent) than that of non-hostelers (73.3 per cent). One-fourth of the non-hostelers (25.2 per cent) and 14.3 per cent of the hostelers had difficulties in few subjects. The remaining hostelers either had difficulties (4.1 per cent) or they had difficulties only casually (1.0 per cent) while only one non-hosteler (0.7 per cent) had found it difficult to follow the lectures. One non-hostelers (0.7 per cent) has not given any response. Chi square test does not show a significant difference in comprehension of hostelers and non-hostelers. The reason cited for not being able to understand lectures was that the teachers did not explain well for 13.3 per cent of the hostelers and 14.8 per cent of the non-hostelers. Other factors account for a very small percentage of causes.

Availability of Help from Teachers

Data shows that 73.4 per cent of the hostelers and 70.4 per cent of the non-hostelers go to teacher for seeking help and guidance. It appears that hostelers are taking more advantage of teachers but the detailed analysis does not necessarily support this. As a matter of fact a higher percentage of non-hostelers (31.9 per cent) than hostelers (16.3 per cent) has said that they visit teachers quite often and the difference is cognisable. However, a considerably higher percentage of hostelers (57.1 per cent) than non-hostelers (38.5 per cent) goes to teachers some time. Chi square test indicates a significant difference between hostelers and non-hostelers as far as their visit to teachers is concerned.

Hostelers' and Non-Hostelers' Opinion About Teachers' Attitude Towards Them

More non-hostelers (68.1 per cent) than hostelers (43.8 per cent) feel that teachers are very helpful to them. Only a small proportion of hostelers (3.1 per cent) and non-hostelers (4.4 per cent) are of the opinion that teachers are not at all helpful. However fifty percent of the hostelers and a little more than one-fourth of the non-hostelers (26.7 per cent) are of the opinion that the teachers do not pay extra attention to them. Chi square test shows a significant difference between hostelers and non-hostelers in regard to their opinion about teachers.

Coaching

Though neither of them need extra coaching, yet the percentage of the hostelers is higher (83.6 per cent) than that of non-hostelers (70.4 per cent) who do not require extra coaching and the difference is cognisable. Reverse is the situation for those who say that they need extra coaching but do not go for that. This response has been given by a higher percentage of non-hostelers (28.1 per cent) than hostelers (15.3 per cent) and the difference is cognisable.

Hostelers' and Non-Hostelers' Participation in Extra-Curricular Activities

Data shows that in activities like sports/NCC participation of hostelers (89.8 per cent) is higher than non-hostelers (61.5 per cent). In regard to participation in students' union, the hostelers do not seem to differ much as 36.7 per cent of the hostelers and 39.3 per cent of the non-hostelers are present. In debates and other literary activities again the hostelers have registered high participation. 46.9 per cent as compared to non-hostelers (30.3 per cent). The overall participation reveals that hostelers are more active than non-hostelers.

Educational Aspirations

Only 9.2 per cent of the hostelers have aspired for graduation whereas 21.5 per cent of the non-hostelers have aspired for this degree. The difference is cognisable.

Occupational Aspirations

Fathers' Occupation and Hostel and Non-Hostel Students

Both hostelers (96.9 per cent) and non-hostelers (96.3 per cent) do not want to follow the occupations of their fathers. There is no difference in percentage of hostelers (3.1 per cent) and non-hostelers (3.7 per cent) who want to follow the occupation of their fathers.

Occupational Choice of Hostelers and Non-Hostelers

Most of the hostelers (49.0 per cent) want to opt for the post of government officers. Only 35.5 per cent of non-hostelers aspire for government officers' posts. This difference is cognisable. The occupation that seems to attract more non-hostelers, is higher profession. As many as 38.5 per cent of non-hostelers as against 30.6 per cent of hostelers aspire for high professional work. Posts of teachers, gram sewak, nurse, typist, clerk etc., attract only a small proportion of students and the proportion of hostellers is smaller (7.1 per cent) than that of non-hostelers (16.3 per cent).

Sectors Preferred for Employment

Government service is the preferred sector for employment for both hostelers and non-hostelers but the proportion of hostelers (94.9 per cent) is a little higher than non-hostelers (88.9 per cent).

Encouragement and Discouragement from Home

Encouragement

Parents are the major source of encouragement for both hostelers and non-hostelers. But the percentage of hostelers (56.1 per cent) is a little higher than that of non-hostelers (47.4 per cent). More non-hostelers (32.6 per cent) than hostelers (23.5 per cent) seem to have been encouraged by siblings.

Discouragement

For both of them, there has not been any source of discouragement. It is found that a huge majority of both hostelers (92.9 per cent) and non-hostelers (93.9 per cent) has not been discouraged in pursuit of education.

Social Life and Out Look of the Students

Exposure to Mass Media

Cinema

Movie-goers are more hostelers (74.5 per cent) than non-hostelers (50.3 per cent). The percentage of non-hostelers (17.0 per cent) who do not see films is also higher than that of the hostelers (3.1 per cent). Since the hostelers are living in the area where cinema halls are generally found they are obviously more likely to see films than non-hostelers most of whom have to come from villages.

Radio

In contrast to cinema, the number of regular radio listeners in hostel is comparatively fewer (7.1 per cent) than that of non-hostelers (23.0 per cent). Chi square test reveals that hostelers and non-hostelers differ significantly as far as radio listening is concerned. Non-hostelers make use of radio more than the hostelers.

Newspaper Reading

The percentage of daily newspaper readers among hostelers is a little lower (56.1 per cent) than that of non-hostelers (60.7 per cent). Another 37.7 per cent of hostelers and 28.9 per cent of non-hostelers read newspapers occasionally. There are 5.1 per cent of hostelers and 9.6 per cent of non-hostelers who read newspapers very rarely and one non-hosteler (0.7 per cent) does not read newspaper. The hostelers on an average read 2.24 newspaper whereas non-hostelers read 1.75 newspapers. Hindi newspaper is very popular among both hostelers and non-hostelers. The percentage, however, is higher of non-hostelers (85.3 per cent) than of hostelers (71.4 per cent) and this difference is cognisable.

Politicisation

Participation in Meeting

It can be observed that more hostelers (47.9 per cent) than the non-hostelers (34.1 per cent) participate in meetings organised by political parties/leaders. Chi square test shows that hosteler's participation is significantly higher than that of non-hostelers.

Participation in Processions

Similarly, in the party processors too, high percentage of hostelites (49.0 per cent) than non-hostelites (31.1 per cent). Chi square test indicates that hostelers have registered significantly higher participation than that of non-hostelers.

Work for Political Party

The scenario is again same, when it comes to doing work for political parties. More hostelers that non-hostelers are active in political work. Only 35.7 per cent of the hostelers have not done any work for any political party, in contrast 65.2 per cent of the non-hostelers. Distribution of slips, pamphlets and canvassing during elections have been done by a higher percentage of hostelites than non-hostelites as first work.

As to the second work, 37.7 per cent of hostelites seem to have done no second work whereas a larger proportion of non-hostelers (68.1 per cent) has not done any second work for political partaies. Less number of hostelers (3.1 per cent) than non-hostelers (9.6 per cent) distributed slips and pamphlets. As against this, more hostelers than non-hostelers canvassed, participated in procession and shouted slogans.

Hostel Students and Political Parties

Almost seven out of every ten hostelers are members of Congress (R) whereas only four out of every ten non-hostelers are members of that party. While a little more than one-tenth of hostelers are not members of any party, somewhat more than a half of the non-hostelers do not belong to any party. While 5.1 per cent of hostelers are oriented to left and 13.3 per cent are oriented to rightist parties, only 3.7 per cent of non-hostelers are members of leftist parties and 4.4 per cent are members of rightist parties. On the whole, 18.4 per cent of hostelers and 8.1 per cent of non-hostelers are members of opposition parties.

Family Members and Political Parties

Like hostelers, their family members are also in large number, members of congress (R). A considerably higher percentage of hostgelers (66.3 per cent) than non-hostelers (31.8 per cent) have said so.

In short, political parties have a strong hold over the hostelers.

The Ideal and the People Hosterlers/Non-Hostelers Admire

Generally, for both hostelers and non-hostelers National leaders are ideals but the proportion of hostlers (54.1 per cent) is a little lower than that of non-hostelers (63.0 per cent). A considerably higher percentage of hostelers (25.5 per cent) than non-hostelers (7.4 per cent) mentioned the name of Scheduled Castes leader as their ideal. As to the second ideal more hostelers (64.0 per cent) than non-hostgelers (60.0 per cent) have mentioned the name of national leaders but the difference is negligible. There is no important difference between hostelers and non-hostelers as far as the third ideal is concerned.

Authority of Parents: Outlook on Marriage

Decision about the Future Career of Hostelers/Non-Hostelers

A majority of both hostelers and non-hostelers decided about their future career by themselves. Only a negligible difference is seen between the percentge of hostelers (70.4 per cent) and that of non-hostelers (67.4 per cent). Fathers played their role only in the case of a small number of students and the proportion of hostelers is 16.3 per cent and that of non-hostelers is 13.3 per cent.

Decision About Marriage

Though, the decision about marriage and the choice of the life prtner is mostly dependent on the parents but in our study the question about marriage is not applicable to 56.1 per cent of hostelers and 57.0 per cent of non-hostelers as they are already married.

Considerations Behind Selection of Life Partner

Economic Status

While smaller percentage of hostelers (4.1 per cent) compared to non-hostelers (8.2 per cent) considers economic status to be very important, a somewhat higher proportion of hostelers (23.5 per cent) than non-hostelers (20.7 per cent) considers it important.

Social Status

More hostelers (22.4 per cent) than non-hostelers (11.9 per cent) consider social status to be very important in marriage while 20.4 per cent of hostelers and 25.2 per cent of non-hostelers consider it important.

Education

There is hardly any difference between hostelers and non-hostelers pertaining toeducation as being considered to be a very important criteria but somewhat more hostelers (31.6 per cent) than non-hostelers (26.7 per cent) considered education to be important in deciding about marriage.

Physical Appearance

No difference seems to exist between hostelers and non-hostelers about physical looks of the partners in marriage being considered to be very important consideration but more hostelers (27.5 per cent) than non-hostelers (23.8 per cent) consider it important.

Girls' House Keeping Ability or the Quality of Job Held By the Boy

A higher proportion of hostelers (36.7 per cent) than non-hostelers (25.9 per cent) considers house keepikng ability of the girl to be very important whereas more non-hostelers (14.1 per cent) than hostelers (7.1 per cent) consider it important.

Girls' Ability to get along with Boys' Parents or the Income of the Boy

While somewhat higher proportion of hostelers (34.7 per cent) considers that it is very important that the girl should be able to get along with boys' parents, only 30.4 per cent of non-hostelers subscribe to this view. Somewhat more than one-tenth of the non-hostelers (11.1 per cent) considers this to be important as against 8.0 per cent of the hostelers.

In short, we may infer that for hostelers very important consideration in marriage is the ability of the girl at house keeping followed by her ability to get along with their parents while for non-hostelers, ability of girls to get along with boys' parents followed by house keeping ability is a very important criteria. Chi square test reveals that as far as the factors like economic status, social status, marriage within caste, education of the partners, income of the boy and ability to get along with boy's parents by girl are concerned the hostelers and non-hostelers do not differ significantly but the factor of the importance of job/ability of house keeping was considered significantly more important by hostelers.

Friendship-Integration and Isolation

Behaviour of the Class Fellows

A majority of both hostelers (63.2 per cent) and non-hostelers (54.1 per cent) feels that being of Scheduled Castes does affect in varying degree the behaviour of the class fellows. The proportion of hostelers (11.2 per cent) who hold that belonging to Scheduled Castes does not affect the behaviour of the class fellows to a large extent, is smaller compared to that of the non-hostelers (15.6 per cent). Compared to non-hostelers (45.9 per cent) a smaller percentage of hostelers (36.7 per cent) feels that the behaviour of their class fellows is not at all affected. This shows that both the hostelers and non-hostelers feel that behaviour of others with them is affected because they are of Scheduled Castes. A higher percentage of hostelers (75.5 per cent) than non-hostelers (63.0 per cent) is of the view that the students know that they belong to Scheduled Castes. It is quite understandable because most of the time the hostelers are in touch with other students.

Students area of Friendship

Castes of Friends

Generally, more hostelers (49.0 per cent) than non-hostelers (40.0 per cent) have first friends of their own castes. As far as second friend is concerned, a considerably higher percentage of hostelers (50.0 per cent) than non-hostelers (37.8 per cent) has friends from their own castes. A little difference exists between hostelers (35.7 per cent) and non-hostelers (43.7 per cent) who have third friend from their own castes. The distribution of friendship brings out that hostelers are more inclined to have friends from their own Scheduled Castes.

Experience of Discrimination

More than three-fifths of the hostelers (64.3 per cent) have not experienced any discrimination on account of their being of Scheduled Castes.

Conclusions

Analysis shows that even less than a half of the Scheduled Castes college students live in the hostels run by mostly colleges. Because of the non-availability of sufficient rooms, the hostelers share room with other students of their own castes. The hostelers generally belong to villages and almost seven-tenths of them are of the districts where the college is located. All the hostelers as well as non-hostelers except three girl students are males. The average age of the hostelers and non-hostelers is 19.3 years.

The hostelers are predominantly Hindus as in the case of most of the non-hostelers. A considerably higher percentage of Balais are hostelers. More parents of hostelers than of non-hostelers are unlettered. More hostelers than non-hostelers are highly educated in comparison to their siblings. Fathers of both hostelers and non-hostelers work in villages and nearly all mothers are housewives. There does not seem to be any remarkable difference in the economic status of the hostelers and non-hostelers. It is not possible for most of the hostelers and non-hostelers to cover the expenses of education with scholarship/freeship only and they have to depend on their parents/relatives also. This is more perceptible in the case of hostelers than non-hostelers. In regard to the parents' responsibility towards others' education in the family, a majority of hostelers and non-hostelers feels that their parents have to bear others educational expenses. More hostelers are scholarship holders while more non-hostelers are freeship recipients. Few of them even earn through jobs.

It is found that the proportion of day-scholars is less than of the hostelers in the final year class. Though a general liking of both is towards Arts stream but compared to hostelers more non-hostelers have offered Arts courses. Compared to hostelers more non-hostelers are Science students. The advice of parents/relatives has been instrumental in selection of college for both hostelers and non-hostelers in large measure. Besides, unavailability of colleges also force them to join the only available one.

The hostelers devote more time to study than non-hostelers as by and larage they are not in a position to spend time because they have to do a great deal of domestic work. Both type of students generally understand the lectures and only a minority does not understand them and the reason generally advanced by them is that the teachers do not explain the subject well. Though teachers may be conveniently available to hostelers, the percentage of hostelers who visit teachers quite often is lower. It may be because more hostelers feel that the teachers do not pay extra attention to them. There is practically no diversity of opinion among hostelers and non-hostelers in regard to taking extra coaching yet they generally do not go for it.

More hostelers than non-hostelers participate in sports/NCC, debates and other literary activities but no remarkable difference is seen in participation in students' union activities.

More hostelers than non-hostelers seem to have higher educational aspirations.

Except a few exception, neither the hostelers nor the non-hostelers wants to follow fathers' occupation. While hostelers aspire, by and large, for government posts, non-hostelers aspire for higher profession. Both the groups in large number gave first preference to government service. A higher percentage of hostelers got encouragement from parents and similar is the situation in regard to non-hostelers.

More hostelers than non-hostelers go for movies frequently

but the percentage of regular radio listeners is more among non-hostelers than hostelers. Newspaper reading is a common activity for both of them. On an average, hostelers read 2.24 newspapers and non-hostelers read 1.75 newspapers. Hindi newspaper is popular among both but percentage of non-hostelers is higher than that of the hostelers who read Hindi newspaper.

Hostelers actively participate in political activities than non-hostelers. A majority of hostelers and non-hostelers recalls the name of national leaders as ideal but the proportion of hostelers is higher. Both hostelers and non-hostelers wish to decide for their future career themselves. Ability of girls at homekeeping is considered very important in marriage by more hostelers but ability of girls to get alongwith boys' parents is very important for non-hostelers. Both hostelers and non-hostelers would go by their parents decision in marriage. Both hostelers and non-hostelers feel that their being of Scheduled Castes does affect in varying degree the behaviour of their class fellows. As to the castes of friends, the non-hostelers show a tendency of selecting friends from non-Scheduled Castes groups in comparison to the hostelers and the hostelites and day-scholars do not differ in their experience of discrimination.

Fourteen

Follow-up

As part of the follow up work we were supposed to pay a monthly visit to each one of the participant village unfortunately our actual performance was much below the said mark. Table 14.1 shows our actual performance.

TABLE 14.1
FOLLOW-UP VISITS TO PARTICIPANTS IN THE 1973 COURSES

Course	*Village**	*Participants*	*Follow-up visits*
1st	Ekpur	23	4 (1973 : 1; 1974 : 2; 1975 : 1)
	Dwipur	3	2 (1973 : 1; * ; 1975 : 1)
2nd	Tripur	24	3 (1973 : 1; 1974 : 1; 1975 : 1)
	Charpur	3	
3rd	Panchpur	21	3 (1973 : 1; 1974 : 1; 1975 : 1)
4th	Chhapur	24	13 (1973 : 1; 1974 : 6; 1975 : 6)

*pseudonyms used.

The aim of the follow-up visits was to consolidate the work that had been done during the course itself. While the participants were setting up their goals they were told that we would be visiting them again. This, we hoped, would not only be an added incentive to better performance, put would provide us feedback on our performance in the courses, besides acting as a bridge with our former trainers.

That these visits helped the participants is, we believe, generally true. They took pride in showing us their achievements. A poor Thakore from Tripur told us that, after some efforts to improve his fields, he finally gave us and handed them over to a relative of his and decided to look for new work. He conducted a rough market survey of his own by accompanying village traders to town and there inquiring about their needs. Eventually he set up a new business. He said, "Every time you came, I heard the Patels telling you all the great improvements they had made after the course. I could not emulate them since I have no irrigation facilities, as you know. So I gave charge of the fields to my brother and started this business." As he spoke he pointed to his clothes and smiled. He was no longer wearing poor clothes.

Our follow-up visits to Tripur and Panchpur were always joyful occasions for both trainees and us. We loved to admire the progress made by the former trainees. Dwipur and Charpur each with only three trainees stood in marked contrast to the other villages and frankly, did not give us much incentive to visit them. [More will be said later about this practice of giving a course to participants from two villages.] Originally, we had planned to cover as many villages as possible. To achieve this we conceived the idea of having satellite villages, that is, a big village where we would concentrate our efforts and a smaller adjoining village with a few participants to act as contact men who would allow the influence of the bigger village to percolate.

Ekpur had a very good start; but, due to natural calamities, drought followed by heavy rain damaged the crops and affected the morale of our trainiess. There was a marked shift in their concern from improving agriculture to an obsession with a tube-well to secure a permanent means of irrigation. But things are beginning to look up again and we hope to call them back for a refresher course in agriculture.

The Charpur course was the first given to lower castes, mainly Thakores and Bharvads who compared to the Patels were economically backward. Unity and co-operation are central in all our courses, but they become the dominant themes when the courses are given to the weaker sections of society. During the course itself ther was a mild attempt to form an irrigation co-operative. Since most of the participants were small farmers they qualified for a government scheme which gave 50 per cent as grant and 50 per cent as loan to small farmers' irrigation co-operatives to sink a tube-well. The follow-up visits showed us the need for greater efforts to induce a sufficient number of them to join the co-operative. It was decided to call them back to the College to consolidate and strengthen the work started during the course.

For the first time follow-up meant more training to build on the foundations laid in the first course. As a result the co-operative was formed and work started to complete all the formalities required to set it up and receive from the Small Farmers Development Agency (SFDA) an outright grant of 50 per cent of the expenditure plus loan facilities for the rest of the money. The scheme looked very attractive to us when it was proposed to the participants by the Chief Officer of the SFDA project in the District. Therefore when the participants decided to go ahead with the scheme, we thought it well within our aims to help them in doing all the paper work and going to various offices. What follows is the story of a long (more than two years by now) and, so far, unsuccessful fight with the bureaucracy.

In January 1974, we went to Charpur and then to the district headquarters to see the SFDA Officer. All the administrative requirements were clearly explained to the participants but, when they got working on the application forms they encountered difficulties with the Talati and Sarpanch of Charpur itself and also at the taluka offices. In February 1974 we personally went to see the SFDA officer and he himself accompanied us to the taluka office. Evidently, there were some mysterious hitch because in the course of the conversation the TDO (Taluka Development Officer) called the SFDA officer apart to talk with him privately. When we were returning from the office the SFDA officer was very apologetic and promised that now things would move fast. Five months later, on July 30, 1974, we were told by the former trainees that all necessary documents had been filled in any duly submitted. Everybody was hopeful.

But even after five months nothing had happened. We found our participants in a pessimistic mood. "We go from office to office and nobody gives us a satisfactory answer. What can we do?", they told us. Again the SFDA officer generously offered to come with us to the taluka offaices. Their the clerk in the Land Development Bank claimed that he had issued the forms but they had not yet been completed. Our participants denied it outrightly. Anyway, the SFDA officer gave orders to the clerk to take the forms and have them filled in by all the members of the co-operative. We accompanied the clerk to Charpur. Charpur the clerk quietly produced from his bag all the forms. He told the participants to see him at the office on Monday.

Twenty days later we again went back to Charpur. By now the participants were really annoyed. "We spend money, time and energy and these clerks do not give us any information." We took them to the same clerk. He said that they had not furnished all the details.

"What is missing now?"

"They are supposed to answer all the questions. Otherwise I shall land into trouble..."

Therefore followed a long discourse on his responsibility and the lack of understanding of these people.

"But now, what is missing? Kindly tell us!"

"I have told them so many times. But these people ..."

We insisted on his giving us an answer. And finally he did. When our participants heard his answer their reaction was immediate :

"Is this what you need? Such a simple thing? The way you explained it to us, it sounded so complicated!"

Since February to April we were stuck up with other village courses. So Charpur was forgotten for a while. Nevertheless, in April we were again at Charpur and it was the same story all over again. The SFDA officer again accompanied us to the TDO's office. There the Extension officer blamed our participants :

"They have not given me the proper information."

"What information do you require?"

"The land ownership deeds."

"But that is precisely what we have been asking this office to give us!"

The SFDA officer again gave orders to the Extension Officer to have all the papers ready immediately.

One week later we were at the TDO's office. Not only the papers were not ready but there was now a new requirement, a blueprint of the area where the well was to be sunk. This had to be issued by the TDO's office and countersigned by the Executive Engineer's office.

"This will take time," they said. For once they had spoken the truth. We followed up constantly on monthly basis but the papers were not ready. It was now October 1975. In the meantime new difficulties had cropped up and we were informed that the site of the well could not be approved because a Patel had his plan approved and his well was nearby. A notification was sent to our people saying, "Your application has been lost. Kindly send us a fresh one." The new one, naturally, had a latter date than the Patel's. Consequently, our men lost not only their turn but also the Rs. 50 paid to the overseer for the blueprint of the well site. Now a new blueprint would be required.

In the process the Cooperative Extension Officer had given the participants a paper which apparently had to be signed by them as part of the procedure. One of them took the paper promising to have it signed later and returned. It was a letter cancelling the application! Armed with it, we went again to the TDO's office. Again the same speeches by them on the incompetence of our participants and polite silence on our part. The letter was handed over to the TDO with the remark—"May be after all it is not entirely the fault of our participants?"

"A foolish thing like this should never have done!" was the only comment he had to make, promising that all the papers would be sent to the District Headquarters within two days. The papers were sent early enough, but with incomplete information. They came back to the TDO's office. It was already two years and seven months and during this period our team visited the place thirteen times, but still we could not see any ray of hope.

The year 1974 was a difficult year for Gujarat and a bad one for us. Popular discontent erupted early in January, giving rise to the so-called Navnirman agitation. Curfew and police firings plagued our city for a long time and it was not until the State Assembly had been dissolved in March that conditions limped back to normalcy. In this period of uncertainty we could not afford to run these courses. These colleges were closed down early in January.

When conditions became normal in mid-March we tried to make up fooro time lost. Two villages that had previouslyagreed to come sent word that they would not since conditions in Ahmedabad "are not safe".

This village was contacted through one of the college students who meant well and wanted his village to prosper. In the agitated circumstances of 1974 the real situation in the village could not be assessed. The Patels (for whom this course was intended) were daily involved the mutual fights and mutual recriminations. Our contact man, though impartial and above party struggles was not taken in a apositive way by other group. His initiative was the initiative of his group, something to be boycotted by the other. Out emotional attachment forwards his village this student did not let us know the reality of the social situation in the village. He believed that he would be able to persuade a sufficiently large number of people to join the course.

TABLE 14.2

1974 COURSES AND THEIR FOLLOW-UP

Course	*Village**	*Participants*	*Follow-up Visits*
5th	Athgam	17	Course not complete
6th	Navgam	25	2 (1974 : 1; 1975; 1)
7th	Dashgam	15	3 (1974 : 2; 1975; 1)
	Giargam	4	2 (1974 : 1; 1975: 1)
8th	Bargam	10	1 (1974 : 1; —)
9th	Bhal region	24	Participants belonged to various villages from the Bhal area. No follow-up work was envisaged.

*pseudonyms used.

But when we reached, we were dismayed at seeing only ten people and wanted to cancel the course. But the ten pleaded with us. "How can we return to our village without the course? We shall be the butt of endless ridicule."

It was fought against all our wishes, for a few days some attempts were made with the group; but we soon gave up. It was our second and, to date, last failure. Later on, we were faced again with a similar situation when participants did not turn up in sufficient numbers. But we politely declined to conduct the course. It is not only a question of design but also of their future influence in the village. What can ten people do against so many odds?

There is a silver lining to every cloud and ours in 1974 was Navgam and its 25 participants whose performance is discussed in an earlier chapter. In our first follow-up visit to Navgam the agricultural expert accompanied us to inspect their fields and to give them further suggestions. Our follow-up visits were as joyful as the course itself. This village has the distinction of having the highest rate of economic increase of all our villages. 1974 was not such a bad year, after all.

It was due to our inexperience and unawareness that heterogeneous caste groups were very difficult to handle that the 7th course was not successful. In this group we had a heterogeneous composition of Rajputs and Scheduled Castes. Another shortcoming in this group was the age of the participants. Our contact man in the village, a student of the college, did most of the recruiting work through Dashgam's Yuvak Mandal (Youth Association) of which he was a leading member. This youth association did an excellent job in recruiting younger people failed to attract the more influential members of their own caste. The course remained mainly a Yuvak Mandal's activity and failed to have much impact with the rest of the village. Fortunately, some of them were old enough to take care of the fields themselves and somehow to salvage this course.

One thing which our participants did learn was how to deal effectively with the bureaucracy. These people knew about soil analysis and had even sent samples through their gramsevak to the government laboratory. No report was received. But after our course they were not ready to take a no for an answer. They appealed to the TDO. He, too, was not very sympathetic at first. But they insisted. "Sir, if justice is not done to us here we shall go to the DDO and if necessary to the State Minister." That was enough to motivate the TDP who transferred the erring gramsevak and sent a more duty-conscious person in his place. One good result of his inter-caste course was that all the castes of the village agreed on the need to grow trees to prevent soil erosion by the wind.

In the course conducted at Giargam, there were only four participants but they were all wonderful : quiet, eager to learn. In our first visit after the course, they could not offer us even water—so undrinkable and muddy was it. In that year (1974) of total drought their economic condition was desperate yet their spirits remained undaunted. First they wanted to know whether it was advisable to start a salt industry since Giargam is on the coast. But there were transportation difficulties and the idea had finally to be given up. Then on their own they made contacts with some traders in the taluka town and started a little industry to perforate semi-precious stones. This brought to them a monthly income of Rs. 150. By the time of the second visit, conditions had improved immensely. Their fields could now be irrigated with canal water and they would no longer have to depend so much on the vagaries of the monsoon.

Our ninth course, properly speaking, does not belong to this project. Since it recruited participants from a number of villages, it could not be considered a village project. We carried out no follow-up work with these participants. This course was organised to make up for the lack of participants in the previous courses and also to prepare the ground for future courses in this area. The two or three participants would not be able to exert much influence in their village but at least they could prepare the way for future courses in their village. And indeed two of the following year's courses were organized by participants of this course.

TABLE 14.3
COURSES AND THEIR FOLLOW-UP

Course	*Village**	*Participants*	*Follow-up visits*
10th	Chaudbad	29	4
11th	Pandarbad	12	1
	Solbad	12	1
12th	Satarbad	23	2
13th	Dashgam-Kharland	37	1

*pseudonyms used.

The recruitment of participants for the courses was relatively easy. The participants of Chaubad and Dashgam-Kharland had been prepared to join the course by the alumni from the Bhal area course. Pandarbad and Solbad came at the invitation of taluka government officials and Satarbad's participation was the outcome of the suggestion of a social worker who was organizing relief work in that area.

If the recruitment work was smooth enough, the courses too made us happy. Our work with Chaudbad, however, did not end with the course. We re-visited the village to consolidate the gains and bring them to fruition. As described earlier, there was a conflict between Hindus and Christians regarding the cultivation of the jointly owned land and there was also a dispute over the bajri grown by the Christians. On the first follow-up visit the participants told us that, due to pressure of work in their fields, nothing had been done as yet about the settlement of the dispute. On our second visit, a joint meeting of the two parties was then called and though the elders were rather reluctant at first and needed coaxing, they finally agreed to come.

The meeting opened with arguments by both parties, the Hindus accusing the Christians of breaking their traditions and conventions and the Christians accusing the elders of obstructionism. We intervened to restore peace and order, and asked the elders to tell us their grievances and what exactly they expected from the Christians.

"They have cultivated that land without our permission, thereby breaking an age-old convention," they said.

"What do you expect from the Christians now?"

"Oh, well, since the plot cultivated belonged to all of us, they have to give us half of the crop."

We then turned to the Christians who were already making violent attempts to argue their case.

"Please, be calm. All we want to know from you is this: Are you ready too give to the rest of the community half of your bajri crop?" "Yes." They had agreed to this both at the end of the course and again today when we saw them before the meeting. We then turned to the elders :

"Does this meet your demands?"

"Yes, it does," was their reply.

We turned to the other group :

"What are your demands?"

"We want to cultivate our land. Why should it be given to a third party?"

"Well, that is the way it has been done so far. Besides, the land will not be properly cultivated by the new association you propose to set up," was the rather apologetic answer of the elders. To keep tempers down we said, "The elders seem to doubt your capacity to cultivate the land. Can you show them that you can do it to the advantage of your whole community?"

Of course, we can! See this year! We have earned relatively more from our piece of land than from the rest which was given to a third party."

This the elders accepted. At this moment we asked mildly :

"Don't you think that it would be worthwhile to give this new association a trial?"

The elders agreed. The other party was now jubilant and in their joy promised that if the whole community tilled the land their income would increase from Rs. 30 to Rs. 1000. "Furthermore", they said, "this will bring unity to the community. We shall indeed retain our separate religious associations, but for social and economic matters we shall have only one which will be in charge of cultivating the land."

The meeting had lasted three hours. Before departing we again made the Christians promise solemnly that they would give the rest of their community half of the bajri crop. The elders, in their turn, gave the new association permission to cultivate the land.

As they pulled their resources together the Vankars decided to cultivate jointly not only the disputed piece of land but also another plot, an old river bed, which was theirs. This plot was being used by the village shepherds for cattle grazing since no body was tilling it. When the shepherds saw that this land which they had come to consider theirs was being tilled by the Vankars, they became violent. the sequence of events is described below.

It was the second day that Vankars were cultivating their fields. There were sixty Vankars when six shepherds approached them. They objected, argued and soon the argument developed into a fight. The sixty Vankars formed two ranks—the first raising their spades to protect themselves from the blows of the shepherds while those in the second rank waited for the staffs to fall on the spades and then catch hold of them. They managed to snatch one—a loss of face which the shepherds could ill afford and so they charged with renewed fury. But in this second attack they lost another staff. That was too great a loss of face and they withdrew. The first battle was over, but not the war. Other forms of harassment were now utilised to break the will of the Vankars. The Sarpanch of the village tried to intervene and asked the Vankars to give back the staffs to the shepherds. They were ready to do so provided the Sarpanch guaranteed them the peaceful possessions of their land. Since this guarantee was not forthcoming, the Vankars now went to the taluka town to see the Mamlatdar. Fortunately for them he himself belonged to the Vankar community. He told them : "Tomorrow the Collector is coming. Wait here and make an official complaint." At Collector's arrival, the Vankars were surprised to know that although they had paid for the land five years ago the deed through no fault of theirs had not yet been finalised. The Collector decided to expedite the matter and finalize the deed of ownership.

In their efforts to unite themselves and to improve their economic situation the Vankars had unwillingly brought newer issues to Chaudbad. For one thing, the principle of secularism was now accepted by both parties : the Hindus continued with their Ram Pir Mandal, the Christians with their Kristi Mandal and a common Mandal was set up to deal with economic and social matters. Then by appealing to the State in their conflict, they had made big inroads into the village autonomy, contributing unknowingly to that operation which political scientists call "state-building". But this encroachment by the State was resented by the dominant caste which tried again to bring pressure on the Vankars to withdraw the case (There was a criminal case pending against the shepherds for their attack on the Vankars) and to settle things amicably. The Vankars agreed on condition that the Rajputs assured them peaceful possession of the land. But the Rajputs were in a dilemma, if they agreed they would be siding with the Scheduled Castes against the Caste groups. If they did not, they would concede to the government their preponderant position in the village. The former alternative appeared acceptable and they agreed to guarantee the Vankars peaceful possession of their land. The Vankars then returned the staffs to the shepherds and peace was restored to the village.

Analysis shows that all of them as a united group had

safeguarded their common interests, surely a new and healthy development. Our participants had always before been on the losing end but once their main problem of the lack of unity among themselves was solved, they acquired bargaining leverage. They accomplished this purpose in their own way and it was very wise.

By simply resisting the attack and winning only a token victory—snatching the stafs—nobody could raise a finger against them. On the other hand they could accuse the shepherds. By calling in the government and, later, withdrawing the case when justice was meted out to the shepherds, the Vankars proved that they were not quarrelsome. All they wanted was justice.

While the Rajputs were discussing whether or not to accept the condition laid down by the Vankars, a leading Rajput is reported to have said : "We better give it to them. The Vankars are no longer what they used to be." Though the social structures are still the same at Chaudbad. But by improving the community life of the Vankars, they had also managed to change their image in the eyes of the other communities, thus making possible a new and justice relationship. And all this without violence.

The second course was given to Patels from two small villages—Pandarbad and Solbad. Pandarbad had some difficulty in sending participants to the course because of a fight going on in the village between Patels and Thakores. "In these circumstances, how can we remain here?" they pleaded with us "Can't you organise the course at a later date?"

But the Solbad participants had a different way. Their objections soon became accusations ending with an ultimatum : "Either we have the course right away or we shall not have it at all." A compromise was worked out that Pandarbad would send two of their number back to the village to consult with their people at home.

Soon the two delegates were back with the Sarpanch himself who brought along two more participants to ensure that his village had equal representation with Solbad. He then called the Pandarbad group and harangued them to uphold the honour of the village. "What do you think we are in the village? Do you think we cannot take care of ourselves? We are not chicken stuff, do you know? You must remain here and do your lessons properly to preserve the honour of the village. If anyone of you comes back to the village before the course is over, I shall personally take care of him. Do you understand?" From this moment onwards not one of them mentioned the idea of returning to the village.

However, the fight between the two communities continued to vitiate the atmosphere at Pandarbad. The drama reached its climax some months later when the Patels murdered the leader of the other community. In a subsequent follow-up visit we found that four of our alumni had left the village, one was in jail (17 people had been imprisoned) and the rest were not in the proper frame of mind to do innovative work in their fields. Their economic performance, all the same, was not worse than that of Solbad. (See Table 14.10).

Looking back at this camp it is clear that little learning could take place under pressure, either ours or the Sarpanch's. At that moment what the Pandarbad participants needed most was to work out their main problem which was the conflict with the other caste. This, of course, could not be done since we had to take care of the other group also. We feel that we need to conduct two separate courses for two villages, even if they be small and near to each other. Five times we had courses of this kind but on previous occasions the number of participants from the second village never exceeed five. Our main attention was given to the majority participants from one village. The smaller village did not usually raise specific concerns which could not be tackled in common. However, this was not the case with Pandarbad. They had a very specific problem which they would never dare to speak about in the presence of the participants from Solbad village. We therefore were at fault. But to our defence we could say that at the time we did not think it was so serious but merely an instance of routine intercaste rivalry transferred to the political arena. Undoubtedly if the course had been given to Pandarbad only, the participants would have certainly spoken more clearly about their problem. Possibly we would have been able to help them find more creataive and constructive ways of resolving a conflict than resorting to murder.

Solbad had none of these difficulties. Still, the impact of the course was not sufficiently deep. There were only 12 participants.

But, the number of those who could really influence the village was too small to be really effective. This, again, was another reason to discontinue the practice of giving a course to two villages at the same time.

The third course has already been fully described. With help from their Rajkot friends, Satarbad began to use the spinning wheels which had been lying idle for a long time. Besides, the monsoon had helped to wash the salinity of their fields and given them hopes of a good harvest of wheat. We analysed that a few had increased their income, they had done it in a significant manner in about six months. At this group's economic situation improves still further, it may very well be that the others will realise the importance of training. It would be at time that we will take up a refresher course as part of our follow-up work.

The last course was held in December for Scheduled Castes of Dashgam. A social service society had formed a Kharland co-operative at Dashgam to buy at a government auction 600 square miles of land reclaimed from the sea. The soil, according to the experts, was very good, except for its salinity which could be removed. The conditions on which this land was bought were that as long as the land needed improvement and as long as the loan utilised to buy the land was not repaid, it would be cultivated on a co-operative basis. When the loan was repaid it would become the exclusive property of the co-operative members. The difficulty was to tide over this period of relative infertility of the land.

As work started on the Kharland the managers of the society complained that the members did not show enough interest in the work of the Kharland co-operative. The participants were finding the whole project as a burden because they had to work without any immediate financial gain. The fact that at a later date this land would be theirs was not enough to motivate them and take them out from the present economic needs.

Hence, an agreement was reached with the representatives of the Social Service Society. The Society's representatives decided to bear all the cultivataion costs for five years. As for the profit from the fields, during the first two years the gross profit would go half to the members (according to the work they put in) and half to the society to meet actual expenditure and, if possible, repay the loan. After the first two years, when the land would hopefully be more fertile, two-thirds of the gross profit would go to the society and one third to the members of the co-operative. After the fifth year, all the cultivation expenditure would have to be paid first and the net profit divided equally between the society and the members of the co-operative.

Just like other courses, the stress was on self-respect and unity. We would call the group to task whenever they ridiculed the others and we even made them solemnly promise to respect each other. This soon created a climate of trust and well-being which brought in its train much enthusiasm and readiness to learn.

In our Research Farm the participants were in for a big shock. The Director told them point blank that they had too much land and that, given their poor economic situation, they could not cultivate it at a profit. "Don't cultivate so much land. Take little and do intensive cultivation. Let the rest remain fallow." This simple advice became the topic of our dialogue for a whole day. The group saw the reason behind it but it drew a different conclusion. "What we must do," they said, "is to cultivate the land on a co-operative basis. It will be difficult to do it with our private plots but we can certainly do it in the Kharland." By the end of the course we have been able to change the thinking of even those who had insisted on being given individual plots in the Kharland for their cultivation. Now they wanted to join the co-operative venture with the Societal Service Society. It is very early still to know whether they have persevered in their resolve. But as one of them said, "If we do, we shall soon come back to see you in a motor car!"

Towards an Evaluation

Evaluation of a project can be attained by ascertaining whether its goals have been achieved or not. The goals of the project and the methods used to achieve them have been explained in previous chapter. For better understanding and simplicity these aims and methods could perhaps be synthesised in two propositions. First, non-formal education leads to personal growth. Second, personal growth leads to rural development.

We need to test these propositions in order to evaluate our work. To test the first proposition the behavioural sciences offer certain tools logically, we should test our assumptions at every stage of our training process. First, do the participants have the characteristics that we attribute to them when they join one training courses? Second, do our training courses effect the behavioural changes they are supposed to bring about? Third, are these behavioural changes — if they take place at all — of a lasting nature?

While testing the second proposition one must be clear about the meaning of rural development. It means the creation of those conditions which are conducive to personal growth. The behavioural sciences can, partly at least, evaluate rural development thus understood. On the other hand, when rural development takes place in the economic field, its evaluation is done by economists.

In this project, economic development has to be measured as a function of personal growth. According to our hypothesis, there is a casual relationship between non-formal education and economic progress. This hypothesis could be tested on an econometric model, whose aim would be the production of quantiative economic statements which would study the relationship between two variables : our non-formal educational inputs and their economic performance. There are various indicators of economic performance through which it can be measured by various indicators such as increase in income, adoption of improved agricultural technology, increase in the producivity of land, increase in the marketed surplus of agricultural produce and changes leading to organisational development (like the setting up of a co-operative or reactivating an existing one).

In this econometric model besides analysing the structural parameters (or the whole complex of features that do not change) the model will have to take into consideration the variables. In any econometric problem (other than the random disturbances) these variables may be what economists call "endogenous" and "exogenous". Endogenous variables are those values or levels which are required to be explained or predicted. The values of these variables are simultaneously determined inside the system and statistical inference methods can be applied to test the hypothesis. In our case these endogenous variables are determined by our own hypothesis. One type of variables will be the educational inputs given by us and the other type of variables will be the economic performance of our trainees as observed through the economic indicators mentioned above. According to our hypothesis, there is a casual relationship between the two.

In order to ascertain the casual relationship of these endogenous variables, one must establish or determine the value of the other variables within the economic structure obtaining in the village where we work. To achieve this, the model will have to lay down certain propositions which will have to be translated into a mathematical form. Then, relevant and appropriate data must be assembled which would be required to carry out tests to observe whether there is a real casual relationship between our educational inputs and the economic performance of the trainees.

Though, this aspect of evaluation is important as it makes a contribution to the behavioural sciences yet the concern here has been almost exclusively with education rather than research. At the start of the project, the problem of recruitment, how to persuade the farmers to come to our college for a ten-day course; our own teaching methods and how best to conduct the courses; and even our own competence were the issues which took the time and effort. Later on, the follow-up work took much of our time and attention. Reflection on our own experience in the light of what experts on rural development had written took away the little free time that our educational activities left us.

Whatever, may be the case, an evaluation of the project needs to be done in order to achieve professional competence. Simplest way to evaluate the performance was by having our sessions taped and then replay. But with this, there was always a doubt at the back of our mind has our training been effective? Has the course really meant much to them? Has it effected any behavioural changes? Can we know to what degree they have been affected the course and how they compare with other groups?

For the present our evalaution has focused on the question of effectiveness of the investment in this project. The obvious way of answering this question would be to set up a formal cost benefit model which would qualify the increase in welfare accruing not to one individual alone but to the whole community. The application of this idea to our project may look ambitious but it expresses concisely the final aim of our course : to train a mini-community which would influence the village community and its neighbouring communities as well.

TABLE 14.4

PARTICIPANTS WHO ANSWERED THE QUESTIONNAIRE BY VILLAGE

Sl. No.	*Date*	*No. of participants* attended	left	completed Course	*No. of participants* interviewed	should have been interviewed	Per-centage	*Village**
1.	Feb, 1973	23	0	23	19[a]	21	90.5	Ekpur
		3	1	2	1	2	50	Dwipur
2.	Mar, 1973	24	0	24	18[b]	22	81.8	Tripur
		5	0	5	4	5	80	Charpur
3.	April, 1973	21	0	21	18[a]	20-	90	Panchpur
4.	May, 1973	22	5	17	11[d]	16	68.7	Chhapur
		2	0	2	2	2	100	
5.	Mar, 1974	17	17	0	0	-	-	Athgam
6.	Apr, 1974	25	0	25	25	25	100	Navgam
7.	May, 1974	15	0	15	12	12	100	Dashgam
		4	0	4	3	4	75	Giarganm
8.	May, 1974	10	10	0	0[g]	-	-	Bargam
9.		24	0	24	0[h]	-	-	Bhal area
		95						
10.	Jan, 1975	29	0	29	28	29	96.5	Chaudbad
11.	Feb, 1975	12	0	12	8[i]	9	88.9	Pandarbad
		12	0	12	11	12	91.7	Solbad
12.	Mar, 1975	23	0	23	20[j]	22	90.9	Satarbad
13.	Dec, 1975	37	0	37	0[k]	-	-	Dashgam-Kharland
		113						
	Total	308	33	275	180	201	89.55	

*Pseudonyms used.

[a]Two had died. [b]Two had left the village. [c]One had left the village. [d]One had left the village. [e]No evaluation was done in this village since the course ended in failure. [f]Those not interviewed include three young men who were still studying in college. [g]No evaluation was done since the course was prematurely terminated and the participants did not set goals for themselves. [h]This course included participants from many villages and, as such did not fall fully under our scope. [i]Those not interviewed include one who was in jail and two who had left the village. [j]One could not be interviewed because he is still under bonded labour. [k]No evaluation has been done so far.

To evaluate the project on the basis of cost-benefit model, we require (a) a clear statement of our project : the number of people trained, the number of villages affected, and the life-time of the project, i.e. the approximate duration of both streams of costs and benefits; (b) a detailed specification of costs and benefits, inclusive of direct and indirect costs and benefits. An example of a direct benefit would be the increase in income; an indirect benefit would be the subsequent increase in the demand of, say, consumer goods; (c) the calculation of the appropriate set of what economists call "shadow prices", or in our language, the prices that should exist in normal circumstances; (d) the use of an appropriate discount rate and the choice of a method to evaluate costs and benefits; (e) the measurement of risk and uncertainty that accompanies many of the elements analysed in any project. This is usually one of the most difficult task, since this element of risk and uncertainty is difficult to quantify.

Due to certain research limitations mentioned earlier, we have been able to prepare only a rough and approximate exercise in cost-benefit analysis.

In presenting this tentative evaluation we shall follow the sequence shown below:

(a) Explanation of our method of data collection and the problems involved; (b) A statement of the problem (number of villages and people trained; time involved); (c) The problem of prices; (d) Specification of costs and benefits; (e) Reflections on other related questions.

Data collection: To check the efficacy of our training our enquiries were limited to our former trainees mostly. Besides, the other sources have also been used, especially the records of co-operatives set up as a result of these courses. Though some visits were also made to their fields to check their efforts at land improvement and to see their compost pits, but the main source of information was the trainees.

Collecting information from them was a relatively easy task, as after a ten-day course, a new relationship of mutual acceptance, mutual openness and co-operation gets established and when they are asked questions, they received us told the truth spontaneously. Table 14.4 shows the results of our efforts. Although 275 completed the course, not all of them fall under the present scheme which is concerned with training a community which is a replica of the village community. This crietrion excludes all those who left their village for good, 13 of them; it also excludes the Bhal area course, since it was given to people coming from many villages. Finally, there was no point in evaluating the last course since it had then just concluded. The main aim of our inquiry was to know whether the participants had done better in their fields as a result of our training. Implicit in their answers was always a comparison between their performance in 1975 and that of previous years.

This raises several questions. How can we be sure that the increase shown is not due to an exceptionally good monsoon? For those interested in knowing the general situation of the fields in our villages, Table 14.5 gives a general picture of the quality of the harvests for the winter crop of 1974-75 and the monsoon crop of 1975, which come under the purview of our evaluation.

Although these details are of interest, but during the interviews we insisted on their telling us only the increases due to the training received. Any farmer knows only too well that the quality and quantity of a harvest depends on how good the season is and therefore, when we asked our participants how much their crops had increased as a result of our course, they could more or less effectively isolate other seasonal factors which affected all the farmers in the same area.

The second bone of contention was that now can we really believe what our participants tell us? The figures might be inflated, to please us? So we insisted on their telling us the truth and we believed their sincerity. Those who had shown no increase, and they were not a few, were not embarrassed to admit the fact, as can be seen in Table 14.12 still, as a precaution, a certain amount of checking was done in the fields on previous visits to the villages to gauge more accurately the extent of their progress.

Moreover, we also verified their truthfulness on consistency of their answers, by comparing the improvements mentioned by them with the inputs given by us in the course. If there was agreement between the two we had further proof that they were telling the truth. Thus, for example, the improvement shown oftener in Ekpur/Dwipur is the introduction of til oil-seeds. This was the subject of a long discussion between them and the agricultural expert; they kept on insisting it would not grow and he, pleading with them just to try it. Another improvement mentioned is in the production of rice stressed by the Director of Xavier Farm to double their production by following the proper method of cultivation. We could go over each of the improvements in this manner. Also, each participant is interviewed separately. To achieve this one member of the team entertains the crowd while the other draws apart the person to be interviewed.

Statement of the problem: There were 214 farmers belonging to 14 different villages to whom a ten-day course was given. The question was to study on the one hand the costs incurred during the training and, on the other hand, the benefit which accrued to the trainees and, through them, to the villages concerned. Table 14.6 gives in summary form data on the villages and trainees involved.

TABLE 14.5
QUALITY OF CROPS DURING THE WINTER 1974-75 AND THE MONSOON OF 1975

*Village**	*Crop*	*Quality*	*Remarks*
Ekpur/Dwipur	Winter	Failed	Drought
	Monsoon	Good	
Tripur	Winter	Good	Subsoil water available.
	Monsoon	Good	However, there were many diseases.
Panchpur	Winter	Poor	Groundnut failed, cotton
	Monsoon	Poor	seed plots failed.
Chhapur	Winter	Poor	
	Monsoon	Poor	
Navgam	Winter	Good	
	Monsoon	Very poor	Monsoon crop failed due to excessive rain
Dashgam/ Giargam	Winter	Very poor	Severe drought
	Monsoon	Good	Very good paddy crop
Chaudbad	Winter	Poor	Drought
Pandarbad/ Solbad	Winter	Poor	Drought
	Monsoon	Good	
Starbad	Winter	Very poor	Severe drought

*Pseudonyms used.

In making this study, we have calculated the benefits received during one year only, i.e., 1975, but no attempt is made to estimate the benefits received during 1973 and 1974 by the villages that had the earlier courses. This implies that we are not concerned with the problem of calculating the future benefits and the question of calculating the discount rate to be applied, and of determining how long the effect of our training lasts. By not estimating the benefits for the year 1973 and 1974 the total amount of benefits resulting from our programme will naturally decrease and by not calculating the discount rate the stream of costs will increase. These limitations have to be borne in mind.

The problem of prices: In determining the costs and benefits of the programme there were many differences on a method of fixing prices which vary considerably not only between city and village markets but also between one village and another. Though, the standard procedure, would have been to determine the so-called shadow prices or the real competitive prices that prevailed in the market; but we have not been able to do so. Hence, we adopted this policy : all costs have been calculated according to the prices current in November 1975, in the village itself. There has been no need to standardise prices to control for inflation, because the farmers never calculate their crops in terms of rupees but in terms of maunds. And the conversion of maunds in rupees has been done according to the prices prevailing in November 1975.

TABLE 14.6
VILLAGES AND TRAINEES INVOLVED IN THE PROJECT

Sl. No.	*Village**	*Date of course*	*Number of Participants*	*Number interviewed*
1.	Ekpur	Feb. 1973	23	19
	Dwipur	Feb. 1973	2	1
2.	Tripur	March 1973	24	18
	Charpur	March 1973	5	4
3.	Panchpur	April-May 1973	21	18
4.	Chhapur	May 1973	17	11
	Satpur	May 1973	2	2
5.	Navgam	April 1974	25	25
6.	Dashgam	April-May 1974	15	12
	Giargam	April-May 1974	4	3
7.	Chaudbad	Jan. 1975	29	28
	Pandarbad	Feb. 1975	12	8
	Solbad	Feb. 1975	12	11
8.	Satarbad	March 1975	23	20
	Total		211	180

*Pseudonyms used.

TABLE 14.7
IMPROVEMENTS INTRODUCED

Course	*Improved method of cultivation*	*Increase use of fertilisers and insecticides*	*Use of H.Y.V.*	*New crops*	*Compost pits*	*Increase in livestock*	*Increase in crops*	*Levelling of land and bunding*	*Increase in income*
1. Ekpur/ Dwipur	10	7 (Rs. 1,600)	7	16	0	3	8 (1,015 mds.)	0	14
2. Tripur & Charpur	17	18 (Rs. 45,900)	12	10	0	3	17 (4,100 mds.)	0	18
3. Panchpur	7	10 (Rs. 54,50)	4	10	0	10	4 (110 mds.)	0	13
4. Chhapur & Satpur	6	7 (Rs. 1,150)	8	8	0	3	6 (460 mds.)	1	7
5. Aathgam									
6. Navgam	16		19	17	20 (1,836 sq.ft.)	2	17 (270 mds.)	25	17
7. Dashgam & Giargam	13	6	9	8	3 (908 sq. ft.)	2	13 (930 mds.)	6	13
8. Chaudbad	14	0	10	13	13 (4,983 sq. ft.)	9	28 (718 mds.)	11	28
9. Pandarbad & Solbad	10	8 (Rs. 1,550)	11	12	4 (506 sq. ft.)	1	7 (700 mds.)	5	9
10. Satarbad	7	1 (Rs. 100)	4	3	2 (260 sq. ft)	0	5 (330 mds.)	13	6
Total	100	57	84	97	43	33	105	61	125

All figures, unless otherwise specified, indicate the number of participants who have introduced improvements.

TABLE 14.8
ADDITIONAL COSTS DUE TO IMPROVEMENTS *(in Rupees)*

(in Rupees)

Course	*Labour*	*Tools*		*Irrigation*	*Manure*	*Fertiliser*	*H.Y.V.*	*Cattle*	*Total cost*	*Gross income*	*Net increased income*
		Tractor bought	*Tractor utilised*								
1. Ekpur-Dwipur	200	-	-	-	1,045	1,600	240	600	3,685	51,555	47,870
2. Tripur-Chhapur	700	4,000	550	6,020	870	47,850	1,550	600	63,140	2,15,800	1,52,660
3. Panchpur	300	-	-	900	150	5,450	1,300	3,700	11,800	95,500	83,700
4. Chhapur-Satpur	500	-	-	850	75	1,150	500	290	3,365	12,200	8,835
5. Aathgam	-	-	-	-	-	-	-	-	-	-	-
6. Navgam	1,850	-	-	-	148	250	300	160	2,703	10,030	7,322
7. Dashgam-Giargam	1,200	-	150	-	1,335	1,050	350	200	4,285	29,140	24,855
8. Chaudbad	1,775	-	750	-	715	-	330	1,150	4,720	25,581	20,861
9. Pandarbad-Solbad	850	-	800	-	75	1,550	450	100	3,825	21,505	17,680
10. Satarbad	650	-	-	-	440	100	-	-	1,190	8,320	7,130
Total	8,025	4,000	2,250	7,770	4,853	59,000	5,020	6,800	98,718	4,69,631	3,70,913

Specification of costs and benefits

Table 14.7 gives an idea of the improvement introduced by the former trainees in their fields. A summary of each trainee's improvements is given in the Appendix. From these figures both the benefits received and the extra costs incurred as a result of our training are calculated as shown in table 14.8. The calculation of benefits is based only on columns 5 and 7 of Table 14.7. Benefits with a longer period of gestation like those of levelling and bunding have not been calculated, since they will come to fruition later.

TABLE 14.9
COST OF EACH COURSE AND NET BENEFIT TO THE PARTICIPANTS (IN RUPEES)

Course	*Village*	*Centre's expenditure*	*Participants' expenditure*	*Total Expenditure*	*Net additional income*
1st	Ekpur Dwipur	14,799.15	325.00	15,124.15	47,870.00
2nd	Tripur Charpur	14,832.95	377.00	15,209.95	1,39,440.00
3rd	Panchpur	14,412.65	460.00	14,872.65	83,700.00
4th	Chhapur Satpur	17,516.70	556.00 540.00	18,612.70	8,835.00
6th	Navgam	15,158.47	1,050.00 600.00	16,808.47	7,322.00
7th	Dashgam Giargam	12,545.80	300.00	12,845.80	24,855.00
10th	Chaudbad	13,385.83	638.00 870.00	14,893.83	20,861.00
11th	Pandarbad Solbad	11,985.39	312.00	12,297.39	17,680.00
12th	Satarbad	12,454.15	575.00 690.00	13,729.15	7,130.00
	Total	1,27,101.00	7,293.00	1,34,394.09	3,57,693.00

This again reduces the stream of benefits. If we now compare the costs incurred in the courses and the additional net income on the trainees (Table 14.9) we have a ratio of 1 : 2.66. In three of the villages the ratio is negative. It is mainly due to the richer villages that this ratio has changed sign.

Our assumption was that through our participants the village as a whole would benefit. These benefits are mentioned separately because they are based on second-hand information and, to that extent, the figures are less reliable. We also estimate the benefits accruing from schemes which have been startaed as a result of our courses, but for these we have not made a cost-benefit analysis. In the case of co-operatives, the turn-over is given as an indication of the progress made by them in such a short time. Similarly, in other schemes an estimate is given of the additional income without calculating the costs.

TABLE 14.10
OTHER BENEFITS

(in Rupees)

Course	*Village*	*Net additional income to others*	*New schemes*	*Total*
1st	Ekpur/Dwipur	37,100.00	10,000.00[a]	
			80,000.00[b]	1,27,100.00
2nd	Tripur/Charpur	4,16,662.00	5,62,561.69[c]	9,79,223.69
3rd	Panchpur	8,765.00	4,17,713.63[d]	4,26,478.63
4th	Chhapur/Satpur	7,242.00		7,242.00
6th	Navgam		2,720.00[e]	2,720.00
7th	Dashgam/Giargam	3,412.00		3,412.00
10th	Chaudbad	11,564.00		11,564.00
11th	Pandarbad/Solbad			
12th	Satarbad	520.00		572.00
	Total	4,85,317.00	10,72,995.32	15,58,312.32

a Additional income from better prices of milk, as a result of collective bargaining.
b Additional income from the introduction of a new varaiety of til seeds.
c Turn over of a multi-purpose co-operative decided upon during the course.
d Turn-over of a Milk Praoducers Co-operative Society planned during the course.
e Additional income from the introduction of compost pits in the village.

Disparities: So far only a tentative analysis of the costs and benefits of our courses has been made. In the process of this analysis several other points of great interest have come to our attention, such as the great disparity in benefits between village and village. The phenomenal increase in the Tripur and Panchpur villages shown in Table 14.10 has to be seen in the context of the data in Table 14.11. The average income of our participants in Tripur before our courses was Rs. 13,900 and that of Panchpur

Rs. 17,680. In short, there were several people sufficient who were economically well off to start ventures in a big way. Panchpur set up a big Milk Producers' Co-operative, borrowed a lot of money to buy buffaloes and within two years it was selling milk worth about Rs. two lakhs. The inputs given in our course were simple. We discussed with our group and the expert from the Sabar Dairy the feasibility of such a venture; we also discussed with an expert in rural credit the availability of loans. As explained in previous chapters this is done when the participants have already been sufficiently enthused and are ready to take risks.

The case of Tripur was different. Ita was an example of how Organisational Development techniques could work in a rural setting. The most gifted participants in this course were highly sophisticated. There was a lot of one-upmanship among them, a lot of mutual suspicion and lack of trust. Though, they were all aware that if they united they could easily set up a co-operative which would benefit everybody in the village; but there was no one to take the initiative. The one who was looked up as a leader by others, an elder among the council of nine elders, excused himself politely. In this scenario, there was little chance for any other learning to take place. What is worse, they were standing in the way of the rest who wanted to learn.

We decided to separate the groups and take the nine elders for a real T-group. In the first session, all the trainers did was to show the nine elders how they were (the elders) saying one thing and actually meaning another. The first two times this feedback was bluntly denied by them. The trainers did not argue and did not even repeat what they had said—they just kept silent after their denial. The third time the same feedback was given to them, no attempt was made to deny it. They just exchanged glances among themselves. In a later session we wrote a summary of the previous sessions and the way we perceived their behaviour. This was received in stunned silence. As we left the hall we overheard one of the leading members exclaim: "We thought we were very clever ! May be we are not so clever after all !"

These were pressure tactics and we were a little apprehensive. Our courage paid rich dividends. The nine elders abandoned the one-upmanship game, Raghavji accepted to become the first secretary of the multipurpose co-operative, the others promised to support him unconditionally, and soon Tripur had an efficient co-operative. Table 14.11 gives an idea of the significance of this decision for the village. It was not only the co-operative's turnover of Rs. four lakhs; more important than this was how much this co-operative had helped to increase the income of the rest of the people. According to our calculations it amounted to Rs. four lakhs, due especially to the ready availability of pesticides, fertilisers and improved seeds.

Tripur and Panchpur were examples of how much could be achieved by proper training and a sound economic position. But these villages had had more than two years to work out all these improvements. We expect a repeat performance in Chaudbad, Dashgam-Kharland and, may be, Satarbad too, even if their previous income was around Rs. 1000. But this would be part of a future evaluation.

Relative performance: If absolute figures stress the fact of inequality the relative increase provides a corrective view of the situation. Table 14.11 shows quite a differnt picture from that emerging from Table 14.10. Of the three villages having a negative cost-benefit ratio, two in Table 14.11 show a very good rate of increase. When this project was started, there was so much about the difficulty of raising the standards of the poor that we were reluctant to train the weaker sections of society. Later, as we mustered enough confidence to organise courses for them, we assumed that the poorer castes would increase their income by about half the rate of the richer ones. The results shown in Table 14.11 not only confirm our faith in the poor but have by far exceeded our fondest hopes. For, indeed, the highest rate of increase is to be found among the Scheduled Castes and Adivasis—those who had the lowest income. These findings are not only a pleasant surprise to us but also of great significance in any strategy to improve the standard of living of the rural poor.

In the last topic we had mentioned the difficulties we encountered in the course given to participants from Satarbad. As the three of us studied these tables, we had to acknowledge that the impression we carried away of this group was erroneous. We thought we had achieved very little but the reality, as it appears from Table 14.11 seems to be different. Barley six months after the course, six participants had already increased their income by 65 per cent. One of them actually had been keeping accounts in the special forms provided by us and proudly showed us the results. Our former impression nevertheless was not altogether mistaken. Table 14.12 shows that participants from Satarbad had increased their income by only 30 per cent while the average for all the courses was 64 per cent. In other words, 14 uninvolved participants could distort the significant performance of six people who were listening, thinking and planning for the future.

TABLE 14.11
RELATIVE AVERAGE INCREASE OF OUR PARTICIPANTS

(in Rupees)

Course	*Village*	*Main caste*	*Previous income average (gross)*	*Additional income average increase (net)*	*Increase %*
1st	Ekpur Dwipur	Patel	7,812	2,394	31
2nd	Tripur Charpur	Patel	13,900	6,929	49.8
3rd	Panchpur	Patel Rajpur Barot	17,683	4,650	26.3
4th	Chhapur	Thakore	3,130	680	21.7
6th	Navgam	Tribals	520	293	56.3
7th	Dashgam Giargam	Rajput Scheduled Castes	4,763	1,657	34.79
10th	Chaudbad	Scheduled Castes	1,180	745	63.84
11th	Pandarbad Solbad	Patel	9,000	1,931	10.34
12th	Satarbad	Scheduled Castes	672	357	53.13

Table 14.12 also provided us with some negative feedback with respect to the performance of Charpur. In spite of the trouble the team took for this village (Chapter 13), the increase was very

disappointing. We made a mistake in helping the Chharpur group. It was mainly because we expected redemption from all their economic ills by a grant from goverenment and not by their own personal efforts. That, we were wrong is proved by the fact that Satarbad, a village with much poorer land and less than average rain (it actually falls under the DPAP), did much better in a shorter span of time.

It's already stated that we have the courses for only one village at a time. Table 14.12 provides evidence to reinforce this strategy. Though, Pandarbad was in the throes of an intercaste fight, yet it had done better than Solbad. Besides, the real reason for this poor performance was the fact that the course was given to a very few participants (only 12) from each village. The percentage of good people is always small and one requires bigger groups to have enough good people who can influence the others, and also to have sufficient leverage in the village. All this is, however, hindsight since our re-collection of this course is full of positive memories. At that time, we would have rated this course very high. There was a great deal of involvement, eagerness to know about agriculture and even after the course some of them corresponded with the Director of Xavier Farm about their difficulties in agriculture. All this suggests the need for periodic evaluation at regular intervals.

In the end, it shows that the earlier courses have been relatively less effective than the later ones. If we exclude Pandarbad and Solbad where the number of participants was not sufficiently large to bring about change, then the average is more than 58 per cent, while the average for the first years is only 31 per cent. This was primarily due to the agricultural technology from the sixth course onwards. The earlier courses, on the other hand, proved very effective in resolving inter-personal conflicts and developing co-operative spirit. At the beginning of our course we intended to have progress among at least 30 per cent of the participants. This objective has been achieved and, in most cases, exceeded. The fact however, still remains that not all the trainees profit from each course.

TABLE 14.12
INDIVIDUAL PERFORMANCE OF OUR PARTICIPANTS

Course	*No.*	*Not increased*	*Increased*	*Percentage*	*Net total Increase (Rs.)*	*Average* Increase (Rs.)*	*Village***
1st	20	6	14	70	47,870	3,419.29	Ekpur/Dwipur
2nd	22	4	18	82	1,52,440	8,468.89	Tripur/Charpur
3rd	18	5	13	72	83,700	6,438.46	Panchpur
4th	13	6	7	54	8,835	1,262.14	Chhapur/Satpur
Grand Average				69.5	73,211	4,897.20	
6th	25	8	17	68	7,322	430.71	Navgam
7th	15	2	13	87	24,855	1,911.92	Dashgam/Giargam
Grand Average				77.5	16,088.50	1,171.32	
10th	28	0	28	100	20,861	745.04	Chaudbad
11th	19	10	9	47	17,680	1,964.44	Pandarbad/Solbad
12th	20	14	6	30	7,130	1,188.33	Satarbad
Grand Average				59	15,223.67	1,299.27	

* Taking into account only those who have registerd an increase.

** Pseudonyms used.

Summary and Conclusions

1. The first tentative cost benefit analysis shows that the benefits resulting from this programme exceed the costs by a ratio of more than two to one.
2. The greatest achievements of our efforts have been the setting up of two very successful co-operatives. With poor farmers, too, we have been successsful. By resolving a factional fight at Chaudbad, two jointly owned fields are now cultivated which before were either not cultivated at all or given for cultivation to a third party. Unfortunately, when we did our evaluation the final figures for the monsoon crop were not yet available, still the bajri crop alone has meant an additional income of Rs. 7,860.
3. With poor farmers, even though the absolute figures are discouraging, the relative rate of increase is very promising indeed.
4. We have definitely failed with smaller groups, as the Pandarbad-Solbad case shows. We have now decided to take up only one village at a time.
5. We have also failed with heterogeneous groups or groups composed of different castes.
6. Another instructive failure has been that of Chhapur where our efforts were mainly directed to securing government grants for our trainees, without insisting sufficiently on their own development.

On the whole, we find that our efforts have been fruitful and in futures, with proper planning, we can do miracles.

Index